4134340

Asian American Psychology

Asian American Psychology

Psychology | The Science of Lives in Context

Edited by Gordon C. Nagayama Hall and Sumie Okazaki

American Psychological Association

Washington, DC

First Printing July 2002
Second Printing July 2003

Published by
American Psychological Association
750 First Street, NE
Washington, DC 20002
www.apa.org

To order
APA Order Department
P.O. Box 92984
Washington, DC 20090-2984
Tel: (800) 374-2721, Direct: (202) 336-5510
Fax: (202) 336-5502, TDD/TTY: (202) 336-6123
Online: www.apa.org/books/
E-mail: order@apa.org

In the U.K., Europe, Africa, and the Middle East, copies may be ordered from
American Psychological Association
3 Henrietta Street
Covent Garden, London
WC2E 8LU England

Typeset in Goudy by AlphaWebTech, Mechanicsville, MD

Printer: Sheridan Books, Ann Arbor, MI
Cover designer: NiDesign, Baltimore, MD
Technical/Production Editor: Jennifer Powers

The opinions and statements published are the responsibility of the authors, and such opinions and statements do not necessarily represent the policies of the American Psychological Association.

Library of Congress Cataloging-in-Publication Data
Asian American psychology : the science of lives in context / edited by
Gordon C. Nagayama Hall and Sumie Okazaki.
    p. cm.
Includes bibliographical references and indexes.
  ISBN 1-55798-902-8 (hardcover : alk. paper)
  1. Asian Americans—Psychology. 2. Asian Americans—Ethnic identity. 3. Asian Americans—Social conditions. 4. United States—Ethnic relations—Research. 5. Psychology—Research—United States. I. Hall, Gordon C. Nagayama. II. Okazaki, Sumie.
E184.O6 A8416 2002
155.8'495073—dc21   2002001965

British Library Cataloguing-in-Publication Data
A CIP record is available from the British Library.

Printed in the United States of America

To Jeanne, Jackie, Kashi, and Koko
—G. C. N. H.

To Allen, Abigail, and Lucy
—S. O.

CONTENTS

CONTRIBUTORS

Kathryn E. Bojczyk, Department of Child Development and Family Studies, Purdue University, West Lafayette, IN

Yulia Chentsova-Dutton, Department of Psychology, Stanford University, Stanford, CA

Gordon C. Nagayama Hall, Department of Psychology, University of Oregon–Eugene

Erin Hardin, Department of Psychology, Ohio State University–Columbus

Gayle Y. Iwamasa, Department of Psychology, DePaul University, Chicago

Frederick Leong, Department of Psychology, Ohio State University–Columbus

Donna K. Nagata, Department of Psychology, University of Michigan, Ann Arbor

Lynn Okagaki, Department of Child Development and Family Studies, Purdue University, West Lafayette, IN

Sumie Okazaki, Department of Psychology, University of Illinois at Urbana–Champaign

Maria P. P. Root, private practice, Seattle, WA

Kristen H. Sorocco, Behavioral Sciences Labs, University of Oklahoma Health Sciences Center, Oklahoma City

Stanley Sue, Department of Psychology, University of California–Davis

Jeanne L. Tsai, Department of Psychology, Stanford University, Stanford, CA

Ying Wong, Department of Psychology, Stanford University, Stanford, CA

FOREWORD

STANLEY SUE

The psychological study of Asian Americans spans only about 40 years, yet several trends in the development of knowledge have occurred. First, in the 1960s, not much was known about Asian Americans, and what was known concerned only Chinese and Japanese Americans, which were the predominant Asian American groups. The popular belief at the time was that Asian Americans were a successful, "model" minority group. Despite the victimization that occurred among Japanese Americans, who were incarcerated during World War II, and the immigrant status of many Chinese in the United States, these two groups were considered successful. In the aggregate, they were perceived as being relatively well educated and hard working, with low rates of divorce, criminality, and mental illness. The few research studies on Asian Americans often attempted to explain their success in the context of Asian cultural values.

Second, during the late 1960s, after the civil rights struggles of African Americans, the quest for civil rights among Asian Americans began to grow. With it came concerns over the stereotyping of Asian Americans as a model minority and the lack of attention and aid given to the real needs of various Asian American groups. Community activists protested social injustices experienced by this population. Social scientists and mental health professionals were appalled at the lack of knowledge about and research conducted on Asian Americans. Some researchers began to challenge the model-minority image by uncovering the problems among Asian Americans that had gone unnoticed. Data on suicide rates, juvenile delinquency, family problems, limited English proficiency, and mental disturbance began to surface. The disputes over the alleged success of Asian Americans also led to questions concerning the validity of cultural theories regarding this population. In the early 1970s, government agencies began to fund research and service programs for Asian Americans, but efforts were inadequate and much smaller than those devoted to African Americans, Latinos, and Native Americans. There was also a growing recognition that Asian Americans were composed of many groups other than Chinese and Japanese Americans. The heterogeneity of the population added to the difficulties in trying to characterize Asian Americans.

Third, the period from the 1970s to the 1990s was characterized by a significant growth in behavioral research on Asian Americans in the fields of psychology, psychiatry, education, anthropology, sociology, social work, nursing, and public health. Baseline knowledge was established about who Asian Americans were. Generalizations about Asian Americans were tempered by the great variability in this population in all sorts of characteristics, such as personality; educational, occupational, and economic well-being; acculturation levels; and cultural values. Awareness grew of the important influence of Asian cultural values, as well as minority group status, on Asian Americans' well-being.

Fourth, I am gratified to see in this new millennium that knowledge of and thinking about Asian Americans have progressed not only in terms of the quantity of the psychological research conducted but also in terms of the quality and sophistication of the work. It is rather passé to say that Asian Americans are not a model minority group; rather, new, complex, and exciting questions are being addressed, as illustrated by the contributors to this book.

Several chapters in this volume provide insight into the effects of cultural values on a wide range of phenomena, such as career development, family socialization, client responses in psychotherapy, and sexual aggression. The authors convincingly argue that culture is a pervasive influence in the lives of Asian Americans. The fact that culture has a strong effect on behavior allows for important tests of the universality of theories that are derived from one culture; that is, are popular theories in psychology culture bound, or are they universally applicable? Some chapter contributors directly address this question.

We also know that Americans live in a multicultural society. This means that Asian Americans are exposed to different cultural values, and through the process of acculturation they may be quite heterogeneous in terms of cultural backgrounds, values, and behavioral patterns. Indeed, some of the most interesting analyses in this book concern the variability within the population of Asian Americans. Heterogeneity is found not only between Asian and European Americans and between various Asian subgroups (e.g., Chinese and Samoan Americans) but also within a particular subgroup. Different models of acculturation and self-identity may be valid for different groups. Adding to the heterogeneity and complexity of Asian Americans is the growth of the population of multiracial individuals (e.g., Asian–African Americans and Asian–European Americans). Given the relatively high rates of interracial marriage among Asian Americans, emerging issues concerning racial–ethnic identity, cultural values, and social relationships among multiracial people are becoming prominent, as noted in this book.

Other indicators of the sophistication of current research on Asian Americans are the discussions of assessment and methodology. In the past, researchers had to use existing measures of personality or mental health that were normed and standardized primarily on European Americans. They often translated the instruments into an Asian language. Results from these studies were reported with admonishments that caution should be exercised in interpreting the results. Some of the contributors to this book have carried matters much further by trying to specify assessment approaches and instruments that have validity with Asian American populations, identifying possible cultural response sets, or comparing outcomes of different assessment strategies. In this way, it is possible not only to identify instruments that are likely to be cross-culturally valid for Asian Americans but also to understand the nature of bias and cultural response sets.

This book is a milestone for psychological research on Asian Americans. Those of us who have spent decades studying Asian Americans can clearly see the advancements in research, the growing numbers of outstanding researchers in this field, and the promise of Asian American research not only in informing us of who Asian Americans are but also in providing implications for theory, research, and practice with all human beings.

PREFACE

The idea for this book arose from a conversation between us over coffee, as we pondered the question of where Asian American psychology is headed. There has been interest in the psychology of Asian Americans at least since 1972, when the Asian American Psychological Association (AAPA) was formed. The idea took root that there is a distinct psychology of Asian Americans that cannot be captured fully by the cross-national studies of United States–Asia comparisons or by the mainstream psychology (implicitly of White middle-class Americans), and psychological research on Asian Americans began. However, much of the initial work in the field proceeded without a cohesive theoretical or conceptual framework.

After 30 years, Asian American psychology, albeit still a young field, has matured into a vibrant, active community of researchers, scholars, and students committed to achieving a richer and more accurate understanding of the psychological experiences of Asian Americans. At the same time, we believe that the field has not yet realized its full potential as a central force in shaping the larger scholarly discourse on cultural psychology. In the past several decades there has been an increasing level of scientific sophistication in examinations of the mechanisms of culture and ethnic minority status in other areas of psychology, including social, cognitive, cultural, and cross-cultural, but this emphasis on mechanisms is only now beginning to influence Asian American psychology. Why not produce a book that captures not only the *zeitgeist* of Asian American psychology but also envisions its potentials?

The purpose of this book, then, is to provide a framework for the conceptual development of Asian American psychology and to help inform future methodological and conceptual directions for the field. In turn, we hope that the innovations and advances in Asian American psychology highlighted in this book will contribute to parallel advances not only in the psychological study of other ethnic minority groups but also in the psychological research of an increasingly multicultural and increasingly global American population.

This book was written for scholars, students, and others who are interested in social scientific approaches to psychological studies of Asian Americans. It is intended for professionals and advanced undergraduate or graduate-level students who have some background in psychological science and research methods, although we welcome scholars or students of any background who are intrigued by the collective efforts of psychological researchers attempting to define the field of Asian American psychology and move it forward. Moreover, the book may serve as a primer on conceptual and methodological issues of importance for an increasing number of researchers who wish to include Asian Americans in their investigations but who lack a background in ethnic minority and cultural studies.

Until the mid-1990s, the only volume on Asian American psychology available was Stanley Sue and James K. Morishima's pioneering text, *The Mental Health of Asian Americans* (1982). There are now several texts available, most notably Laura Uba's (1994) *Asian Americans: Personality Patterns, Identity, and Mental Health*; the *Handbook of Asian American Psychology*, edited by Lee C. Lee and Nolan W. Zane (1998); the more clinically oriented *Working With Asian Americans: A Guide for Clinicians*, edited by Evelyn Lee (1997); and *Psychotherapy and Counseling With Asian American Clients: A Practical Guide*, by George K. Hong and MaryAnna D. Ham (2001); *Relationships Among Asian American Women*, edited by Jean Lau Chin (2000); *A Postmodern Psychology of Asian Americans: Creating Knowledge of a Racial Minority*, by Laura Uba (2002); and *Asian American Mental Health: Assessment, Theories, and Methods*, edited by Karen S. Kurasaki, Sumie Okazaki, and Stanley Sue (in press). Although the growing number of books on Asian American psychology is to be celebrated, none of the available texts provide a focused discussion of the advancing science of this emerging field. At a time when we see a dramatic increase in the number of students pursuing Asian American psychology as their primary research and clinical focus, we hope this book fills such a gap. It is our hope that this volume will stimulate new ideas and serve as a catalyst for more scholars and students to engage in innovative efforts to study Asian American individuals and communities.

The selection of the topics in this book was driven not necessarily by comprehensiveness of the coverage of topics but by their potential for the greatest innovation within the field. The contributors of the chapters are all respected scholars who are known for their expertise and innovations in their respective areas. Many of the topics included in this volume (e.g., career psychology, violence, older adults, multiracial populations) are understudied areas within Asian American psychology, with much potential for future development. Conversely, we are somewhat limited in some ways by the selective coverage in not being able to explore the full potential of Asian

American psychology. It is not our intention to indicate that areas and issues not showcased in this book have reached their maturity, with no promise for future development. To the contrary, as much as has been published regarding Asian American mental health and clinical assessment, for example, many more innovations are needed to answer some of the most basic questions regarding the provision of culturally competent services to this population. There are other excellent books available on this topic (e.g., see Hong & Ham, 2001; Lee & Zane, 1998), which we hope interested readers will seek out.

Finally, this volume is the product not only of a collaborative effort between us, the editors, but also of the chapter contributors and others who enthusiastically participated in the collective dialogue regarding the current state and the future of Asian American psychology. In the summer of 2000, the chapter contributors gathered for a special afternoon "think tank" meeting, under the auspices of the annual AAPA convention, that was dedicated to exchanging ideas sparked by the issues raised in the chapters. The chapter contributors had circulated their manuscript drafts prior to the meeting and, along with the larger audience of scholars and students of Asian American psychology, engaged in a mutual critique of and dialogue about each topic area. We were delighted to witness a lively exchange of views and visions of where Asian American psychology stood and the potentials that can be realized in the years to come. Comments and feedback from the session were incorporated into the chapters; thus, this book represents the collective wisdom and hopes of the field. The chapter contributors exhibited not only a sophisticated level of scholarship but also grace and patience in their willingness to write and rewrite their chapters through rounds of feedback and reviews. We extend our thanks to Yu-wen Ying and the two anonymous reviewers for their thoughtful reviews, and special thanks are due to Mary Lynn Skutley, Susan Reynolds, Kristine Enderle, Chris Davis, and Jennifer Powers at APA Books for their support of and faith in this book.

REFERENCES

Chin, J. L. (Ed.). (2000). *Relationships among Asian American women*. Washington, DC: American Psychological Association.

Hong, G. K., & Ham, M. D. (2001). *Psychotherapy and counseling with Asian American clients: A practical guide*. Thousand Oaks, CA: Sage.

Kurasaki, K. S., Okazaki, S., & Sue, S. (Eds.). (in press). *Asian American mental health: Assessment theories and methods*. Dordrecht, Netherlands: Kluwer Academic.

Lee, E. (Ed.) (1997). *Working with Asian Americans: A guide for clinicians*. New York: Guilford Press.

Lee, L. C., & Zane, N. W. S. (Eds.). (1998). *Handbook of Asian American psychology*. Thousand Oaks, CA: Sage.

Sue, S., & Morishima, J. K. (1982). *The mental health of Asian Americans*. San Francisco: Jossey-Bass.

Uba, L. (1994). *Asian Americans: Personality patterns, identity, and mental health*. New York: Guilford Press.

Uba, L. (2002). *A postmodern psychology of Asian Americans: Creating knowledge of a racial minority*. Albany, NY: SUNY Press.

Asian American Psychology

INTRODUCTION: THE WHO, WHAT, AND HOW OF ASIAN AMERICAN PSYCHOLOGY

SUMIE OKAZAKI AND GORDON C. NAGAYAMA HALL

In the 1999 article "Science, Ethnicity, and Bias: Where Have We Gone Wrong?" Stanley Sue bemoaned the inadequacy of ethnic minority research in psychology with respect to quality, quantity, and funding. Sue believed that ethnic minority research has been hindered by psychology's selective enforcement of scientific principles, namely, its overemphasis on internal validity at the cost of external validity. Sue also remarked that much of ethnic minority research is frequently criticized as descriptive and simple in design rather than theory driven and methodologically sophisticated; such criticisms may arise partly because of lack of understanding of the field. The nascent field of Asian American psychology has enjoyed a remarkable rise in conceptual and methodological sophistication within the past 10 years, yet such progress remains largely unnoticed. The chapters in this volume demonstrate the active and rigorous ways in which scholars in Asian American psychology are tackling the scientific challenges particular to the studies of this population. Before we introduce the organization and the contributions of the seven chapters of this book, however, we lay the groundwork by introducing the terminology and the challenging complexities of studying Asian American individuals and communities.

A NOTE ABOUT TERMS

In this book we use the term *Asian Americans* to refer to people of Asian ancestry residing in the United States. A significant portion of the research studies discussed in these chapters, as well as the conclusions we draw from them, are concerned with the general psychological experiences of the broad population of Asian Americans. On rare occasions, studies conducted with Canadians of Asian ancestry (Asian Canadians) have bearing on the topics at hand. Given the similarity of the American and Canadian societies on relevant dimensions (e.g., the ethnic minority status of people of Asian ancestry, the relative affluence of the two nations, their similar cultural values), people residing in Canada and the United States (but not in Mexico) are referred to collectively as *North Americans*. It should be noted that a cultural conceptualization of the major issues in Asian American psychology often requires references to psychological constructs (e.g., values, meaning systems, behavioral practices) rooted in Asian cultures and references to studies conducted in Asia. We use the term *overseas Asians* to refer to people residing in Asia of Asian ancestry to distinguish them from Asian Americans.

Some of the studies discussed in the chapters are also specific to a subpopulation group, such as Chinese Americans or Vietnamese Americans, and are noted as such. The literature contains occasional references to subgroups of Asian Americans or overseas Asians referenced by regions of Asia. *Southeast Asia* refers collectively to the nations in the Indochinese peninsula (Vietnam, Cambodia, Laos, and Thailand). *South Asia* refers to the countries in the Indian subcontinent (India, Bangladesh, Pakistan, Sri Lanka, Nepal, Myanmar, and Bhutan), although the majority of the studies conducted with South Asians primarily concern Asian Indians. *East Asia* refers to China, Korea, and Japan. The categorization of Filipinos, or the people who trace their roots to the Philippines, is a long-running and unresolved debate. In area studies, the Philippines is classified as a part of Island Southeast Asia. Some scholars consider the Filipinos to be Pacific Islanders, but most often the Filipinos are treated in a separate category from East Asian, South Asian, or Southeast Asian groups.

Until the 2000 census, the U.S. Bureau of the Census had grouped Pacific Islanders together with Asian Americans under the general category of *Asian and Pacific Islanders*. The Asian American designation in this book does not include the Pacific Islander cultures (e.g., Hawaiian, Samoan, Guamaian) or people from these cultures. Because almost all of the literature covered in this book does not reference Pacific Islanders (unless specifically noted), statements about the Asian American individuals or groups cannot be extended to Pacific Islander populations.

Finally, in the past much research in Asian American psychology has been conducted in the context of comparing Asian Americans with the majority group that represents the mainstream American culture. Although researchers in the field express varying preferences for referring to this group as *White American*, *European American*, or *Caucasians*, in this book the term *European American* is used to refer to people residing in the United States of European ancestry to parallel the terms currently used to refer to ethnic minorities in the United States (e.g., *Asian American*, *African American*).

WHO ARE ASIAN AMERICANS?

While sharing their Asian ancestry and vestiges of Asian cultural heritage to varying degrees, Asian Americans compose an ethnic minority group that defies simple descriptions. Asian Americans are a rapidly growing population that has become a sizable presence in many major metropolitan areas across the United States, such as New York, San Francisco, Los Angeles, Houston, and Chicago. The Asian American population in the United States increased by 72% during the 1990s, making Asian Americans one of the fastest growing American ethnic groups (U.S. Bureau of the Census, 2002).[1] The Asian American population is projected to more than triple within the next 50 years, at which time it will compose 9% of the U.S. population (U.S. Bureau of the Census, 2000).

However, attempts to characterize Asian Americans through even the simplest demographics quickly reveal the sources of this population group's enormous heterogeneity. Currently consisting of approximately 4% of the total U.S. population, Asian Americans trace their roots to 1 or more of 24 Asian countries of origin or ethnic groups. The largest proportions of Asian Americans in the U.S. population in 2000 were of Chinese ancestry (2.7 million), followed by Filipino (2.4 million), Asian Indian (1.9 million), 1.2 million Vietnamese, 1.2 million Korean, and 1.1 million Japanese (U.S. Bureau of the Census, 2002). The continuing influx of new immigrants from Southeast and South Asia as well as from East Asian countries provides a backdrop for a diversity among Americans of Asian ancestry on multiple dimensions, such as national origin, language, nativity, generational status, religion, acculturation to mainstream American values and customs, and so on.

The heterogeneity of Asian Americans' cultural characteristics may be inferred from the demographics. The majority (61%) of Asian Americans in 1997 were born in foreign countries (U.S. Bureau of the Census, 1999), suggesting that this population group has many individuals who trace direct cultural roots to their Asian cultural heritages and traditions. On the other

---

[1]For the first time, Census 2000 allowed respondents to indicate more than one category on the question on race. As a consequence, population statistics concerning race can be calculated for "Asian alone," which refers to the persons who indicated only Asian race, or for "Asian in combination," which refers to persons who indicated at least one other race in addition to the Asian category (e.g., "Asian and White"). The statistics cited in this section are for the total number of persons who endorsed either Asian alone or in combination with other races.

hand, Asian Americans' median age in 2000—32.7 years—was younger than the non-Hispanic White population median of 35.3 years (U.S. Bureau of the Census, 2002). Because younger generations of Asian Americans are influenced by American cultural influences (e.g., through school, peers, popular media) to a greater extent than their immigrant parents or grandparents, a sizable segment of the Asian American population is likely to be highly bicultural.

In fact, the umbrella term *Asian American* and the pan–Asian American ethnic identity (i.e., a sense of shared identity and common fate with Americans of various Asian national origins) are relatively recent developments arising from the minority coalition politics of the civil rights era. In Asia, pan-Asian consciousness is not salient. Some Asian Americans—in particular, recent immigrants—do not develop a pan–Asian American identity, and consequently their attitudes and behavior are influenced primarily by specific cultural traditions (e.g., Chinese, Asian Indian, Hmong). On the other hand, a distinct Asian American culture (as defined and redefined by scholars of Asian American studies, Asian American writers and artists, mainstream and ethnic media, and political and social pan-Asian organizations) has emerged in the past several decades alongside the development of pan–Asian American consciousness and identity. The identity, cultural practices, and behavior of some segments of the Asian American populations (e.g., the American-born or the younger generation cohorts) are thus distinctly Asian American. However, it is difficult to argue that there is such a thing as a monolithic Asian American culture that influences the psychological experiences and behavior of all individuals of Asian ancestry.

Although the educational and occupational achievements of many Asian Americans have been the basis of portrayals of Asian Americans as a "model minority" group, Asian Americans have faced discrimination in American society. In many ways, little has changed from the 1940s, when Japanese Americans, most of whom were American citizens, were deemed a threat to the national security because of suspected cooperation with Japan's World War II efforts, to the late 1990s, when naturalized citizen Wen Ho Lee was placed in solitary confinement on suspicion of providing U.S. military secrets to China. In neither case were the government's suspicions substantiated. Although significant numbers of American citizens of Asian ancestry have made important contributions to American society for more than 100 years, Asian Americans are often treated as perpetual foreigners in the United States. Experiences with subtle or overt forms of discrimination and racism, as well as the feelings of displacement and isolation that may arise from the minority status that Asian Americans hold in contemporary American society, are central themes in much of Asian American studies. Within Asian American psychology, the psychological impact of the minority status experience is most frequently examined in the context of conceptualizing and assessing ethnic identity.

Adding to the challenges of understanding a population group with heterogeneous characteristics and a heterogeneous history is the fact that profiles of the Asian American population have shifted rapidly over the relatively short period of the past few decades. The changes will continue as members of the various Asian American communities constantly remake and redefine themselves in response to the shifts in economic, social, and political circumstances. For example, the high rate of interracial marriages among Japanese Americans in the 50 years since World War II has forced institutions that have traditionally served Japanese Americans, such as the Japanese American Citizens League and San Francisco's Japantown Cherry Blossom Beauty Queen Pageant, to contend with the growing presence of biracial and multiracial Japanese Americans and the renegotiation of the community's racial meanings (King, 1997). The civil unrest in Los Angeles following the Rodney King trial verdict brought on a self-examination of the Korean American community's place within larger American racial ideologies and class (Abelmann & Lie, 1995). Although the larger discipline of Asian American studies has documented some of these complex changes occurring at the community level, the field of Asian American psychology is just at the initial stages of grappling with how such changes influence the psychological functioning of individuals as well as the communities.

LOCATING ASIAN AMERICAN PSYCHOLOGY

It is not an uncommon experience for Sumie Okazaki, whose research specialty is Asian American mental health, to be introduced by colleagues as a cross-cultural psychologist. But is Asian American psychology a part of cross-cultural psychology? What is Asian American psychology's relation to cross-cultural, cultural, and ethnic minority (or multicultural) psychology? Indeed, if cross-cultural psychology can be understood as consisting "mostly of diverse forms of comparative research (often explicitly and always at least implicitly) in order to discern the influences of various cultural factors, many of them related to ethnicity, on those forms of development and behavior" (Segall, Lonner, & Berry, 1998, p. 1102), then such an appellation may be fair and appropriate. After all, cross-cultural psychology has a historical association with two-culture contrasts with a focus on quantitative (and what some would characterize as reductionist) methods, and many of the empirical researchers in Asian American psychology use similar designs and analytic strategies. In addition, methods and theories in Asian American psychology research have borrowed heavily from conceptual frameworks and terminologies of the cross-cultural psychology tradition. For example, methods such as back-translation (to ensure the accuracy of the translation process) and terms such as *etic* (culture universal) and *emic* (culture specific), which originated in cross-cultural psychology, are frequently used in Asian American psychology research.

Although a significant portion of Asian American psychology has followed the comparative paradigms of the cross-cultural psychology tradition (with an explicitly comparative design documenting similarities and differences between Asian Americans and European Americans), cultural psychology's emphasis on a meaning-based view of culture has also influenced studies of Asian Americans' experience. Cultural psychology's explicit recognition of cultural systems as "dynamic, heterogeneous, and interpenetrating" (Miller, 1999, p. 89), and its efforts to avoid essentializing or stereotyping cultures as overly static and uniform, lend themselves to various forms of ethnographic or qualitative inquiries (e.g., focus group studies, narrative analysis) that have been used in Asian American psychology.

Last, Asian American psychology research is practiced within the larger narrative of the increasingly multicultural, contemporary American societal context. Multicultural psychology is a rapidly developing force within the field (Sue, Bingham, Porché-Burke, & Vasquez, 1999). In this regard, the experiences of immigration, acculturation, and racial and ethnic identification are the thematic currents that flow beneath all Asian American psychological research. Placing Asian American psychological experience within the racial ideologies of contemporary America requires that one study not only the Asian cultural roots of behavior but also the impact of an ethnic minority status and its consequences.

The boundaries among the fields of cross-cultural psychology, cultural psychology, and ethnic minority or multicultural psychology certainly are amorphous and permeable. Scientific advances in Asian American psychology demand that boundaries (true or imaginary) be crossed and redefined. As exemplified by recent work in career psychology with Asian Americans (see chapter 5, by Frederick Leong and Erin Hardin), recent efforts in Asian American psychology have been made to simultaneously identify and examine psychological constructs and processes that are unique to Asian Americans as well as those that transcend cultural or ethnic membership. The conceptual and methodological challenges of such ventures, described in the various chapters of this book, are myriad.

ABOUT THIS BOOK

The main purpose of this book is to present a picture of a developing science of Asian American psychology. To this end, the chapters are presented in order of increasing specificity with respect to the themes and topics. Chapters 1 and 2, which focus on methodology and cultural orientation, address broad themes that cut across the various subpopulations of Asian Americans. Chapters 3 and 4 deal with early development and aging and address topics that are particularly salient for certain age cohorts within the Asian American population. Chapters 5, 6, and 7, on career psychology, violence, and multiracial populations, respectively, focus on more narrow subdisciplines or topics within psychology. These chapters offer specific demonstrations of the universal themes discussed in earlier chapters.

In chapter 1, Sumie Okazaki focuses on methods of inquiry in Asian American psychology. She notes that Asian American psychology in its first decades relied heavily on single-occasion, self-report methodology but that the field is ripe for incorporating laboratory paradigms (such as priming cultural cognition and identities) and multimethod assessment of outcome variables. A broader array of methods is needed to advance an understanding of the complex ways in which multiple cultures and identities of Asian Americans affect their psychological experience and behavior.

In chapter 2, Jeanne L. Tsai, Yulia Chentsova-Dutton, and Ying Wong discuss conceptual and methodological issues in advancing our understanding of Asian Americans' ethnic identity, acculturation, and cultural orientation, which may be some of the most central questions in Asian American psychology. They illustrate the multiplicity of ethnic identification and cultural orientation of Asian American individuals with several examples from their own work, in which they have used multiple innovative methods.

Lynn Okagaki and Kathryn E. Bojczyk review in chapter 3 the current state of knowledge in Asian American parenting and development, focusing on parent–child relationships and academic achievement. They note that past research on parenting and achievement has relied on Western theoretical perspectives and that incorporation of Asian frameworks is needed to advance the conceptualization of Asian American models of development. They argue for a new generation of studies in other central topics in development, such as the impact that racial discrimination and bicultural socialization have on Asian American children.

In chapter 4, Gayle Y. Iwamasa and Kristen H. Sorocco discuss strategies to improve the cultural appropriateness of methods for research with Asian American older adults. The effectiveness of various data collection methods, such as surveys, focus groups, and interviews, are examined. Iwamasa and Sorocco stress the importance of establishing and maintaining a collaborative relationship with community-based organizations to gather data from this often-neglected segment of the Asian American population.

Fred Leong and Erin Hardin consider in chapter 5 the cultural validity and cultural specificity of career development literature for Asian Americans. Research that examines the cross-cultural validity of Western-based theories of career development for Asian Americans is valuable; however, Leong and Hardin argue that to arrive at a comprehensive model of career development in Asian Americans one must conduct research that incorporates ethnic-specific variables such as the role of the minority status, acculturation, and culturally based self-construals.

In chapter 6, Gordon C. Nagayama Hall examines interpersonal violence in Asian American communities. Hall reviews culture-specific risk factors and protective factors for Asian Americans and critiques existing models of violence for inadequate attention paid to specific factors affecting the Asian American population. Hall's proposed comprehensive ecological model for understanding Asian American perpetrators and victims of violence is a promising conceptual advance in an often-neglected area of Asian American psychology.

Maria P. P. Root discusses in chapter 7 the conceptual and methodological issues surrounding multiracial identity research, which is a burgeoning topic within the field of Asian American and other ethnic minority-related psychology. Root suggests that interview methods, supplemented by questionnaires, may be best suited for capturing the identities that change over time and across situations as well as the ecological context in which multiracial identity is developed and maintained.

The book closes with an epilogue by Hall, Okazaki, and Donna Nagata that summarizes the key issues and themes that characterize the current state of Asian American psychology as well as their vision for the future of the field. It is our hope that this volume will be a valuable resource to students and professionals who engage in psychological research with Asian American and other diverse populations.

REFERENCES

Abelmann, N., & Lie, J. (1995). *Blue dreams: Korean Americans and the Los Angeles riots*. Cambridge, MA: Harvard University Press.

King, R. C. (1997). Multiraciality reigns supreme? Mixed race Japanese Americans and the Cherry Blossom Queen Pageant. *Amerasia, 23*, 113–128.

Miller, J. G. (1999). Cultural psychology: Implications for basic psychological theory. *Psychological Science, 10*, 85–91.

Segall, M. H., Lonner, W. J., & Berry, J. W. (1998). Cross-cultural psychology as a scholarly discipline: On the flowering of culture in behavioral research. *American Psychologist, 53*, 1101–1110.

Sue, D. W., Bingham, R. P., Porché-Burke, L., & Vasquez, M. (1999). The diversification of psychology: A multicultural revolution. *American Psychologist, 54*, 1061–1069.

Sue, S. (1999). Science, ethnicity, and bias: Where have we gone wrong? *American Psychologist, 54*, 1070–1077.

U.S. Bureau of the Census. (1999). *Profile of the foreign-born population in the United States: 1997* (current population reports, series P23–195). Washington, DC: U.S. Government Printing Office.

U.S. Bureau of the Census. (2000). Census Bureau projects doubling of nation's population by 2100: January, 2000. Retrieved March 18, 2002 from http://www.census.gov/Press-Release/www/2000/cb00-05.html

U.S. Bureau of the Census. (2002). *The Asian population: 2000* (Census 2000 Brief No. C2KBR/01-16). Retrieved March 13, 2002 from http://www.census.gov/population/www/cen2000/briefs.html

1

BEYOND QUESTIONNAIRES: CONCEPTUAL AND METHODOLOGICAL INNOVATIONS IN ASIAN AMERICAN PSYCHOLOGY

SUMIE OKAZAKI

As we stand at the cusp of the 21st century, I cannot help but marvel at the progress of Asian American psychology that has occurred within the past 10 years. Between 1991 and 2000, there was a substantial increase in the number of psychology publications concerning Asian Americans. As shown in Figure 1.1, the number of articles in the PsycINFO database in which *Asian American* was listed as a keyword increased steadily; there was more than a twofold increase over the past 10 years.[1] The rise in the number of empirical publications in which Asian Americans constitute all or a substantial portion of the research participants, as well as the rise in the number of dissertations that have examined this population, are particularly notewor-

Preparation of this chapter was supported in part by a grant from the National Institute of Mental Health (MH01506). I thank Nancy Abelmann, Donna Nagata, and Yu-wen Ying for comments on an earlier version of this chapter.
[1]Singelis (2000) also noted a similar trend with respect to a burgeoning of interest in cross-cultural psychology and the twofold increase between 1987 and 1997 in the number of publications in which *culture* is listed as a keyword.

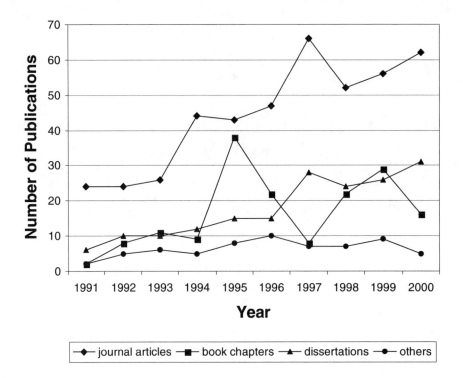

Figure 1.1. Number of publications in which *Asian American* is listed as a keyword in the PsycINFO electronic database, by type, 1991–2000.

thy. A relatively recent phenomena that has contributed to this trend is the increase in publications in some of the leading mainstream psychology journals (e.g., *Journal of Personality and Social Psychology, Personality and Social Psychology Bulletin, Psychological Science*) as well as in cross-cultural journals (e.g., *Journal of Cross-Cultural Psychology*) that describe studies in which Asian Americans[2] were participants.

The recent studies I review in this chapter represent some of the most innovative methodological and conceptual approaches to examining the psychological phenomena involving multiple layers of identities and self-concepts in bicultural individuals. It is notable that in many of the studies experimental paradigms were used to examine the effects of making one aspect of multiple identities salient, whereas in others measurement techniques that go beyond the typical correlational designs of paper-and-pencil questionnaires were used. In contrast to studies in which Asian Americans are conceptualized as occupying the midpoint in psychological space between

[2]Some of the studies discussed in this chapter involved Asian Canadian participants; thus, the group to which I am referring technically comprises individuals of Asian descent residing in North America. For the sake of simplicity, however, I refer to them as *Asian Americans*.

overseas Asians and European Americans (e.g., Heine & Lehman, 1997, 1999; Kim & Markus, 1999), the set of studies I review in this chapter follow the tradition of social cognition research in which aspects of the multiple identities of bicultural Asian American individuals are the focus of investigation (e.g., Gardner, Gabriel, & Lee, 1999; Hetts, Sakuma, & Pelham, 1999; Shih, Pittinsky, & Ambady, 1999). It is important to note that the findings from these studies suggest the powerful effects of seemingly innocuous manipulations (e.g., having research participants respond to questions about either ethnicity or gender prior to completing the main experimental task) on various cognitive and behavioral outcome measures. The fluid and multiplex nature of Asian American ethnicity that emerges from this line of research has enormous implications not only for the development of a theory of Asian American psychological experience but also for an understanding of the subtle but powerful effects of ecological contexts in which psychologically relevant data are collected.

In this chapter, I highlight conceptual contributions of recent methodological innovations that portray a more dynamic and multidimensional understanding of the psychological experience of Asian Americans. It should be noted that this chapter is strictly focused on quantitative approaches. Qualitative approaches are discussed extensively elsewhere in this book (i.e., chapters 4 and 7). I first build a case for why it is desirable, and perhaps even imperative, to expand the range of methods used to investigate the psychological experience of Asian Americans.

METHODS OF INQUIRY

In thinking about the current state of Asian American psychology, particularly with respect to the range of methodological techniques that are used to investigate various facets of the psychological experience of Asian Americans, one can view the cup as half empty (i.e., why an overreliance on one approach is limiting) as well as half full (i.e., what might be gained by expanding the repertoire of experimental methods).

Narrow Range of Methods

Asian American psychology has traditionally relied on single-occasion, paper-and-pencil self-report questionnaires as the primary method for obtaining data on behavior (broadly defined). Several factors contribute to this research tradition: (a) the relative ease of collecting data with written self-report measures (e.g., the convenience of sampling college students or community residents and the relatively low cost of data collection and analyses); (b) Asian American psychology's roots in cross-cultural and personality psychology, subdisciplines that also have traditionally relied on written self-report measures; and (c) until recently, the fact that researchers with Asian American interests were primarily based in clinical, counseling, or other applied programs rather than in experimental psychology programs. Moreover, even within more applied subfields, Asian American psychology has lagged behind mainstream clinical investigations in which assessments of behavior by means of multiple methods (e.g., behavioral observations or indexes, clinical diagnostic interviews, physiological or neuropsychological assessments) have long been the standard. In another example, longitudinal or prospective designs, in which data are collected from the same participants on more than one occasion, are rare in Asian American psychology. This is particularly noteworthy because many variables of central concern to Asian American psychology (e.g., ethnic identity development, acculturation) are conceptualized as dynamic processes that unfold over time (Nagata, 1994) and thus would be most appropriately studied longitudinally. In sum, although the knowledge base regarding the psychology of Asian Americans in the past 25 years has greatly expanded (Uba, 1994), this progress has been limited by a relative uniformity in the method of inquiry.

Indeed, little has been written about general research methods and strategies specific to Asian American psychology, although much has been written about the particular methodological challenges of conducting ethnic minority psychology research (e.g., Bernal & Castro, 1994; Okazaki & Sue, 1995; Rogler, 1999; S. Sue, 1999). One notable exception to this is the chapter on research methods in the *Handbook of Asian American Psychology*, in which Tanaka, Ebreo, Linn, and Morera (1998) astutely asked "What methodologies are appropriate for Asian American psychology?" (p. 37). Tanaka et al. oriented their discussions to these crucial questions: "What does the researcher assume when he or she sets out to study Asian American populations, and what do Asian American research participants believe about the extent to which their 'Asian Americanness' serves as a guide to their behavior?" (p. 22). In constructing a response to their own question, Tanaka et al. called for the assessment of individual differences in the participants' conscious ethnic identification as Asian American and the simultaneous analysis of participants and their social ecology. Specifically with respect to the assignment of any given individual to the Asian American ethnic group, Tanaka et al. suggested that information be collected from multiple sources, including other individuals in the participants' in-group, to corroborate the self-identification. Tanaka et al. also discussed the myriad ways a social context (e.g., political climate, who asks the question, in what form) affects the salience of one identity over another (such as a case in which an individual asserts that she is Laotian to one person and a few minutes later says that she is an American to another). Tanaka et al.'s discussion of the multiplicity and fluidity of Asian Americans' ethnicity serves as a springboard for my analysis later in this chapter of innovative techniques for studying the effects of priming specific identities.

Potential Gains

The use of multiple methods will potentially enable Asian American psychology researchers to address a fundamental question regarding the accurate assessment of well-being and distress. Past studies of Asian American self-reports of distress and well-being have yielded paradoxical results. Some studies have shown that Asian Americans, as well as overseas East Asians, tend to report more affective distress, less well-being, and less happiness compared to North Americans (e.g., Cheung & Song, 1989; Diener, Suh, Smith, & Shao, 1995; Kuo, 1984; Okazaki, 1997, 2000; Ying, 1988).[3] Other studies have characterized overseas East Asians and Asian Americans as expressing distress primarily through the cultural idiom of somatic symptoms (Lin, 1989). It is notable that a recent psychiatric epidemiology interview study of Chinese American community residents suggests lower rates of mood disorders (Takeuchi et al., 1998) but higher rates of neurasthenia (a condition characterized by physical and mental fatigue, dizziness, headaches and other pains, problems with concentration and memory, sleep disturbance; Zheng et al., 1997) in this population compared to national data. There is considerable theoretical and empirical evidence suggesting that the self-report of health and psychological states is mediated by culturally learned cognitive processes that shape the interpretation of physiological and psychological events (Angel & Thoits, 1987). However, because "objective" non-self-report measures of response to stress have rarely been collected alongside self-report measures in Asian American populations, reconciling these findings has been difficult.

Few studies to date have systematically attempted to address a fundamental methodological issue that may explain the patterns of Asians' and Asian Americans' reports of distress and well-being. Some studies have focused on investigating the context as well as the content of self-reports (e.g., Okazaki, 2000; Park, Upshaw, & Koh, 1988), and a handful of studies conducted by Tsai and colleagues (Tsai & Levenson, 1997; Tsai, Levenson, & Carstensen, 2000; Tsai, Levenson, & McCoy, 2000) have compared physiological or biological measures of stress and arousal between Chinese Americans and European Americans. Researchers who have collected both behavioral data and self-reports of social anxiety among Asian American and European American college students have found that, whereas self-report trait measures of social anxiety show ethnic differences, behavioral measures do not (Okazaki, Liu, Longworth, & Minn, in press; D. Sue, Ino, & Sue,

---

[3]However, a growing body of evidence suggests that internal phenomenological states such as emotions are less central as motivational determinants of behavior and self-judgments among individuals from collectivistic cultures (see Suh, 2000). This line of argument questions the differential significance of self-reported subjective states across culture and suggests that research focusing on emotional well-being and emotional distress with Asians and Asian Americans may be misplaced.

1983; D. Sue, Sue, & Ino, 1990). A systematic analysis of the varying contexts and the different channels of expression of distress by Asian American individuals may begin to disentangle the variance in the rates and expressions of distress in this population.

What I hope to contend, through a closer look at the results and methods of recently published experimental studies with Asian American participants, as well as selected studies in which nonquestionnaire assessments have been used, is that there is a need for a better integration between Asian American psychology (which has largely focused its efforts on clinical and counseling concerns) and experimental traditions in psychology that are most relevant to the study of Asian Americans, including developmental and social psychology and affective science. A larger issue underlying such a discussion, on which I touch in the concluding section of this chapter, is how Asian American psychology can make a distinctive contribution in relation to other disciplines that study Asian American populations. In the next section I highlight some innovative paradigms and assessment methods that have intriguing implications for Asian American psychology. The review is organized into two sections: (a) experimental methods in the social cognition literature that manipulate the salience of ethnic or cultural identity (i.e., the "input") and (b) various methods that measure behavioral "output" through ways other than paper-and-pencil questionnaires.

LESSONS FROM SOCIAL COGNITION

Recent developments in the multiplicity of the self arose in the tradition of laboratory-based experimental social psychology. In this section I first present some theoretical frameworks regarding implicit cognition in relation to cultural selfhood and then review studies featuring Asian American individuals that illustrate the relative ease with which thoughts, feelings, and behavior associated with particular cultural or ethnic identities are activated.

Automaticity and Implicit Cognition

Following Bargh's (1997) assertion that much of one's everyday social behavior is driven by automatic processing that bypasses consciousness, Cohen (1997) argued from a cultural psychologist's perspective that many of these unconscious rules for behavior are indeed cultural scripts. According to this line of reasoning, how individuals behave, without much conscious deliberation, when given certain social cues likely reflects a preconscious that is highly enculturated. For example, Cohen has studied the culture of honor in the American South, whose cultural script demands that insults and affronts be answered (often violently) lest a Southern man "lose face." In a series of laboratory experiments, Cohen, Nisbett, Bowdle, and Schwarz (1996) showed that, unlike Northerners, who responded to insults with amusement, Southerners responded to similar insults with anger, hostility, and dominance and with significant increases in cortisol (a hormone associated with stress and arousal) and testosterone (a hormone associated with aggression and competition) levels. However, when pressed to explain, the research participants were not able to articulate why they did what they had done, which suggests that they were following a shared but unarticulated cultural script. Such a lack of ability to introspect accurately and to articulate the reasons for one's behavior is consistent with Brislin's (1993) notion that elements of a culture are widely shared but often unarticulated among its members.

More relevant to the present discussion is that Cohen (1997) suggested on methodological grounds that the investigation of automatic processing may serve as an important tool for examining "shared—yet hidden—cultural truths" (p. 121), because members of a culture may not always have cognitive access to the cultural scripts that guide their behavior. In addition, there are many ways in which verbal reports belie true feelings or beliefs, and this goes beyond mere social desirability or outright lying. Individuals are exposed to multiple, and often conflicting, ideologies of the cultures and subcultures to which they belong. Some of the ideologies and cultural values are broad platitudes (i.e., things people say but do not necessarily believe), whereas others are things people may believe but on which they do not necessarily act (Cohen, 1997). Bypassing the consciously mediated verbal behavior, Cohen advocated the use of an automatic-processing paradigm as a possible way to uncover cultural values and behavior.

A widely used method for studying implicit or automatic processing is some form of a priming procedure. *Priming* refers to the effects of a prior context on the interpretation of new information. Experimenters typically construct the priming context and the target stimulus, which requires a response, in such a way that participants do not consciously connect the two. Most of the studies I review in this section involved priming of some aspect of one's cultural or ethnic identity.

Priming Cultural Cognition

Predating most of the studies that have focused on priming cognition associated with the self, Hong, Chiu, and Kung (1997) proposed a new research paradigm for examining the mechanisms through which culture exerts its influence on social cognition. Hong et al. (1997) asserted that the relationship between culture and social cognitive processes is mediated in part by activation of individuals' cultural meaning system (which is an organized network of interrelated cognitive elements that represent culturally shared ideas, values, beliefs, etc.). They tested the idea that an exposure to relevant cues will activate some components of the cultural meaning system in individuals, which in turn affect their social judgments. In a series of experiments, Hong Kong Chinese university students (who were presumed to have developed both Chinese and Western cognitive networks) were first shown a series of pictures that were strongly associated with either Chinese or American culture to activate a specific cultural meaning system. In a subsequent, ostensibly unrelated task the participants were asked to respond to items assessing Chinese values or were given a measure of attributional style (in which participants were shown a picture depicting a fish swimming in front of a school of fish and asked to make attributions regarding the lone fish's behavior). As expected, the results indicated that exposing participants to cultural materials accentuated culturally patterned judgments. Those who were first exposed to Chinese pictures endorsed Chinese values to a greater extent and gave more external attributions to the fish's behavior than participants who were first exposed to neutral pictures or to American pictures. Hong, Morris, Chiu, and Benet-Martínez (2000) recently formalized their view of how culture is internalized in the form of a loose network of domain-specific knowledge structures, and the frame switching that consequently occurs in bicultural individuals, as the *dynamic–constructivist approach* to culture and cognition. Hong and Chiu (2001) emphasized that the dynamic–constructivist approach views culture as a dynamic open system that is spreading across space and changing over time, thus allowing for studies of within-culture variabilities and multiculturalism.

Priming Cultural Self-Cognition

There is emerging evidence that (a) people of various cultural backgrounds hold construals of both the independent or private self and the interdependent or collectivistic self, and (b) although the dominant cultural ideology may strongly determine the self-construal that is chronically accessible to a given person, the accessibility of a specific type of self-construal is amenable to situational influence. Trafimow and colleagues (Trafimow, Silverman, Fan, & Law, 1997; Trafimow, Triandis, & Goto, 1991) have used priming paradigms to demonstrate a fundamental mechanism surrounding multiple aspects of the self-concept. In their studies, priming the private self (e.g., by having participants think about how they differ from others or by having participants read a story that emphasized the individuality of the protagonist) increased the retrieval of private self-cognitions (e.g., "I am honest"). In contrast, priming the collective self (e.g., by having participants think about how they are similar to others or by having participants read a story that emphasized the family relationship of the protagonist) increased the retrieval of collective self-cognitions (e.g., "I am a Roman Catholic"). It is interesting that this priming effect was obtained with bilingual Chinese individuals residing in both the United States and Hong Kong but only when they generated self-cognitions in English (Trafimow et al., 1997), suggesting that the use of *I* in the English language may have a particular effect on self-cognitions.

Hong, Ip, Chiù, Morris, and Menon (2001) also manipulated the salience of the individual self ("I"), collective self ("we"), and cultural identity (being an American or being a Chinese) among Hong Kong Chinese, American, and Chinese American participants and then assessed their subsequent spontaneous self-statements. Chinese and American participants generated similar patterns of self-descriptions when no cultural identity was activated. When their Chinese cultural identity was primed, the Chinese and Chinese Americans were more likely to generate self-descriptions that focused on their collective duties rather than their individual rights. In contrast, when their American cultural identity was primed, Americans and Chinese Americans were more likely to generate self-descriptions that focused on their individual rights.

Using a similar method, Gardner and colleagues (Brewer & Gardner, 1996; Gardner et al., 1999) have observed the effects of priming the independent or interdependent self-construals on agreements with ambiguous statements, self-descriptions, endorsement of collectivistic or individualistic values, and social judgments. Gardner et al. (1999) used two types of tasks to prime self-construals among European American and Hong Kong Chinese participants. One of the priming procedures involved a word search task in which participants searched for independent pronouns (e.g., *I, mine*) or interdependent pronouns (e.g., *we, ours*) in a text passage. Another procedure involved a story task in which participants read a story with an independent or interdependent theme. Among the European American participants, those who were primed with independence endorsed more individualistic values on a values inventory and made social judgments that emphasized the importance of personal choice, whereas those who were primed with interdependence endorsed more collectivist values and made social judgments that focused on social obligations to others. The results were replicated in a follow-up study in which the same procedure was used to compare European American participants and Hong Kong Chinese participants. Moreover, situational activation of self-construals appeared to shift individuals away from the default cultural orientation when the individuals were primed with a cultural theme that was not chronically encouraged by their cultural context; that is, European American participants who were primed with independence did not differ in their relatively individualistic stance from their peers who were not primed at all (which presumably reflects the cultural default of individualism), but European Americans who were primed with interdependence shifted to become much more collectivistic. Similarly, Chinese participants who were primed with interdependence did not differ in their relatively collectivistic stance from Chinese who were not primed at all (reflecting the cultural default of collectivism), but those who were primed with independence became much more individualistic.

Hetts and colleagues conducted a series of studies in which they assessed the implicit self-concepts of people who differed in degree of exposure to individualistic culture (Hetts et al., 1999; Pelham & Hetts, 1999). In two studies, the researchers compared recently immigrated Asian Americans, U.S.-born Asian Americans, and U.S.-born European Americans, all currently residing in the United States. In another study in the series, they examined the self-concepts of Japanese students residing in Japan who either had or had not lived in North America. They also used two paradigms for priming the individualistic and the collectivistic self. In one method, response latency to a word identification task following collectivistic and individualistic primes (words such as *me* or *us*) was used as an index of implicit self-regard. In this task, participants were shown a prime for 200 ms on a computer screen, followed by a 100-ms buffer, then the target word (*good* or *bad*), and were instructed to press a key as quickly as possible to indicate which of the two target words appeared. In another priming paradigm, participants completed a survey that asked them to perform two different tasks in alternating fashion. On every other item, participants were asked to respond to an attitude item that served as a prime for the individualistic self (e.g., "I am very sensitive to my inner thoughts and feelings") or the collectivistic self (e.g., "My friends are very important to me"). Each attitude item (prime) was followed by a word fragment completion task in which participants generated three words by providing three different missing first letters to the same word fragment (e.g., *OOD* can have responses such as *GOOD*, *FOOD*, and *MOOD*). The serial position of the target words preselected for positive or negative valence (e.g., *good, bad, fine, poor*) that followed the individualistic or collectivistic primes was viewed as reflecting the relative accessibility of the positive or negative implicit cognition surrounding participants' individualistic or collectivistic self-regard.

The results showed that recently immigrated Asian Americans tended to show relatively faster access to positive collectivistic implicit self-regard (as elicited by collectivistic primes) and relatively slower access to individualistic self-regard (as elicited by individualistic primes) compared to American-born Asian Americans and European Americans (Hetts et al., 1999). The Japanese participants' results mirrored this pattern: Those who had lived abroad showed more positive individualistic self-regard than those who had never left Japan. Of note is that the researchers had also gathered a more traditional written self-report measure of the independent and interdependent selves (Kato & Markus, 1993). On this explicit measure of self-construal, the participants tended to endorse self-evaluations that were consistent with their current cultural context, so that Asian American immigrants appeared to quickly adopt explicit self-evaluations that were consistent with the values of an individualistic culture. However, their implicit or nonconscious beliefs appeared to reflect the values of an interdependent upbringing. For recently immigrated Asian Americans, then, Hetts et al.'s (1999) study points to a striking contrast between their explicitly reported self-construal (relatively independent self) and their implicit self-construal (relatively interdependent self).

Echoing Cohen's (1997) support for the use of implicit measures to study culture, Pelham and Hetts (1999) argued that the traditional approaches (namely, questionnaires) to the measurement of aspects of the self-concept tend to assess explicit, consciously considered evaluations of the self that are most responsive to the normative demands of the respondents' current cultural context. It is therefore possible that the reason why some studies have failed to document ethnic differences between Asian Americans and European Americans on explicit measures of the self may be because the participants' responses are driven primarily by normative cultural demands placed by American individualistic cultural demands. In contrast, Pelham and Hetts argued that implicit, automatic appraisal of the independent or interdependent self may be relatively slower to acculturate to a cultural context. They presumed that nonconscious beliefs reflect the long-term influence of the respondents' cultural upbringing rather than the effects of a current cultural context. More studies are needed to replicate and extend Hetts et al.'s (1999) findings, but the notion of dynamic interplay between the implicit and explicit cultural cognitions in Asian Americans presents an added dimension to the way the process of acculturation in Asian Americans is understood.

Priming Ethnic Identity

Whereas the studies reviewed thus far have focused on the cultural aspect of the Asian American self, Ambady and colleagues (Ambady, Shih, Kim, & Pittinsky, 2001; Pittinsky, Shih, & Ambady, 1999; Shih et al., 1999) have pitted the effects of priming ethnic versus gender identity on math performance in Asian American women and children. Their studies follow Steele's (1997) work on the effects of stereotype threat on academic performance in negatively stereotyped groups. Steele argued that minority group members experience a threat that others' judgments or their own actions may negatively stereotype them in a domain that is important to their self-regard (e.g., "I'm a good student"); this threat in turn is thought to negatively affect their performance in that domain. For example, African Americans must contend with negative stereotypes about their abilities in many scholastic domains, as do women in the fields of math and science. Steele and Aronson (1995) showed that African American students underperformed compared to European American students when they were told that a test was diagnostic of their abilities. Moreover, merely asking African American students to record their race prior to the test was enough to impair their test performance (Steele & Aronson, 1998).

Shih et al. (1999) argued that past research on self-stereotyping focused almost exclusively on one dimension of people's identity (e.g., race, gender, age) even though people generally carry with them multiple identities whose salience may be triggered by different contexts and goals. For Asian American women, there are competing stereotypes regarding math and verbal performance that are associated with being Asian ("Asians are good in math but have poor English verbal skills") and with being female ("women are poor in math but good on verbal tasks"). Shih et al. examined the effects of implicit activations of gender and ethnic identities on math performance in Asian American women. They manipulated the salience of gender or ethnic identity (or, in the control group, neither) in Asian American female undergraduates by asking them to first respond to a questionnaire about living in single-sex or coed dorms (gender identity) or about their family's generational status and non-English language use (ethnic identity) prior to administering difficult math questions. Women in the Asian-identity-salient condition outperformed women in the control condition, who in turn outperformed those in the female-identity-salient condition. These performance differences persisted despite the fact that female-identity-salient women attempted just as many questions and were just as confident as other participants and despite the fact that the participants were not aware that their identity salience was being studied or manipulated. The results were replicated with Asian American girls in two age groups (lower elementary school and middle school) but not in Asian American girls in upper elementary school grades (3–5; Ambady et al., 2001). Consistent with the model, Asian American boys in lower elementary and middle schools performed better on a math test when their Asian or gender identity was activated, compared to the control condition in which no identity was activated (Ambady et al., 2001).

In another study, Pittinsky et al. (1999) studied the affective correlates of various facets of individuals' social identities. The researchers first manipulated the adaptiveness of ethnic or gender identity on Asian American women by administering a math test or a verbal test. Next, the participants were asked to recall and write about memories associated with their gender and their ethnicity and to rate how positive or negative each memory was for them. The results revealed that Asian American women who took the math test recalled more positive ethnicity-related memories than gender-related memories, whereas women who took the verbal test recalled more positive gender-related memories than ethnicity-related memories.

Shih and colleagues (Ambady et al., 2001; Pittinsky et al., 1999; Shih et al., 1999) did not conduct tests of potential mechanisms mediating the "stereotype boost" effect of ethnicity priming in Asian Americans. However, Cheryan and Bodenhausen (2000) suggested that the boosting effect may have been obtained because Shih et al.'s (1999) ethnicity-priming manipulations were subtle and indirect, thereby activating in the Asian Americans confidence and private expectations for success. Cheryan and Bodenhausen repeated the math performance experiment with Asian American women, this time priming a public, external expectation of success through the use of the Collective Self-Esteem Scale (Luhtanen & Crocker, 1992). The results showed that Asian American women, for whom the public ethnicity-based performance expectancies had presumably been made salient, performed more poorly on a difficult math task than did Asian American women whose gender or personal identity had been primed. Moreover, the tests of mediators revealed that the negative effects of an ethnicity prime on math performance appeared to be due to the reduced ability of those participants to concentrate on the problems at hand.

Summary

The studies reviewed in this section collectively point to the intriguing dynamics of the multiple identities held by Asian Americans. The studies in which culturally fostered selves were primed (e.g., Gardner et al., 1999; Hetts et al, 1999) show that, regardless of one's cultural background, each individual has distinct sets of self-cognitions associated with the private or independent self and the collective or interdependent self and that the likelihood of retrieval of each type of self-cognition can be shifted by experimental priming or through cultural reinforcements. The studies in which an Asian American identity (and its associated stereotypes) was primed (Ambady et al., 2001; Cheryan & Bodenhausen, 2000; Pittinsky et al., 1999; Shih et al., 1999) show that ethnic identity salience has various affective and behavioral consequences. Moreover, the direction of this stereotype effect (beneficial or deleterious) may depend on whether the expectancies are held privately or publicly. Regarding methodology, the results from social cognition research highlight the malleability of the self with the use of relatively simple priming procedures. The powerful effects of such seemingly innocuous manipulations (e.g., having respondents answer questions about ethnicity) should make one reflect on how instruments such as value inventories and other presumed indexes of culture are used to gather data, particularly with Asian Americans, whose independent and interdependent self-construals are likely to be activated alternately in various cultural contexts.

Before researchers wholly embrace the model of Asian American selfhood as a conglomeration of various identities that are alternately sampled according to context, however, it is important to question the premise of these theories. For example, are there limitations to applying Hong et al.'s (2000) dynamic–constructivist model of culture and cognition to Asian Americans, whose ethnic identity may also include their identity as minority individuals? Is it possible that Asian Americans develop an Asian American cultural knowledge structure that is distinct from their Asian or American knowledge structures? What if there are competing Asian and American primes in a given social context? There is much room for conceptual development in Asian American psychology within this research tradition.

MEASUREMENT APPROACHES

Another way potential methodological advances can be made in Asian American psychology is through the expansion of the types of data that are collected. In this section I review selected studies of three domains of behavior that are currently understudied with respect to Asian Americans.

Informant Report

The use of multiple informants to corroborate self-reports of behavioral and emotional problems is common in studies of children and adolescents (Achenbach, McConaughy, & Howell, 1987) and has received some attention in the study of adult personality (e.g., Biesanz, West, & Graziano, 1998; Watson & Clark, 1991). In most studies of adult psychopathology and mental health, reports from an informant are not routinely collected, and Asian American research is no exception. However, it would be particularly valuable to examine the degrees of agreement between self- and other-ratings of traits and behaviors that are viewed as normative versus abnormal for Asian Americans; such research might illuminate the processes underlying help seeking for, and clinical judgment of, psychopathology in Asian American individuals. For example, it would be important to find out if the same behavior (such as social withdrawal) in Asian American and non-Asian individuals is perceived differently by their peers, family members, and clinicians. This, of course, is a complex question to answer, because of multiple factors (including characteristics of target individuals and informants, biases inherent in person perception processes, and cultural norms and ethnic stereotypes) that are likely to be operating in the self- and other-perception processes. Nevertheless, collecting data from multiple sources in addition to self-report for Asian American individuals is apt to yield findings with important clinical implications.

In a study of depression and social anxiety among college students, I (Okazaki, in press) collected both self- and informant ratings of symptoms for 160 Asian Americans and 177 European Americans. The data revealed that, on average, Asian American targets' levels of self-reported social anxiety and depression were underestimated by their peer informants to a greater extent than those of European American targets. Of note is that the greatest discrepancy in symptom ratings for Asian American targets and their informants occurred among those who were rated by European American informants.

Assessment of Nonverbal Behavior

In a parallel to the paucity of research on Asian Americans that involves informant reports, studies that involve analyses of nonverbal behavior in Asian American individuals are rare. This may be partly due to the relatively small number of researchers trained in the analyses of nonverbal behavior who apply such skills to Asian American research or the relatively high cost of gathering and analyzing nonverbal behavior (e.g., a laboratory with one-way mirrors, video recording and coding facilities). Although some cross-cultural studies of emotional expression or behavioral inhibition have compared overseas East Asian and North American infants and toddlers and involved coding videotaped nonverbal behavior (e.g., Camras et al., 1998; Chen et al., 1998; Kisilevsky et al., 1998), comparable studies have not been conducted with Asian American infants, toddlers, or children.

Nonetheless, analyses of nonverbal behavior have a potential to clarify some long-held assumptions (and stereotypes) regarding the way Asian American individuals behave within the context of family or various American institutions (e.g., work and school settings). There are anecdotal reports as well as cultural stereotypes of Asians and Asian Americans being more stoic, less emotionally expressive, and less assertive (Tseng & Wu, 1985). Clinical texts on assessing and treating the Asian American population also suggest that Asian American clients tend to be emotionally inexpressive (Tsui & Schultz, 1985) and suppress feelings in ways that may be perceived as "superficial" or "inscrutable" (Wu, 1994; Yi, 1995). Early cross-cultural research by Ekman (1972) and Friesen (1972) has documented differences between Japanese and American individuals in regard to "display rules" (i.e., when to show what type of emotion to whom), but no similar studies of display rules have been conducted since. It is thus important to empirically examine whether there are indeed cross- and within-ethnic factors that are associated with different cultural rules for nonverbal displays of specific emotions.

To date, only two studies with Asian Americans have attempted to examine cultural display rules using systematic coding of nonverbal behavior. Tsai, Levenson, and McCoy (2000) examined the emotional responses of 48 Chinese American and 50 European American college-age dating couples during conversations about conflict areas in their relationships, either in the presence of an authority figure or by themselves. Physiological responses and self-report ratings of emotion were collected from each partner along with videotaped expressive behavior. Expressive behavior was coded with the Specific Affect Coding System (Gottman, 1989) to assess couples' second-by-second emotional behavior (anger, contempt, disgust, fear, sadness, affection, humor, validation, and satisfaction, plus an additional code for shame). Tsai, Levenson, and McCoy found that Chinese American and European American couples did not differ in most measures of emotional responding but that Chinese Americans displayed less positive emotionally expressive behavior.

Okazaki et al. (in press) addressed whether Asian American–European American ethnic differences on self-report of social anxiety extend to observed behavior and reports of anxiety-related emotions during a 3-minute social performance task. Forty Asian Americans and 40 European Americans completed the Social Phobia and Anxiety Inventory (Turner, Beidel, Dancu, & Stanley, 1989) and rated their emotions while anticipating the task and immediately after the task. Their videotaped behavior was coded using microlevel behavioral codes. Results indicated that Asian Americans scored higher than European Americans on the Social Phobia and Anxiety Inventory and on self-reports of anxiety-related emotions, but the two ethnic groups did not differ on the microlevel behavioral codes. Moreover, the self-report and behavioral measures of social anxiety converged moderately for European Americans but not among Asian Americans. The findings were consistent with other studies in which both behavioral data and self-reports of social anxiety were collected among Asian American and European American college students and in which ethnic differences were found on self-report trait measures of social anxiety but not on behavioral measures (D. Sue et al., 1983, 1990).

Together, the studies by Tsai, Levenson, and McCoy (2000) and Okazaki et al. (in press) point to more commonalities than differences between Asian American and European American college-age individuals in their nonverbal behavior during stressful laboratory tasks. Further studies with non-college-age Asian American individuals using behavioral assessment are likely to provide more definitive answers regarding the parameters by which Asian American individuals differ in their cultural display rules and expressive behavior.

Physiological Measures

One of the most remarkable recent advances in emotion research is the emergence of affective neuroscience (see Davidson & Sutton, 1995). Specific developments in electrophysiological studies of psychopathology and emotion hold great promise for serving as markers for subjective distress. For example, Davidson and colleagues have demonstrated that a pattern of decreased activity in the left anterior brain distinguished between subclinically depressed and nondepressed participants (e.g., Davidson, Chapman, & Chapman, 1987), between clinically depressed and nondepressed participants (Henriques & Davidson, 1991), and between remitted depressives and never-depressed participants (Henriques & Davidson, 1990). Davidson, Marshall, Tomarken, and Henriques (2000) also demonstrated that social phobics show a marked increase in right-sided activation of anterior temporal and lateral prefrontal brain regions while they anticipated making a public speech. Heller, Nitschke, and Lindsay (1997) proposed that activity in anterior regions of the brain is associated with the valence of an emotion (e.g., pleasant vs. unpleasant), whereas the right posterior region is associated with the arousal aspect of emotional experience. There have also been advances in the use of cardiovascular activity patterns mediated by the sympathetic nervous system

(R. Sinha, Lovallo, & Parsons, 1992) and facial electromyograph measurements (Cacioppo, Martzke, Petty, & Tassinary, 1988) to differentiate among specific positive and negative emotions. In sum, psychophysiological measures can potentially index affective processes that are not reflected in self-reports because of deception, social desirability, or other self-presentation concerns and biases (Tomarken, 1995), and thus they have great potential as an assessment tool for psychopathology (Iacono, 1991).

However, very few studies have involved psychophysiological measurements with Asian or Asian American participants, even though it has been recognized that there are sociodemographic group differences (e.g., age, gender, and ethnicity) in psychophysiological activity (Anderson & McNeilly, 1991). In a study that measured both self-report of subjective–affective experiences and psychophysiological indicators, Lazarus, Opton, and Tomita (1966) found that self-ratings of distress during benign and stressful films were essentially identical for Japanese and American college students; however, skin conductance responses to benign films were higher in Japanese participants than in their American counterparts, and American participants' skin conductance responses to stressful films correlated more highly with stressfulness of the film than did those of the Japanese participants. Moss, Davidson, and Saron (1985) recorded brain activity using electro-encephalograms in 12 Japanese and 12 Western women during eyes-open and eyes-closed rest periods before and after the performance of a series of cognitive tasks. Japanese women showed greater relative right-sided parietal activation during the eyes-closed condition, and this ethnic difference was due to greater left-hemisphere activation among the Western women. A recent study of physiological arousal among Cambodian refugees and Vietnam veterans showed that Cambodians with posttraumatic stress disorder showed patterns of general nonspecific hyperarousal, whereas the Vietnam veterans showed inhibited arousal responses to stressful stimuli (Kinzie et al., 1998).

However, in a study of Chinese American and European American dating couples, Tsai and Levenson (1997) found that, compared to European Americans, Chinese Americans tended to report less intense emotions while maintaining similar levels of physiological responding. In two others studies comparing Chinese Americans and European Americans, Tsai and colleagues (Tsai, Levenson, & Carstensen, 2000; Tsai, Levenson, & McCoy, 2000) also found no ethnic differences in mean levels of physiological responding with respect to cardiovascular, electrodermal, respiratory, and somatic activities in response to emotional stimuli. Because only a handful of studies have been conducted in which psychophysiological measures were used to compare Asians and non-Asians, it is too early to infer any sort of pattern with respect to the ways in which ethnocultural groups are similar or different in their physiological responding as well as their experience and interpretation of physiological changes. It should be noted that ingenious work on the physiological consequences of exposure to racism and stereotype threat has been conducted on African Americans (e.g., Blascovich, Spencer, Quinn, & Steele, 2001; Jones, Harrell, Morris-Prather, Thomas, & Omowale, 1996); these studies may serve as a model for similar work with the Asian American population.

Making Sense of Multiple Sources of Data

Once one begins to collect data with multiple sources and multiple methods, questions arise regarding the interpretation of consistency among the various measures. In their seminal article, Campbell and Fiske (1959) suggested an analysis of intercorrelations of measures in a multitrait–multimethod matrix as a way to establish the convergent and discriminant validity of the constructs being assessed. However, studies involving multiple methods have generally found relatively low correlations between ratings by different types of informants (e.g., parents, teachers, clinicians) for child and adolescent problems (Achenbach et al., 1987) and imperfect correlations among self-report, overt behavior, and physiological measures surrounding emotions (Lang, 1968). The limited evidence available to date shows that even the modest degree of correspondence between self-reports and observer or informant ratings of distress observed with European Americans may not hold for Asian Americans (e.g., Okazaki, in press; Okazaki et al., in press). It goes without saying that such findings need to be replicated with other non-college-age Asian American samples and with other measurement approaches. Nevertheless, these findings also indicate a need to re-examine the ways researchers interpret the accumulated knowledge regarding Asian Americans based only on self-report. Achenbach et al. (1987) and Lang (1968) have suggested that the constructs that yield poor covariation among multiple measures may be best construed as having a multidimensional structure and that different methods or different informants validly contribute different information. Consequently, it is possible that self-reports of various psychological constructs in Asian Americans are painting only a very limited picture of their multidimensional experience. Put another way, there is a great potential for gaining a much fuller, multidimensional understanding of the ways Asian Americans experience and communicate distress and well-being with the use of multiple methods.

CONCLUDING REMARKS

From a methodological perspective, Asian American psychology in its first 25 years has been narrow in its scope. The field, however, is ripe for expansion, and I have suggested some ways an increased methodological diversity may contribute to new insights into the psychological mechanisms underlying the unique aspects of being Asian American. Many of the methods I have reviewed are admittedly laboratory based and require greater resources than are typically needed to carry out a small-scale survey study (e.g., specialized skills such as systematic coding of videotaped behavior, or specialized equipment for acquiring and analyzing behavioral, physiological, or biological measures). In many instances, laboratory-based methods may be viewed as impractical for studying a population that is highly heterogeneous, largely immigrant, geographically scattered, and constantly changing. The alternative suggestion would be to cross-fertilize and to establish more collaboration with mainstream experimental psychology, yet that could also be viewed as counter to the goal of indigenizing psychology and making methods more culturally appropriate. Mainstream psychology has been criticized as "culture-bound and culture-blind" and in need of indigenization (D. Sinha, 1997, p. 131). S. Sue (1999) also argued that an overemphasis on internal validity and tight experimental control in scientific psychology has acted as a deterrent to the advancement of Asian American and ethnic minority psychology.

Researchers certainly must take care not to become overly enamored by the seductive beckoning of the latest technologies and paradigms of experimental psychology. Methodological discussions are productive insofar as they generate testable hypotheses that further an understanding of aspects of Asian American psychology—or, to borrow the words of Miller and Kozak (1993), "Cute technology begs the question of which patterns of which data are theoretically interesting" (p. 38).[4] However, I contend that a reexamination of Asian American psychology within the context of emerging methods and paradigms from the experimental tradition in psychology is worthwhile. Reflections on why researchers study Asian American psychology the way they do parallel an epistemological question of how they know what they know about individuals who are classified (most typically by researchers) as Asian American, and this "how" concerns the way professionals practice psychology within the larger contexts of the methods practiced in other related and overlapping subdisciplines within Asian American studies and in cross-cultural, cultural, and ethnic minority psychology. The question of what unique contributions the field of Asian American psychology can make is fundamentally related to the characterization of psychology as a discipline committed to the data-based scientific study of behavior. Stanovich (1998) contended that, in principle, psychology progresses by the investigation of solvable empirical problems and that psychologists propose and test falsifiable theories through systematic empiricism. In doing so, scientific psychology strives for the logic of control and manipulation that characterizes a

---

[4]The context in which this remark by Miller and Kozak (1993) appeared was a discussion regarding what new technological advances (such as facial display coding and topographic scalp electroencephalogram mapping) can and cannot do to advance theories of physiology in emotion.

true experiment. Stanovich acknowledged that questions in some areas of psychology are more difficult than others to solve and that many of the important variables studied by psychologists (e.g., birth order, sex, age) cannot be manipulated. Nevertheless, there are lessons to be learned from experimental approaches to Asian American psychology, particularly when one suspects that the predominant methodology of relying on self-reports may be subject to the same influences one is interested in examining. The studies reviewed in this chapter suggest that cultural socialization shapes the communication of distress and well-being and that there are implicit effects on response tendencies of being asked about culture and ethnicity. Finally, the challenge remains to integrate the data obtained from experimental methodological approaches with the more ethnographic, narrative data of the lived experiences of Asian American individuals.

In closing, I echo the position taken by Tanaka et al. (1998), that the question of what is the most appropriate way for psychologists to study and understand the psychological experience of Asian American individuals (that cannot be captured by existing theories and methods) must necessarily be paired with the question of what makes the psychological experiences of Asian American individuals distinct from those of non–Asian Americans. Of course, there is no definitive answer to such a broad question, but I suggest that the key lies in recognizing the advantages of capturing the constructs of central interest (e.g., identity, biculturalism, effects of minority status) on multiple levels through multiple methods. Although deriving a big picture from data from multiple sources and multiple methods will take much time and resources, such an approach is likely in the end to yield a richer, more complex picture of the multiplicities inherent in the experiences of individuals who cross cultures in many ways. Hermans and Kempen (1998) argued that a conception of cross-cultural differences as cultural dichotomies (e.g., individualistic vs. collectivistic, independent vs. interdependent, West vs. East), which has served as a working model for contemporary cross-cultural psychology, is becoming increasingly irrelevant in a globalizing society. The challenges of capturing the psychological experience of Asian American individuals (with the appreciation that Asian America is in constant flux) are quite formidable in a context of pervasive influence of intercultural contacts and global hybridization, but it behooves all psychology professionals to reflect on and to improve on this process.

FUTURE RESEARCH DIRECTIONS

- The dynamic–constructivist approach (Hong et al., 2000) and other recent social cognition research with Asian Americans suggests that Asian Americans respond differently on various psychological outputs (e.g., self-descriptions, value endorsements, social judgments, math performance) depending on the particular aspect of their cultural or ethnic identity that is situationally activated. Research is needed to examine the ecological validity of these laboratory paradigms that simulate social contexts and cues.

- Recent advances in social cognition represent novel ways of conceptualizing and testing a particular model of bicultural identity. However, this approach appears to presume that Asian–collective and American–individualistic aspects of culture are mutually exclusive and cannot be simultaneously activated; that is, that one can be either Asian or American, depending on the context, but not both. Alternative models that allow for an Asian American identity or Asian American cultural knowledge structure should be considered and tested.

- Asian Americans' patterns of responding do not converge across multiple methods and contexts in the same manner that they do for European Americans. This may indicate that the meaning of the different tasks, and observers' or informants' interpretations of these tasks, may vary because of cultural or ethnic factors. Further work is needed to examine the sociocultural mechanisms that contribute to the patterns of responding to different methods that are used in psychological research.

REFERENCES

Achenbach, T. M., McConaughy, S. H., & Howell, C. T. (1987). Child/adolescent behavioral and emotional problems: Implications of cross-informant correlations for situational specificity. *Psychological Bulletin, 101,* 213–232.

Ambady, N., Shih, M., Kim, A., & Pittinsky, T. L. (2001). Stereotype susceptibility in children: Effects of identity activation on quantitative performance. *Psychological Science, 12,* 385–390.

Anderson, N. B., & McNeilly, M. (1991). Age, gender, and ethnicity as variables in psychophysiological assessment: Sociodemographics in context. *Psychological Assessment, 3,* 376–384.

Angel, R. J., & Thoits, P. (1987). The impact of culture on the cognitive structure of illness. *Culture, Medicine and Psychiatry, 11,* 465–494.

Bargh, J. A. (1997). The automaticity of everyday life. In R. S. Wyer, Jr. (Ed.), *The automaticity of everyday life: Advances in social cognition* (Vol. 10, pp. 1–61). Mahwah, NJ: Erlbaum.

Bernal, M. E., & Castro, F. G. (1994). Are clinical psychologists prepared for service and research with ethnic minorities? Report of a decade of progress. *American Psychologist, 49,* 797–805.

Biesanz, J. C., West, S. G., & Graziano, W. G. (1998). Moderators of self–other agreement: Reconsidering temporal stability in personality. *Journal of Personality and Social Psychology, 75*, 467–477.

Blascovich, J., Spencer, S. J., Quinn, D., & Steele, C. (2001). African Americans and high blood pressure: The role of stereotype threat. *Psychological Science, 12*, 225–229.

Brewer, M. B., & Gardner, W. L. (1996). Who is this "we"? Levels of collective identity and self representations. *Journal of Personality and Social Psychology, 71*, 83–93.

Brislin, R. (1993). *Understanding culture's influence on behavior*. New York: Harcourt Brace Jovanovich.

Cacioppo, J. T., Martzke, J. S., Petty, R. E., & Tassinary, L. G. (1988). Specific forms of facial EMG response index emotions during an interview: From Darwin to the continuous flow hypothesis of affect-laden information processing. *Journal of Personality and Social Psychology, 54*, 592–604.

Campbell, D. T., & Fiske, D. W. (1959). Convergent and discriminant validation by the multitrait–multimethod matrix. *Psychological Bulletin, 56*, 81–105.

Camras, L. A., Oster, H., Campos, J., Campos, R., Ujiie, T., Miyake, K., et al. (1998). Production of emotional facial expressions in European American, Japanese, and Chinese infants. *Developmental Psychology, 34*, 616–628.

Chen, X., Hastings, P. D., Rubin, K. H., Chen, H., Cen, G., & Stewart, S. L. (1998). Child-rearing attitudes and behavioral inhibition in Chinese and Canadian toddlers: A cross-cultural study. *Developmental Psychology, 34*, 677–686.

Cheryan, S., & Bodenhausen, G. V. (2000). When positive stereotypes threaten intellectual performance: The psychological hazards of "model minority" status. *Psychological Science, 11*, 399–402.

Cheung, F. M., & Song, W. (1989). A review on the clinical applications of the Chinese MMPI. *Psychological Assessment, 1*, 230–237.

Cohen, D. (1997). *Ifs* and *thens* in cultural psychology. In R. S. Wyer, Jr. (Ed.), *The automaticity of everyday life: Advances in social cognition* (Vol. 10, pp. 121–131). Mahwah, NJ: Erlbaum.

Cohen, D., Nisbett, R. E., Bowdle, B. F., & Schwarz, N. (1996). Insult, aggression, and the Southern culture of honor: An "experimental ethnography." *Journal of Personality and Social Psychology, 70*, 945–960.

Davidson, R. J., Chapman, J. P., & Chapman, L. J. (1987). Task-dependent EEG asymmetry discriminates between depressed and non-depressed subjects. *Psychophysiology, 24*, 585.

Davidson, R. J., Marshall, J. R., Tomarken, A. J., & Henriques, J. B. (2000). While a phobic waits: Regional brain electrical and autonomic activity in social phobics during anticipation of public speaking. *Biological Psychiatry, 47*, 85–95.

Davidson, R. J., & Sutton, S. K. (1995). Affective neuroscience: The emergence of a discipline. *Current Opinion in Neurobiology, 5*, 217–224.

Diener, E., Suh, E. M., Smith, H., & Shao, L. (1995). National differences in reported subjective well-being: Why do they occur? *Social Indicators Research, 34*, 7–32.

Ekman, P. (1972). Universals and cultural differences in facial expressions of emotion. In J. Cole (Ed.), *Nebraska Symposium on Motivation* (Vol. 9, pp. 207–283). Lincoln: University of Nebraska Press.

Friesen, W. V. (1972). *Cultural differences in facial expression in a social situation: An experimental test of the concept of display rules.* Unpublished doctoral dissertation, University of California, San Francisco.

Gardner, W. L., Gabriel, S., & Lee, A. Y. (1999). "I" value freedom, but "we" value relationships: Self-construal priming mirrors cultural differences in judgment. *Psychological Science, 10,* 321–326.

Gottman, J. M. (1989). *The Specific Affect Coding System (SPAFF).* Unpublished research manual, University of Washington, Seattle, WA.

Heine, S. J., & Lehman, D. R. (1997). The cultural construction of self-enhancement: An examination of group-serving biases. *Journal of Personality and Social Psychology, 72,* 1268–1283.

Heine, S. J., & Lehman, D. R. (1999). Culture, self-discrepancies, and self-satisfaction. *Personality and Social Psychology Bulletin, 25,* 915–925.

Heller, W., Nitschke, J. B., & Lindsay, D. L. (1997). Neuropsychological correlates of arousal in self-reported emotion. *Cognition & Emotion, 11,* 383–402.

Henriques, J. B., & Davidson, R. J. (1990). Regional brain electrical asymmetries discriminate between previously depressed and healthy control subjects. *Journal of Abnormal Psychology, 99,* 22–31.

Henriques, J. B., & Davidson, R. J. (1991). Left frontal hypoactivation in depression. *Journal of Abnormal Psychology, 100,* 535–545.

Hermans, H. J. M., & Kempen, H. J. G. (1998). Moving cultures: The perilous problems of cultural dichotomies in a globalizing society. *American Psychologist, 53,* 1111–1120.

Hetts, J. J., Sakuma, M., & Pelham, B. W. (1999). Two roads to positive regard: Implicit and explicit self-evaluation and culture. *Journal of Experimental Social Psychology, 35,* 512–559.

Hong, Y., & Chiu, C. (2001). Toward a paradigm shift: From cross-cultural differences in social cognition to social–cognitive mediation of cultural differences. *Social Cognition, 19,* 181–196.

Hong, Y., Chiu, C., & Kung, T. M. (1997). Bringing culture out in front: Effects of cultural meaning system activation on social cognition. In K. Leung, U. Kim, S. Yamaguchi, & Y. Kashima (Eds.), *Progress in Asian social psychology* (Vol. 1, pp. 139–150). Singapore: Wiley.

Hong, Y., Ip, G., Chiu, C., Morris, M. W., & Menon, T. (2001). Cultural identity and dynamic construction of the self: Collective duties and individual rights in Chinese and American cultures. *Social Cognition, 19,* 251–268.

Hong, Y., Morris, M. W., Chiu, C., & Benet-Martínez, V. (2000). Multicultural minds: A dynamic constructionist approach to culture and cognition. *American Psychologist, 55,* 709–720.

Iacono, W. G. (1991). Psychophysiological assessment of psychopathology. *Psychological Assessment, 3*, 309–320.

Jones, D. R., Harrell, J. P., Morris-Prather, C. E., Thomas, J., & Omowale, N. (1996). Affective and physiological responses to racism: The roles of Afrocentrism and mode of presentation. *Ethnicity and Disease, 6*, 109–122.

Kato, K., & Markus, H. R. (1993, June). *Development of the Interdependence/Independence Scale: Using American and Japanese samples.* Paper presented at the 5th annual convention of the American Psychological Society, Washington, DC.

Kim, H., & Markus, H. R. (1999). Deviance or uniqueness, harmony or conformity? A cultural analysis. *Journal of Personality and Social Psychology, 77*, 785–800.

Kinzie, J. D., Denney, D., Riley, C., Boehnlein, J., McFarland, B., & Leung, P. (1998). A cross-cultural study of reactivation of posttraumatic stress disorder symptoms: American and Cambodian psychophysiological response to viewing traumatic video scenes. *Journal of Nervous and Mental Disease, 186*, 670–676.

Kisilevsky, B. S., Hains, S. M. J., Lee, K., Muir, D. W., Xu, F., Fu, G., et al. (1998). The still-face effect in Chinese and Canadian 3- to 6-month-old infants. *Developmental Psychology, 34*, 629–639.

Kuo, W. H. (1984). Prevalence of depression among Asian-Americans. *Journal of Nervous and Mental Disease, 172*, 449–457.

Lang, P. J. (1968). Fear reduction and fear behavior: Problems in treating a construct. In J. M. Shlien, H. F. Hunt, J. D. Matarazzo, & C. Savage (Eds.), *Research in psychotherapy* (pp. 90–102). Washington, DC: American Psychological Association.

Lazarus, R. S., Opton, E., Jr., & Tomita, M. (1966). A cross-cultural study of stress reaction patterns in Japan. *Journal of Personality and Social Psychology, 4*, 622–633.

Lin, T. Y. (1989). Neurasthenia revisited: Its place in modern psychiatry. *Culture, Medicine, and Psychiatry, 13*, 105–129.

Luhtanen, R., & Crocker, J. (1992). A collective self-esteem scale: Self-evaluation of one's social identity. *Personality and Social Psychology Bulletin, 18*, 302–318.

Miller, G. A., & Kozak, M. J. (1993). Three-systems assessment and the construct of emotion. In N. Birbaumer & A. Ohman (Eds.), *The structure of emotion: Psychophysiological, cognitive and clinical aspects* (pp. 31–47). Seattle, WA: Hogrefe & Huber.

Moss, E. M., Davidson, R. J., & Saron, C. (1985). Cross-cultural differences in hemisphericity: EEG asymmetry discriminates between Japanese and Westerners. *Neuropsychologia, 23*, 131–135.

Nagata, D. K. (1994). Assessing Asian American acculturation and ethnic identity: The need for a multidimensional framework. *Asian American and Pacific Islander Journal of Health, 2*, 108–124.

Okazaki, S. (1997). Sources of ethnic differences between Asian American and European American college students on measures of depression and social anxiety. *Journal of Abnormal Psychology, 106*, 52–60.

Okazaki, S. (2000). Asian American–European American differences on affective distress symptoms: Do symptom reports differ across reporting methods? *Journal of Cross-Cultural Psychology, 31*, 603–625.

Okazaki, S. (in press). Self–other agreement on affective distress scales in Asian Americans and European Americans. *Journal of Counseling Psychology.*

Okazaki, S., Liu, J. F., Longworth, S. L., & Minn, J. Y. (in press). Asian American–European American differences in expressions of social anxiety: A replication and extension. *Cultural Diversity and Ethnic Minority Psychology.*

Okazaki, S., & Sue, S. (1995). Methodological issues in assessment research with ethnic minorities. *Psychological Assessment, 7*, 367–375.

Park, K. B., Upshaw, H. S., & Koh, S. D. (1988). East Asians' responses to Western health items. *Journal of Cross-Cultural Psychology, 19*, 51–64.

Pelham, B. W., & Hetts, J. J. (1999). Implicit and explicit personal and social identity: Toward a more complete understanding of the social self. In T. R. Tyler, R. M. Kramer, & O. P. John (Eds.), *The psychology of the social self: Applied social research* (pp. 115–143). Mahwah, NJ: Erlbaum.

Pittinsky, T. L., Shih, M., & Ambady, N. (1999). Identity adaptiveness: Affect across multiple identities. *Journal of Social Issues, 55*, 503–518.

Rogler, L. H. (1999). Methodological sources of cultural insensitivity in mental health research. *American Psychologist, 54*, 424–433.

Shih, M., Pittinsky, T. L., & Ambady, N. (1999). Stereotype susceptibility: Identity salience and shifts in quantitative performance. *Psychological Science, 10*, 80–83.

Singelis, T. M. (2000). Some thoughts on the future of cross-cultural social psychology. *Journal of Cross-Cultural Psychology, 31*, 76–91.

Sinha, D. (1997). Indigenizing psychology. In J. W. Berry, Y. H. Poortinga, & J. Pandey (Eds.), *Handbook of cross-cultural psychology: Vol. 1. Theory and method* (2nd ed., pp. 129–169). Boston: Allyn & Bacon.

Sinha, R., Lovallo, W. R., & Parsons, O. A. (1992). Cardiovascular differentiation of emotions. *Psychosomatic Medicine, 54*, 422–435.

Stanovich, K. E. (1998). *How to think straight about psychology* (5th ed.). New York: Longman.

Steele, C. M. (1997). A threat in the air: How stereotypes shape intellectual identity and performance. *American Psychologist, 52*, 1613–1629.

Steele, C. M., & Aronson, J. (1995). Stereotype threat and the intellectual test performance of African Americans. *Journal of Personality and Social Psychology, 69*, 797–811.

Steele, C. M., & Aronson, J. (1998). Stereotype threat and the test performance of academically successful African Americans. In C. Jencks & M. Phillips (Eds.), *The Black–European test score gap* (pp. 401–427). Washington, DC: Brookings Institution.

Sue, D., Ino, S., & Sue, D. M. (1983). Nonassertiveness of Asian Americans: An inaccurate assumption? *Journal of Counseling Psychology, 30*, 581–588.

Sue, D., Sue, D. M., & Ino, S. (1990). Assertiveness and social anxiety in Chinese-American women. *Journal of Psychology, 124*, 155–163.

Sue, S. (1999). Science, ethnicity, and bias: Where have we gone wrong? *American Psychologist, 54*, 1070–1077.

Suh, E. M. (2000). Self, the hyphen between culture and subjective well-being. In E. Diener & E. M. Suh (Eds.), *Subjective well-being across cultures* (pp. 63–86). Cambridge, MA: MIT Press.

Takeuchi, D. T., Chung, R. C.-Y., Lin, K.-M., Shen, H., Kurasaki, K., Chun, C., et al. (1998). Lifetime and twelve-months prevalence rates of major depressive episodes and dysthymia among Chinese Americans in Los Angeles. *American Journal of Psychiatry, 155*, 1407–1414.

Tanaka, J. S., Ebreo, A., Linn, N., & Morera, O. F. (1998). Research methods: The construct validity of self-identity and its psychological implications. In L. C. Lee & N. W. S. Zane (Eds.), *Handbook of Asian American psychology* (pp. 21–79). Thousand Oaks, CA: Sage.

Tomarken, A. J. (1995). A psychometric perspective on psychophysiological measures. *Psychological Assessment, 7*, 387–395.

Trafimow, D., Silverman, E. S., Fan, R. M.-T., & Law, J. S. F. (1997). The effects of language and priming on the relative accessibility of the private self and the collective self. *Journal of Cross-Cultural Psychology, 28*, 107–123.

Trafimow, D., Triandis, H. C., & Goto, S. G. (1991). Some tests of the distinction between the private self and the collective self. *Journal of Personality and Social Psychology, 60*, 649–655.

Tsai, J. L., & Levenson, R. W. (1997). Cultural influences of emotional responding: Chinese American and European American dating couples during interpersonal conflict. *Journal of Cross-Cultural Psychology, 28*, 600–625.

Tsai, J. L., Levenson, R. W., & Carstensen, L. L. (2000). Autonomic, subjective, and expressive responses to emotional films in older and younger Chinese Americans and European Americans. *Psychology and Aging, 15*, 684–693.

Tsai, J. L., Levenson, R. W., & McCoy, K. (2000). *Cultural similarities and differences in emotional responding: Chinese American and European American dating couples during conflict.* Unpublished manuscript.

Tseng, W., & Wu, D. Y. H. (Eds.). (1985). *Chinese culture and mental health.* Orlando, FL: Academic Press.

Tsui, P., & Schultz, G. L. (1985). Failure of rapport: Why psychotherapeutic engagement fails in the treatment of Asian clients. *American Journal of Orthopsychiatry, 55*, 561–569.

Turner, S. M., Beidel, D. C., Dancu, C. V., & Stanley, M. A. (1989). An empirically derived inventory to measure social fears and anxiety: The Social Phobia and Anxiety Inventory. *Psychological Assessment, 1*, 35–40.

Uba, L. (1994). *Asian Americans: Personality patterns, identity, and mental health.* New York: Guilford Press.

Watson, D., & Clark, L. A. (1991). Self- versus peer ratings of specific emotional traits: Evidence of convergent and discriminant validity. *Journal of Personality and Social Psychology, 60*, 927–940.

Wu, J. (1994). On therapy with Asian patients. *Contemporary Psychoanalysis, 30*, 152–168.

Yi, K. (1995). Psychoanalytic psychotherapy with Asian clients: Transference and therapeutic considerations. *Psychotherapy, 32*, 308–316.

Ying, Y. (1988). Depressive symptomatology among Chinese-Americans as measured by the CES–D. *Journal of Clinical Psychology, 44*, 739–746.

Zheng, Y.-P., Lin, K.-M., Takeuchi, D., Kurasaki, K. S., Wang, Y., & Cheung, F. (1997). An epidemiological study of neurasthenia in Chinese-Americans in Los Angeles. *Comprehensive Psychiatry, 38*, 249–259.

2

WHY AND HOW RESEARCHERS SHOULD STUDY ETHNIC IDENTITY, ACCULTURATION, AND CULTURAL ORIENTATION

JEANNE L. TSAI, YULIA CHENTSOVA-DUTTON, AND YING WONG

I can't explain it. It's so much . . . being Hmong is too broad to explain.
It comes with a lot of aspects. That's as far as I can get.
—Hmong college student

As the number of immigrants, refugees, and American-born ethnic minorities living in the United States and Canada continues to grow, North American psychologists and other social scientists have become increasingly interested in culture and how it shapes one's interactions with others, responses to one's environments, and feelings about oneself and others. At first blush, cultural processes may appear too broad to explain and difficult to study, resulting in sentiments similar to those expressed by the Hmong college student quoted at the beginning of this chapter. However, research conducted in the late 20th century on ethnic identity, acculturation, and cultural orientation has moved researchers closer to identifying the many aspects

We thank Yu-Wen Ying for reading an earlier version of this chapter.

of culture that might influence human behavior. Therefore, as the 21st century begins, we are optimistic that researchers will go much farther in understanding the mechanisms of cultural influence than they have in the past. In this chapter we present new conceptual and methodological approaches to studying ethnic identity, acculturation, and cultural orientation that may help researchers achieve this end. First, however, we define our terms and discuss why these constructs are worthy of further scientific pursuit.

WHAT ARE ETHNIC IDENTITY, ACCULTURATION, AND CULTURAL ORIENTATION?

Ethnic identity (the degree to which one views oneself as a member of a particular ethnic group), *acculturation* (the process of adjusting to a different culture), and *cultural orientation* (one's feelings toward and levels of engagement in different cultures) are similar in a number of ways. All three constructs describe individuals' relationships to their cultural environments, span multiple domains of life experience (e.g., language, activities), and are dynamic and constantly changing. In addition, researchers have primarily used self-report inventories such as the Multigroup Ethnic Identity Measure (Phinney, 1992), the General Ethnicity Questionnaire (Tsai, Ying, & Lee, 2000), and the Suinn–Lew Asian Self-Identity Acculturation Rating Scale (Suinn, Rickard-Figueroa, Lew, & Vigil, 1987) to measure these constructs. Because of these similarities, these terms are often used interchangeably in the literature.[1]

These constructs, however, are distinct in significant ways, making critical the accurate use of these terms. Whereas ethnic identity requires conscious endorsement, acculturation and cultural orientation do not; that is, an individual may be very oriented to American culture in terms of the customs and traditions he or she practices, but he or she may not explicitly identify with American culture. Also, whereas *acculturation* refers to the adjustment of immigrant and refugee groups, *ethnic identity* and *cultural orientation* also apply to American-born ethnic minorities. Given the similarities among the three constructs, we discuss all of them in this chapter; however, where appropriate, we focus on them separately.

WHY SHOULD RESEARCHERS STUDY THESE CONSTRUCTS?

Although ethnic identity, acculturation, and cultural orientation are constructs that have received much attention in the literature, many critical

---

[1]We are not discussing *racial identity*, or "the quality of one's identification with one's racial group," because of its emphasis on "racial oppression and racism" (Alvarez & Helms, 2001). Although we strongly believe that racial identity assumes an important role in the psyche of Asian Americans and other multicultural individuals, given space constraints we limit the focus of this chapter to constructs that are related to the influence of cultural practices and beliefs and identification with such practices and beliefs.

questions remain unanswered. Before we describe these questions in detail we discuss the reasons why they are worthy of continued pursuit.

To Examine a Central Aspect of Identity or Self-Concept

> It means a lot for me to be Hmong. It's one of the most important parts of my life. It's a daily thing I have to live with, being a Hmong person.
> —Hmong college student

Over the centuries, belonging to a particular ethnic group has remained an important part of how individuals view and describe themselves (Smith, 1986). By identifying oneself in terms of one's ethnic or cultural group, an individual retains his or her connection to an existing community as well as to a larger historical context (Takei, 1998). Over the course of an individual's life, ethnic identity may also link earlier and later stages of that life. For example, Luborsky and Rubinstein (1990) found that in a sample of 45 Irish, Italian, and Jewish widowers living in Philadelphia, the majority reported that their ethnic identities provided a way for them to retain connections with their life experiences before the deaths of their wives. Although much of the literature suggests that the development of ethnic identity peaks during adolescence, (Phinney, 1990), Simic (1987) and Myerhoff (1978) have argued that ethnic identity may also assume a central role in old age, when older adults are perceived by younger adults as cultural carriers and transmitters.

To Reveal the Psychology of Immigrant, Refugee, and Other Multicultural Groups

In light of the tremendous amount of migration that has occurred in the past few decades and the concomitant emergence of multicultural societies, it has become increasingly important to understand the psychology of multicultural individuals, or people who have been influenced by different cultural traditions. Such knowledge is critical if such individuals are to be integrated successfully into U.S. society and if the intercultural conflict and distress that result from adapting to a new culture are to be reduced. For example, several studies have demonstrated that many Asian American families suffer from intergenerational conflict, or tension between immigrant parents and their children due to generational differences in American cultural orientation (Drachman, Kwon-Ahn, & Paulino, 1996; Ying & Chao, 1996). To address this issue, Ying (1999) devised an intervention (Strengthening of Intergenerational/Intercultural Ties in Immigrant Chinese American Families) that aims to facilitate cultural understanding between Asian immigrant parents and their American-born children. With a pilot sample of 15 parents living in the San Francisco Bay area, the intervention was found to improve parental reports of their senses of efficacy and their relationships with their children.

Research on ethnic identity, acculturation, and cultural orientation may also reveal how multicultural individuals view specific interventions, which may in turn affect their rates of compliance with mental health treatment. For instance, evidence suggests that overseas-born Asian Americans are significantly less compliant with psychotherapy treatments than are American-born Asians (Sue, Fujino, Hu, Takeuchi, & Zane, 1991). This may be due to their distinct models of cultural orientation. Previous findings suggest that American-born Chinese have bidimensional models of cultural orientation; that is, their orientations to Chinese and American cultures are uncorrelated with each other (Tsai et al., 2000). Thus, American-born Chinese may view compliance with American treatments as not affecting how Chinese they are. Immigrant Chinese Americans, however, have unidimensional models of cultural orientation; that is, their Chinese and American orientations are inversely related to each other (Tsai et al., 2000). Thus, immigrant Chinese Americans may believe that complying with American treatments may decrease how Chinese they are. As a result, American-born Chinese may be more likely than immigrant Chinese to comply with American interventions.

To Uncover Heterogeneity Within Cultural Groups

Given the increasing diversity of the U.S. population, it is likely that variation within groups will become larger than variation among groups. Unfortunately, scholars interested in cultural influences on human behavior often overlook the enormous variation that exists within cultural groups, which may result in cultural stereotyping or the misattribution of group differences to culture. Studies of ethnic identity, acculturation, and cultural orientation are important because they highlight and elucidate such within-group differences. For example, across a series of studies, Jeanne L. Tsai and colleagues have demonstrated that within Asian American groups, place of birth has a significant impact on individuals' models of cultural orientation (Tsai, 2001; Tsai et al., 2000) and have demonstrated the effects of cultural orientation on various measures of psychological well-being (Tsai, Ying, & Lee, 2001; Ying, Lee, & Tsai, 2000).

To Elucidate the Mechanisms of Cultural Influence

Ethnic identity, acculturation, and cultural orientation are deserving of study because they reveal the mechanisms of cultural influence in two ways. First, studying these constructs ensures that differences among groups are due to cultural variables rather than to variables confounded with culture (e.g., socioeconomic status [SES]; Triandis, Kashima, Shimada, & Villareal,

1986). For instance, Tsai and Levenson (1997) compared reports of emotion made by Chinese Americans and European Americans living in the San Francisco Bay area during emotional conversations with their romantic partners and found that, consistent with Chinese values of emotional moderation, Chinese Americans' reports of emotion were less variable than those of European Americans. These differences could have been due to a variety of group differences (e.g., familiarity with the experimental setting). Therefore, to ensure that the differences were due to cultural variables, the authors looked at the correlation between acculturation to American culture and reports of emotion among Chinese Americans. As expected, the less acculturated to American culture Chinese Americans were, the less variable were their reports of emotion.

Second, because measures of ethnic identity, acculturation, and cultural orientation include multiple aspects of culture (e.g., language, social affiliation, and attitudes), they can illuminate the specific means by which cultural values, customs, and norms are transmitted to and influence the individual. For example, Ying, Lee, and Tsai (2000) found that for American-born Chinese living in a region in which there is a significant Chinese-speaking community, cultural orientation in the domain of language predicted participants' sense of coherence (the degree to which the world is experienced as manageable, meaningful, and comprehensible; Antonovsky, 1987), whereas cultural orientation in the domains of social affiliation and attitudes did not. By comparison, for immigrant Chinese living in the same community, cultural orientation in all three domains influenced sense of coherence. These findings suggest that for American-born Chinese, language is the primary mediator through which culture may influence individuals' experiences of their environments, whereas for immigrant Chinese, cultural influences are also transmitted through social affiliation and attitudes.

Given the importance of studying ethnic identity, acculturation, and cultural orientation, it is not surprising that the number of publications on ethnic identity, acculturation, and cultural orientation from 1990 to 1999 (2,867 journal articles and chapters) is more than twice as large as that of the previous decade (1,409 journal articles and chapters).[2] In all likelihood, this number will continue to increase in the decades to come. In the next section we briefly review what is known about these constructs, particularly as they pertain to Asian Americans. Rather than provide a comprehensive review of existing studies, we describe dominant themes in the literature to lay the foundation for the main purpose of our chapter, which is to propose ways in which researchers should study ethnic identity, acculturation, and cultural orientation in the future.

---

[2]To calculate these figures we searched the PsycINFO database, using *acculturation, assimilation, cultural orientation,* and *ethnic identity* as keywords. We included non-English publications but excluded dissertations.

WHAT IS CURRENTLY KNOWN?

The existing literature on ethnic identity, acculturation, and cultural orientation in Asian Americans has revolved around three main topics: (a) the applicability to Asian Americans of popular models of ethnic identity development; (b) the dimensionality for Asian Americans of cultural orientation and acculturation; and (c) the relationships among ethnic identity, acculturation, cultural orientation, and various indicators of mental health. To study these topics, most researchers have measured ethnic identity, cultural orientation, and acculturation with self-report questionnaires.

Applicability to Asian Americans of Ethnic Identity Development Models

Phinney (1989, 1990) has proposed a model of ethnic identity development that is based on Marcia's (1993) model of identity formation in adolescents. According to Phinney's model, individuals move from one stage of identity development to another; these transitions are a function of individuals' psychological maturity and exposure to different life experiences. During late childhood and adolescence, individuals are at either the *diffuse* stage (where there is a lack of commitment toward, and no exploration of, one's ethnic identity) or the *foreclosed* stage (where there is commitment to an ascribed ethnic identity, without exploration of the meaning of that identity). Individuals may enter the *moratorium* stage, where they re-examine their ethnic identity and explore its meanings before committing to the same or a different ethnic identity. After intense exploration, individuals may commit to an ethnic identity, at which point they have entered the *achieved* stage. On the basis of a content analysis of participants' essays on the topic of growing up Asian American, Ying and Lee (1999) found that the ethnic identity development of a sample of 342 American-born and immigrant Asian American adolescents living in the San Francisco Bay area followed Phinney's model. These results are consistent with those of Phinney and Chavira (1992), which also demonstrated that Phinney's model is applicable to Asian American high school students living in Los Angeles. More longitudinal studies, however, are needed to determine definitively whether individuals move from one stage to the next over time.

Dimensionality of Cultural Orientation and Acculturation

The two most popular models of cultural orientation and acculturation are the *unidimensional* model and the *bidimensional* model. The unidimensional model was initially developed to describe the process by which European immigrants became more American during the late 1800s and early 1900s (Gordon, 1964). This model assumes that one cultural orientation is inversely related to the other (i.e., the more oriented one is to Culture A, the less oriented he or she is to Culture B). The bidimensional model was a product of the increased ethnic consciousness brought forth by the civil rights movement and reflected an emerging emphasis on the value of multiculturalism. This model assumes that cultural orientations are independent of each other (i.e., the degree to which one is oriented to Culture A is unrelated to the degree to which one is oriented to Culture B). Berry (1980) provided a classification of acculturation strategies that incorporates both models; in his scheme, immigrants may be strongly oriented to their host culture and only weakly oriented to their heritage culture (assimilation), strongly oriented to the heritage culture and only weakly oriented to the host culture (separation), weakly oriented to both cultures (marginalization), and strongly oriented to both cultures (integration). Because both unidimensional and bidimensional models have received various criticisms (see Tsai & Chentsova-Dutton, in press), researchers have attempted to determine the conditions under which each model is applicable.

In our own studies of Chinese Americans living on the West coast (Tsai et al., 2000) and of Hmong Americans living in the Midwest (Tsai, 2001), we tested the unidimensional and bidimensional models by measuring the relationship between reported orientation to Chinese/Hmong culture and reported orientation to American culture. Our findings suggest that place of birth (a proxy for cultural exposure and experience) may determine which model best describes self-reported cultural orientation. More specifically, our findings suggest that American-born Asians have a bidimensional model of cultural orientation, whereas overseas-born Asian Americans have a unidimensional model of cultural orientation.

Ryder, Alden, and Paulhus (2000) also tested the unidimensional and bidimensional models, but they used an approach that was different from Tsai et al.'s (2000). Ryder et al. examined whether the unidimensional or bidimensional models best described different measures of psychological and social functioning in three samples of Chinese living in Canada (greater than 50% of these samples were immigrants). They administered separate self-report measures of unidimensional cultural orientation–acculturation, bidimensional cultural orientation–acculturation, and various measures of psychological and social functioning and found that the bidimensional model better captured relations between cultural orientation–acculturation and the various psychological indexes than did the unidimensional model. It is interesting that Ryder et al. also found that although orientations to host and native cultures were negatively correlated in the first generation, they were not correlated in subsequent generations, supporting the findings of Tsai et al. (2000). Recently, Abe-Kim, Okazaki, and Goto (2001) found that a multidimensional model best characterized the relationships between levels of acculturation and cultural variables such as individualism–collectivism, loss of face, and impression management for a sample of Asian American college students. Similarly, Lieber, Chin, Nihira, and Mink (2001) found that bidimensional approaches to acculturation and ethnic identity were better predictors of life satisfaction among Chinese immigrants than were unidimensional models. Thus, these studies suggest that specific relationships between cultural orientation and psychological and social functioning may be lost if one assumes only a unidimensional perspective.

Relationships Between Ethnic Identity, Acculturation, and Cultural Orientation and Mental Health

Over the past 20 years, much research has focused on the relationship between ethnic identity, acculturation, cultural orientation, and various indicators of psychological well-being. The focus of these studies has been on which stage of ethnic identity, type of acculturation strategy, or type of cultural orientation is related to the most positive psychological outcome. Although the findings have been mixed, for the most part they support Phinney's (1990) model of ethnic identity development, Berry's (1980) model of acculturation, and the assumption that high levels of orientation to different cultures is optimal. For example, in a sample of predominantly American-born Asian, African American, and Hispanic minority adolescents, Martinez and Dukes (1997) found that individuals with an achieved ethnic identity had higher levels of self-esteem than those who were still exploring or had not yet examined their ethnic identities. Another study found that orientation to Vietnamese culture was associated with increased self-esteem for adult Vietnamese immigrants living in Australia (Nesdale, Rooney, & Smith, 1997), and another found that decreased identification with Vietnamese culture was associated with increased levels of depression for mostly foreign-born Vietnamese American college students living in the Midwest.

Consistent with Berry's (1995) model, integrated acculturation appears to be associated with higher levels of psychological adjustment than other acculturation strategies (Berry & Kim, 1988; Szapocznik & Kurtines, 1980; Ward & Kennedy, 1994). In a similar study, Ying (1995) investigated the relationship between cultural orientation strategies and well-being for a community sample of Chinese American adults living in San Francisco and found that being oriented to both cultures was more psychologically adaptive than being oriented to only one. For example, participation in Chinese and American activities was associated with less depression, greater life satisfaction, more positive affect, and less negative affect than was exclusive participation in Chinese activities. Leiber et al. (2001) found that being bicultural (i.e., being highly acculturated and having a strong Asian identity) was associated with higher SES, which together enhanced positive life satisfaction in Chinese immigrants.

Findings from other studies, however, tell a different story. Phinney, Madden, and Santos (1998) found no relationship between cultural orientation and levels of depression, anxiety, and self-esteem in a sample of Armenian, Mexican American, and Vietnamese (mostly immigrant) adolescents living in Los Angeles. Verkuyten and Lay (1998) reported that ethnic identity was unrelated to personal self-esteem (feelings of regard for the self), life satisfaction, and mood for Chinese adolescents living in the Netherlands who were second generation or who had migrated to the Netherlands before the age of 2 years. Vollebergh and Huiberts (1997) found in a sample of students in the Netherlands that included Asian secondary school students that minority students who demonstrated integrated acculturation did not differ from those with separated acculturation in reported levels of depression, stress, or well-being. Leiber et al. (2001) found that separated and bicultural individuals did not differ in reported quality of life in the domains of friendship, finances, or community. Thus, although many studies support popular models of ethnic identity development, acculturation, and cultural orientation, some studies do not. Single-item measures of ethnic identity were most frequently used in these studies. Thus, it is possible that the construct of ethnic identity was not sampled adequately to demonstrate relationships between ethnic identity and psychological health. A host of other factors, such as heterogeneity in Asian groups and in their cultural contexts, may also account for these findings; however, it also is possible that popular models of ethnic identity development, acculturation, and cultural orientation should be revised to account for recent findings.

Researchers clearly have learned a substantial amount about ethnic identity, acculturation, and cultural orientation from studies conducted in the past few decades. Researchers should continue to examine whether existing models of ethnic identity, acculturation, and cultural orientation apply to Asian Americans and how different stages of ethnic identity and types of acculturation–cultural orientation affect psychological and social functioning. There are many other questions, however, that remain to be answered, all of which stem from existing studies and methods of examining ethnic identity, acculturation, and cultural orientation. We dedicate the rest of this chapter to a discussion of these questions. We begin with the methodological questions and end with conceptual ones. For each question we present possible solutions; in some cases we illustrate these solutions with findings from our own research.

HOW SHOULD RESEARCHERS STUDY ETHNIC IDENTITY, ACCULTURATION, AND CULTURAL ORIENTATION IN THE FUTURE?

Methodological Questions

In this section we introduce three methodological questions that deserve further study: (a) What instruments should be used? (b) can researchers move beyond self-report measures? and (c) are there other ways of measuring changes in ethnic identity, acculturation, and cultural orientation?

What Instruments Should Be Used?

With the exception of the Suinn–Lew Asian Self-Identity Acculturation Rating Scale, the lack of commonly accepted measures of ethnic identity, acculturation, and cultural orientation makes comparison of results across studies virtually impossible. Agreement among researchers about which instruments to use with specific cultural groups clearly would overcome this problem. It is unfortunate that no studies have empirically examined whether one instrument is better than another for use with a particular cultural group. Furthermore, one's research question will determine which instrument is the most appropriate one to use. For example, if researchers are interested in examining individuals' feelings about their relationships to their ethnic groups, or the meaning of ethnic group membership, it makes sense to use interviews rather than forced-choice questionnaires. However, if researchers are interested in specific behaviors, they may choose to use questionnaires, which are more efficient and less time and labor intensive. In this case, researchers should clearly articulate to their participants the exact behaviors of interest. For instance, if researchers are examining the effects for members of different cultural groups of socializing with European Americans on attitudes toward American culture, then they should clearly articulate the specific form of socialization to which they are referring. Two different cultural groups may report socializing "a lot" with European Americans, but for one group *socializing* may refer to talking with coworkers, whereas for the other group *socializing* may refer to dating European Americans. This example illustrates a common problem of equivalence in measuring aspects of cultural orientation by means of self-report measures. What are the ways to surmount such problems? In the next section we describe methodological innovations that may aid researchers in assessing constructs such as "socializing" in different cultural groups.

Can Researchers Move Beyond Self-Report Measures?

Most measures of ethnic identity, acculturation, and cultural orientation are self-report questionnaires. Although these instruments have the advantage of easy administration, they also experience the common biases of self-report (e.g., invalid responses due to limited self-understanding or the desire to give socially acceptable responses). Thus, assessments of ethnic identity, acculturation, and cultural orientation that include more than the target individual's perspective and that are behavioral are needed.

One possible method is the *Q-sort technique*, which has been used successfully in the assessment of personality (Block, 1971; Westen & Shedler,

1999). With Q-sort techniques an individual must determine how well various statements describe him- or herself or another person. Each statement is given a particular weight, based on how characteristic the statement is of the target individual. Moreover, individuals are given a fixed distribution so that only a limited number of statements can receive a given weight. This technique may be used to identify patterns of ethnic identification and cultural orientation. For example, Davis (1997) used this method in his study of a Basque sample to examine the relative importance their ethnicity, language, and geographic location assumed in their lives. This method can also be used to create composite profiles of individuals' ethnic identification or cultural orientation; that is, in addition to having individuals sort statements about themselves, other people in their lives (e.g., family members, close friends, coworkers) may also sort statements about them. Individual profiles may be averaged to create a composite profile of the individual, which may be more accurate than any one profile. Finally, this technique could be used to compare individuals' perceptions of themselves with others' perceptions of them. For example, this technique might allow researchers to measure disparities between how Asian American children view themselves and how their parents view them.

Another promising method is the *sociometric task*, which is often used by developmental psychologists to assess the status of children and adolescents within peer groups. Like Q-sort techniques, sociometric techniques allow one to obtain more comprehensive assessments that are based on participants' self-reports and the reports of others. This method also can provide information regarding the relative position of individual members in terms of their cultural orientations. One problem with existing instruments is that they do not indicate a clear reference group. As a result, when rating oneself, an individual may compare him- or herself with a recently immigrated Chinese American, whereas another may compare him- or herself with a fourth-generation American-born Chinese American. In sociometric tasks the reference group is clear, which ensures that participants are using the same criteria when making their ratings. For example, the effects of socializing for members of different cultural groups can be examined in reference to specific social environments. Two principal sociometric methods have been validated and widely used (Frederickson & Furnham, 1998; Maassen, Goossens, & Bokhorst, 1998). In one method, children are asked to provide a certain number of nominations of their peers with whom they would most (or least) like to undertake a particular activity. In the other method, children are asked to provide ratings or forced-choice evaluations of each of their peers. For our purposes, a group of individuals may be asked to nominate which of their peers are the "most Chinese" and which are the "most American" to obtain a rating of cultural orientation for each of the group members.

Behavioral and physiological measures of ethnic identity, acculturation, and cultural orientation should also be used, particularly to capture the emotional aspects of these dimensions. For example, using the Facial Action Coding System (Ekman, 1978), we coded the emotional facial behavior of American-born and overseas-born Hmong college students during the 10-s period after they were asked "What does it mean to be Hmong?" and "What does it mean to be American?" Although the two groups did not differ in their reported pride in being Hmong or American (as assessed by a self-report inventory), they did differ in their facial behavior. More American-born Hmong than overseas-born Hmong frowned in response to the question "What does it mean to be American?" (36% of American-born Hmong compared to 9% of overseas-born Hmong); $\chi^2(1, N = 42) = 4.59, p < .05$. This difference puts in doubt the validity of the self-report findings. For example, it is possible that more American-born Hmong than overseas-born Hmong felt concerned about being American, perhaps because they are more aware of their status as minorities. Thus, behavioral coding may capture the complexity of participants' feelings about their cultural identity that their responses to cultural orientation inventories cannot. Physiological measures (e.g., heart rate, skin conductance activity) may also be used to capture the emotional responses of participants when asked about their ethnic identity, acculturation, and cultural orientation (see Tsai & Levenson, 1997, for more information). Of course, in future studies researchers must first determine the conditions under which behavioral and physiological measures have greater predictive value than self-report methods.

Are There Other Indicators of Change in Cultural Orientation?

Most of the existing research assesses changes in cultural orientation in terms of participation in cultural activities, feelings about the culture, and other domains of life experience. However, cultural exposure also changes one's values, beliefs, and conceptions of the world. For example, Ying (1988, 1990) has examined the conceptions of depression held by unacculturated members of the Chinese American community in San Francisco's Chinatown. She found that, consistent with a lack of separation between mind and body in Chinese culture, this sample of Chinese Americans viewed the somatic, affective, and interpersonal aspects of depression as inseparable. This is in stark contrast to European Americans, who clearly differentiate among the somatic, affective, and interpersonal aspects of depression. Recently, Ying, Lee, Tsai, Yeh, and Huang (2000) examined the conceptions of depression held by a sample of bicultural Chinese American college students. They found that this sample of Chinese Americans held conceptions of depression that resembled those of European Americans, suggesting that with increased exposure to American culture Chinese Americans adopt European American conceptions of depression. In future work a variety of techniques (e.g., similarity and consensus tasks) should be used to measure how cultural orientation and acculturation affect the way individuals perceive and understand their worlds and what values and beliefs they hold.

Conceptual Questions

Armed with the answers to the methodological problems described earlier, researchers may be able to address central questions about ethnic identity, acculturation, and cultural orientation that have hitherto received limited attention. We discuss these questions next.

Are Researchers' Notions of "Ethnic Identity" Culturally Constructed?

Markus and Kitayama (1998) argued that cultural values, norms, and traditions influence how one views what it means to be a person. In Western cultures people are "rooted in traits and motives," (p. 65) whereas in Asian cultures people are situated in a web of social roles and interpersonal relationships. For example, Kanagawa, Cross, and Markus (2001) asked Japanese and American participants to respond to the question "Who am I?" 20 times. Americans described themselves in terms of pure psychological attributes (e.g., "I am outgoing") and attitudes (e.g., "I am not a racist") more than Japanese, whereas Japanese described themselves in terms of activities ("I have a part-time job") more than did Americans. It is possible that studies of ethnic identity are based on Western cultural assumptions about what it means to be a person that may not apply to members of other ethnic groups. For instance, in examining identity, American psychologists emphasize traits rather than social roles. However, it is possible that for Asian Americans social roles may be an important part of identity or self-perceptions.

To examine whether Asian Americans and European Americans differ in their social roles, Tsai, Chentsova-Dutton, Idzelis, Miranda, and Hama (2001) compared 144 Chinese American (American-born and immigrant) and 170 European American descriptions of the roles that composed their lives. At the time of the study, the participants were all living in the San Francisco Bay area. Participants completed Cowan and Cowan's Pie (1975); in this task, participants were asked to list all of the roles that composed their lives. They were then asked to divide a 360-degree Pie, which represented the totality of their lives, into separate pieces that reflected the significance of each role in their lives. Participants completed two Pies: one that reflected their current lives and another that reflected how they would ideally like their lives to be. When we compared the roles that participants assumed in their lives, we found interesting differences between Chinese Americans and European Americans. Chi-square analyses revealed that a greater percentage of Chinese Americans than European Americans mentioned the daughter/son role as composing part of their identities (Chinese Americans: 89.6%, European Americans: 81.4%), $\chi^2(1, N = 316) = 4.15$, $p < .05$. Moreover, among participants who did mention the daughter/son role, Chinese Americans allotted a significantly greater portion of their Pie to it than did European Americans, $F (1, 257) = 8.72, p = .003$ (scores were transformed into square roots to meet parametric assumptions; European Americans: 6.34 [SD = 2.07], Chinese Americans: 7.20 [SD = 2.62]). To illustrate this difference, Pies of 1 participant from each group are shown in Figure 2.1.

Moreover, the more "Chinese" Chinese Americans reported being (based on their responses to the General Ethnicity Questionnaire–Chinese version, a measure of orientation to Chinese culture; Tsai et al., 2000), the more they defined themselves in terms of the daughter/son role ($r = .24, p < .01$). In addition, in their ideal Pies, compared to European Americans, a significantly greater percentage of Chinese Americans mentioned the daughter/son role, $\chi^2(1, N = 316) = 3.08, p < .05$, one-tailed, and, among those who did, Chinese Americans reported that they would like their roles as daughters and sons to assume larger pieces of the Pie than did European Americans. (Scores were transformed into square roots to meet parametric assumptions; Chinese Americans: 7.79 [SD = 2.40], European Americans: 6.93 [SD = 2.18]; $F[1, 253] = 9.00, p < .01$.) These group differences are consistent with descriptions of Chinese culture as placing greater value than American culture on familialism and filial piety. Thus, thinking of identity as comprising roles rather than traits revealed interesting differences between Chinese and European Americans that may not have emerged had identity been defined in terms of traits only. Future research should begin to explore the other ways in which Western cultural assumptions may obscure an understanding of identity in Asian American groups.

What Does It Mean to Be a Member of a Particular Ethnic or Cultural Group?

In our questionnaires, we routinely ask our respondents to indicate their ethnicity or cultural heritage, or to rate how oriented they are to a particular culture, across different life domains (e.g., activities). Do we know, however, what our respondents mean when they indicate that they are "very Asian"? Does "being American" mean the same thing for members of different ethnic groups in the United States? Moreover, researchers often do not account for the fact that the meaning of ethnic identities may change over time. For instance, the term *Asian American* arose from an acknowledgement that individuals of various Asian cultures, although different along a number of dimensions, share a common status as a minority group in the United States. When the term emerged in the 1960s it held primarily political significance; since then, however, the term has gained cultural, social, and psychological significance. For example, Kibria (1997) found that since the creation of the term *Asian American*, second-generation Korean and Chinese Americans living in Los Angeles and Boston have begun to view other Asian Americans as viable marital partners with whom they share common cultural values as well as a common status.

Chinese American Female

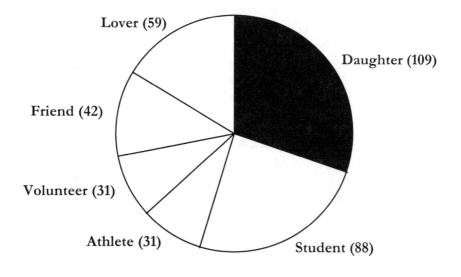

Lover (59)

Daughter (109)

Friend (42)

Volunteer (31)

Athlete (31)

Student (88)

European American Female

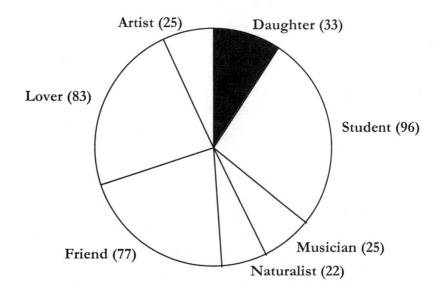

Artist (25)

Daughter (33)

Lover (83)

Student (96)

Friend (77)

Musician (25)

Naturalist (22)

Figure 2.1. Pies of a Chinese American female participant (top) and European American female participant (bottom). Numbers in parentheses are degrees.

Remarkably few studies have asked these questions, despite the fact that the answers to them are extremely important to an understanding of ethnic identity, acculturation, and cultural orientation. For example, if members of various American ethnic groups view differently what "being American" means, one cannot compare their responses to an American identity questionnaire unless one lets the participants know ahead of time what one means by "being American."

In several studies, we and our colleagues have attempted to understand the meaning of ethnic identity for Asian American and European American groups. For example, Tsai, Mortensen, Wong, and Hess (in press) compared American-born and immigrant Hmong and European American notions of what it means to "be American." Participants (all of whom lived in the Midwest) were asked to describe what "being American" meant to them. Their responses were coded with a system devised by Tsai (2001). A sample of codes and representative examples are provided in Table 2.1. Whereas Hmong viewed "being American" more in terms of customs and traditional behaviors, European Americans viewed "being American" more in terms of ethnic diversity and patriotism (see Figure 2.2).

These findings also held for Chinese Americans and European Americans living in California. We speculate that because Asian Americans are a minority in the United States and must adjust to mainstream American culture, the term *American* conjures up notions of mainstream customs and traditions. European Americans, however, are members of the majority culture; as a result, the meaning of being American is abstract and based on themes that they learned in school. It is interesting that both Asian Americans and European Americans described "being American" in terms of political ideology, which may speak to the pervasiveness of notions that the United States is a symbol of democracy and freedom. Thus, although the meaning of "being American" for Asian Americans and European Americans is similar in one way, it is different in others. It is likely that the meanings of "being American" or "being Chinese" also show significant within-group variability due to factors such as specific cultural background, reasons for migration, and time spent in the United States.

In the pie study described earlier, Tsai, Chentsova-Dutton, et al. (2001) found further suggestion that the meaning of "being American" might differ across ethnic groups. Whereas for European Americans an American orientation was significantly and positively correlated with the brother/sister role ($r = .26$, $p < .05$), it was negatively, although not significantly, correlated with the brother/sister role for Chinese Americans ($r = -.12$, $p > .20$). This is contrary to notions that American culture places more emphasis on independence and less emphasis on social relationships than does Chinese culture. It is possible that Chinese Americans, in trying to emulate American values of independence and individualism, actually become more stereotypically "American" than their European American counterparts. In

TABLE 2.1
Sample Codes and Representative Examples

Code	Representative example
Customs/traditional behavior	Having the American lifestyle
Ethnic diversity	The whole melting pot idea
Patriotism	To be proud is the essence of America
Political ideology	We have equal rights

any case, these findings, like those of Tsai et al. (2000), suggest that one should not assume that cultural terms, or the cultures themselves, have the same meaning across ethnic groups. In future studies researchers should invest substantial time understanding what ethnic identity, cultural orientation, acculturation, and other related constructs mean to research participants and ensuring that participants know what one means when one uses such terms.

Do These Processes Vary By Context, Domain, and Group?

Context. We have discussed how ethnic identity may be influenced by historical changes; however, it may also be influenced by more immediate forces, such as changes in situational or environmental social context. Social contexts vary in terms of how salient cultural values and norms are. For instance, the degree to which one feels oriented to Chinese culture may depend on whether one is surrounded by European Americans or by Chinese immigrants, whether one is speaking Chinese or English (Yang & Bond, 1980), or whether one is in the presence of an authority figure or a peer. In future studies researchers also need to examine the role of minority status in the development of ethnic identity by comparing Asian Americans residing in primarily Asian communities (e.g., Hawaii) versus in primarily European American communities. In addition, individuals may be more concerned about being evaluated and providing socially desirable responses in some contexts than in others. Unfortunately, few studies have explicitly examined the effect of social context on self-perceptions of ethnic identity, cultural orientation, and acculturation in Asian Americans.

Although the social context can be manipulated in ways that are obvious to participants (e.g., having another person present), it may be also informative to understand how changes in the social context may unconsciously or nonconsciously influence ethnic identity, acculturation, and cultural orientation. One way to assess the nonconscious influence of the social context is to use priming techniques. In previous literature, priming techniques have been used to elicit culturally consistent or stereotypically consistent behavior. For instance, Shih, Pittinsky, and Ambady (1999) found that when they primed Asian American identity by asking participants living on the East coast a variety of questions about their ethnicity, language proficiency, and

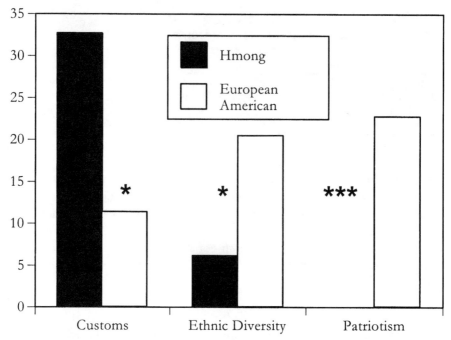

Figure 2.2. Percentages of respondents who mentioned customs/traditional behavior, ethnic diversity, patriotism, and political ideology when asked "What does being American mean to you?" *$p < .05$. **$p < .001$. (From Tsai et al., in press)

family history, Asian American females performed significantly better on math tests (consistent with the stereotype of Asian Americans as having superior quantitative skills) than when their identities were not primed. Similar techniques may also be used to illustrate how perceptions of ethnic identity, cultural orientation, and acculturation may be influenced by the social context. For example, Hong, Chiu, and Kung (1997) found that exposure to Chinese cultural icons through priming increased endorsement of Chinese values in Hong Kong students.

Berry (1995) emphasized that the process of acculturation and cultural adjustment depends on the larger socioenvironmental context. Specifically, he predicted that immigrants will have an easier time adjusting to their host culture if that culture is tolerant of cultural diversity and has resources to accommodate the immigrant groups. Similarly, the meaning of ethnic identity may be shaped by the larger socioenvironmental context. For instance, in our study of Asian American–European American differences in the meaning of American identity (Tsai, Mortensen, Wong, & Hess, in press), we included two samples: one from Minneapolis, where the vast majority of the population (88.2%) is European American, and another from the San Francisco Bay area, where 40.3% of the population is European American (U.S. Bureau of the Census, 1990). We found greater differences in the meaning of "being American" between Asian Americans and European Americans in the Minneapolis sample than between Asian Americans and European Americans in the San Francisco Bay area sample, perhaps because there is a more homogeneous mainstream American culture in the Midwest than on the West coast. Future research should explicitly examine how the socioenvironmental context influences ethnic identity, cultural orientation, and acculturation processes.

Finally, North American researchers often overlook the fact that the United States and Canada are not the only countries that house many ethnic groups. Europe, Russia, and China, for example, all include numerous Asian ethnic groups. Although studying ethnic identity in these countries poses additional difficulties, such studies may offer valuable insights about how individuals of Asian descent in North America are similar to or different from those in other parts of the world. For example, Lee, Falbo, Doh, and Park (2001) found that Koreans living in China are less likely to be bicultural (i.e., equally oriented to Korean culture and their host culture) than are Koreans living in the United States. The authors attributed this difference to the greater openness of American culture (relative to Chinese culture) to members of different cultural backgrounds.

Domain. Ethnic identity, acculturation, and cultural orientation have been described in the literature as comprising multiple domains. Although some of these domains are conceptually derived, there have been recent attempts to characterize the domains empirically through factor analysis (Roberts et al., 1999; Tsai et al., 2000). The domains that have been frequently described in the literature include cultural knowledge (Boski, 1992), positive and negative feelings toward one's ethnic group (Der-Karabetian & Ruiz, 1997), social affiliation preferences (Constantinou & Harvey, 1985), participation in culturally relevant activities (Phinney, 1990), linguistic preferences (Olmedo & Padilla, 1978; Ying, 1995), and political and ideological views and activity (Constantinou & Harvey, 1985).

Some domains may be more susceptible to acculturative processes than others (Ying, 1995). This domain-specific acculturation pattern has been termed *selective acculturation*. As immigrants or minority individuals adjust to life in their host culture, they may become highly oriented to the host culture in some of these domains but only weakly or not at all oriented in others. For example, an immigrant may learn to speak and understand English in order to succeed in his job, but outside of work he may continue to socialize exclusively with friends from his native culture. In fact, Ying (1995) found that immigrant Chinese American adults living in San Francisco were more likely to adopt American activities and speak English than to become close friends with Americans. Thus, rather than view acculturation as a general process, researchers should examine the domain-specific nature of acculturation. In addition, they should study other domains of life experience (e.g., political ideology, religious practices, values) in which individuals may actually become more rather than less oriented to their native cultures as they spend more time in their host cultures. Measures of such domains are becoming increasingly available (Wolfe, Yang, Wong, & Atkinson, 2001).

Groups. To advance an understanding of culture, researchers must broaden their samples. Most studies of ethnic identity, acculturation, and cultural orientation, including our own, have limited themselves to ethnic minority student populations. This may not only reflect the greater convenience of studying students compared to nonstudents, but it may demonstrate a bias toward Western models of development; that is, most models of identity development are at least partly based on Erik Erikson's theories, which portray identity formation as the major task of adolescence and young adulthood (Erikson, 1963). Remarkably little is known about ethnic identity, acculturation, and cultural orientation at other stages of the human life span, despite some evidence that ethnic identity has renewed meaning in old age (Simic, 1987). Thus, longitudinal studies are sorely needed to reveal how ethnic identity, acculturation, and cultural orientation change over time. In addition, although researchers often recognize the influence of ethnic identity on minority group members, they fail to acknowledge its influence on the majority group. Astonishingly little research has explored White or European American identity. This research is critical if researchers are to distinguish the effects of culture from those of minority–majority status and examine the generalizability of acculturation processes across different cultural contexts.

Moreover, the participants in our research studies are a select sample. Given that they are students and that research participation is voluntary, it is likely that individuals who participate in our studies are the ones most familiar with European American culture. Because individuals who are marginalized or separated from mainstream European American society are reluctant to participate in studies conducted by mainstream American institutions, we do not know how applicable our models of ethnic identity, acculturation, and cultural orientation are to them. Thus, to broaden the scope of our knowledge, researchers should actively try to include less acculturated individuals in their studies.

FUTURE RESEARCH DIRECTIONS

Much has been learned about ethnic identity, acculturation, and cultural orientation in the past few decades. Previous research has begun to answer basic questions about these constructs. Much more work is needed, however, if researchers are to learn more about a central aspect of identity, understand the psychology of multicultural groups, examine the tremendous variation that exists within groups, and reveal the mechanisms of cultural influence. In this chapter we suggested that researchers should

- Use greater care when using the terms *ethnic identity*, *acculturation*, and *cultural orientation* and when choosing specific instruments.
- Expand measures of these constructs to include behavioral and physiological methods and measures that do not rely solely on participants' reports (e.g., Q-sorts, sociometric tasks).
- Examine other indicators of change in cultural orientation, such as conceptions and beliefs.
- Consider cultural variation in notions of ethnic identity and the meaning of group membership.
- Consider how ethnic identity, acculturation, and cultural orientation processes vary by context (the immediate as well as the larger sociocultural context), domain (political ideology, values, and practices), and group (age, culture, and minority status).

It is our hope that in the years to come these methodological and conceptual directions will allow researchers to answer more difficult questions about how people relate to their cultural groups and cultural contexts.

REFERENCES

Abe-Kim, J., Okazaki, S., & Goto, S. (2001). Unidimensional versus multidimensional approaches to the assessment of acculturation for Asian American populations. *Cultural Diversity and Ethnic Minority Psychology, 7,* 232–246.

Alvarez, A., & Helms, J. E. (2001). Racial identity and reflected appraisals as influences on Asian Americans' racial adjustment. *Cultural Diversity and Ethnic Minority Psychology, 7,* 217–231.

Antonovsky, A. (1987). *Unraveling the mystery of health: How people manage stress and stay well.* San Francisco, CA: Jossey-Bass.

Berry, J. W. (1980). Acculturation as varieties of adaptation. In A. Padilla (Ed.), *Acculturation: Theory, models and some new findings* (pp. 9–25). Boulder, CO: Westview Press.

Berry, J. W. (1995). Psychology of acculturation. In N. R. Goldberger & J. B. Veroff (Eds.), *The culture and psychology reader* (pp. 457–488). New York: New York University Press.

Berry, J. W., & Kim, U. (1988). Acculturation and mental health. In P. R. Dasen, J. W. Berry, & N. Sartorius (Eds.), *Health and cross-cultural psychology: Towards applications* (pp. 207–236). London: Sage.

Block, J. (1971). *Lives through time.* Berkeley, CA: Bancroft.

Boski, P. (1992). In the homeland: National self-identity and well-being of Poles in Poland and in America. In S. Iwawaki, Y. Kashima, & K. Leung (Eds.), *Innovations in cross-cultural psychology* (pp. 199–213). Amsterdam: Swets & Zeitlinger.

Constantinou, S. T., & Harvey, M. E. (1985). Dimensional structure and intergenerational difference in ethnicity: The Greek Americans. *Sociology and Social Research, 69,* 234–254.

Cowan, C. P., & Cowan, P. A. (1975). *The PIE*. Unpublished instrument. Available from Department of Psychology, University of California, Berkeley, 3210 Tolman Hall, Berkeley, CA, 94720-1650.

Davis, T. C. (1997). Patterns of identity. *Nationalism and Ethnic Politics, 3,* 61–88.

Der-Karabetian, A., & Ruiz, Y. (1997). Affective bicultural and global–human identity scales for Mexican-American adolescents. *Psychological Reports, 80,* 1027–1039.

Drachman, D., Kwon-Ahn, Y. H., & Paulino, A. (1996). Migration and resettlement experiences of Dominican and Korean families. *Families in Society, 77,* 626–638.

Ekman, P. (1978). *Manual for the Facial Action Coding System.* San Francisco, CA: Human Interaction Laboratory.

Erikson, E. (1963). *Childhood and society* (3rd ed.). New York: Norton.

Frederickson, N. L., & Furnham, A. F. (1998). Use of sociometric techniques to assess the social status of mainstreamed children with learning disabilities. *Genetic, Social, and General Psychology Monographs, 124,* 381–433.

Gordon, M. M. (1964). *Assimilation in American life.* New York: Oxford University Press.

Hong, Y., Chiu, C., & Kung, T. (1997). Bringing culture out in front: Effects of cultural meaning system activation on social cognition. In K. Leung, U. Kim, S. Yamaguchi, & Y. Kashima (Eds.), *Progress in Asian social psychology* (Vol. 1, pp. 139–149). New York: Wiley.

Kanagawa, C., Cross, S. E., & Markus, H. R. (2001). "Who am I?" The cultural psychology of the conceptual self. *Personality and Social Psychology Bulletin, 27,* 90–103.

Kibria, N. (1997). The construction of "Asian American": Reflections on intermarriage and ethnic identity among second-generation Chinese and Korean Americans. *Ethnic and Racial Studies, 20,* 523–544.

Lee, R. M., Falbo, T., Doh, H. S., & Park, S. Y. (2001). The Korean diasporic experience: Measuring ethnic identity in the United States. *Cultural Diversity and Ethnic Minority Psychology, 7,* 207–216.

Lieber, E., Chin, D., Nihira, K., & Mink, I. R. (2001). Holding on and letting go: Identity and acculturation among Chinese immigrants. *Cultural Diversity and Ethnic Minority Psychology, 7,* 247–273.

Luborsky, M., & Rubinstein, R. L. (1990). Ethnic identity and bereavement in later life: The case of older widowers. In J. Sokolovsky (Ed.), *The cultural context of aging: Worldwide perspectives* (pp. 229–240). New York: Bergin & Garvey.

Maassen, G. H., Goossens, F. A., & Bokhorst, J. (1998). Ratings as validation of sociometric status determined by nominations in longitudinal research. *Social Behavior and Personality, 26,* 259–274.

Marcia, J. E. (1993). The ego identity status approach to ego identity. In J. E. Marcia, A. S. Waterman, D. R. Matteson, S. L. Archer, & J. L. Orlofsky (Eds.), *Ego identity: A handbook for psychosocial research* (pp. 3–21). New York: Springer-Verlag.

Markus, H. R., & Kitayama, S. (1998). The cultural psychology of personality. *Journal of Cross-Cultural Psychology, 29*, 63–87.

Martinez, R. O., & Dukes, R. L. (1997). The effects of ethnic identity, ethnicity, and gender on adolescent well-being. *Journal of Youth and Adolescence, 26*, 503–516.

Myerhoff, B. (1978). A symbol perfected in death: Continuity and ritual in the life and death of an elderly Jew. In B. Myeroff & A. Simic (Eds.), *Life's career—Aging: Cultural variations on growing old* (pp. 163–206). Beverly Hills, CA: Sage.

Nesdale, D., Rooney, R., & Smith, L. (1997). Migrant ethnic identity and psychological distress. *Journal of Cross-Cultural Psychology, 28*, 569–588.

Nguyen, L., & Peterson, C. (1993). Depressive symptoms among Vietnamese-American college students. *Journal of Social Psychology, 133*, 65–71.

Olmedo, E. L., & Padilla, A. M. (1978). Empirical and construct validation of a measure of acculturation for Mexican Americans. *Journal of Social Psychology, 105*, 179–187.

Phinney, J. S. (1989). Stages of ethnic identity development in minority group adolescents. *Journal of Early Adolescence, 9*, 34–49.

Phinney, J. S. (1990). Ethnic identity in adolescents and adults: Review of research. *Psychological Bulletin, 108*, 499–514.

Phinney, J. S. (1992). The Multigroup Ethnic Identity Measure: A new scale for use with diverse groups. *Journal of Adolescence, 7*, 156–176.

Phinney, J. S., & Chavira, V. (1992). Ethnic identity and self-esteem: An exploratory longitudinal study. *Journal of Adolescence, 15*, 271–281.

Phinney, J. S., Madden, T., & Santos, L. J. (1998). Psychological variables as predictors of perceived ethnic discrimination among minority and immigrant adolescents. *Journal of Applied Social Psychology, 28*, 937–953.

Roberts, R. E., Phinney, J. S., Masse, L. C., Chen, Y. R., Roberts, C. R., & Romero, A. (1999). The structure of ethnic identity of young adolescents from diverse ethnocultural groups. *Journal of Early Adolescence, 19*, 301–322.

Ryder, A. G., Alden, L. E., & Paulhus, D. L. (2000). Is acculturation unidimensional or bidimensional? A head-to-head comparison in the prediction of personality, self-construal, and adjustment. *Journal of Personality and Social Psychology, 79*, 49–65.

Shih, M., Pittinsky, T. L., & Ambady, N. (1999). Stereotype susceptibility: Identity salience and shifts in quantitative performance. *Psychological Science, 10*, 80–83.

Simic, A. (1987). Ethnicity as a career for the elderly: The Serbian–American case. *Journal of Applied Gerontology, 6*, 113–126.

Smith, A. D. (1986). *The ethnic origins of nations.* New York: Basil Blackwell.

Sue, S., Fujino, D., Hu, L., Takeuchi, D., & Zane, N. (1991). Community mental health services for ethnic minority groups: A test of the cultural responsiveness hypothesis. *Journal of Consulting and Clinical Psychology, 59*, 533–540.

Suinn, R. M., Rickard-Figueroa, K., Lew, S., & Vigil, P. (1987). The Suinn–Lew Asian Self-Identity Acculturation Scale: An initial report. *Educational and Psychological Measurement, 47*, 401–407.

Szapocznik, J., & Kurtines, W. M. (1980). Biculturalism and adjustment among Cuban Americans. In A. Padilla (Ed.), *Recent advances in acculturation research: Theory models and some new findings* (pp. 139–157). Boulder, CO: Westview.

Takei, M. (1998). Collective memory as the key to national and ethnic identity: The case of Cambodia. *Nationalism and Ethnic Politics, 4*(3), 59–78.

Triandis, H. C., Kashima, Y., Shimada, E., & Villareal, M. (1986). Acculturation indices as a means of conforming cultural differences. *International Journal of Psychology, 21*, 43–70.

Tsai, J. L. (2001). Cultural orientation of Hmong young adults. *Journal of Human Behavior in the Social Environment, 3–4*, 99–114.

Tsai, J. L., & Chentsova-Dutton, Y. (in press). Models of cultural orientation: Differences between American-born and overseas-born Asians. In K. Kurasaki, S. Okazaki, & S. Sue (Eds.), *Asian American mental health: Assessment theories and methods.* Dordrecht, the Netherlands: Kluwer Academic.

Tsai, J. L., Chentsova-Dutton, Y., Idzelis, M., Miranda, C., & Hama, Y. (2001). *Chinese-Americans and European-American self-identification.* Manuscript in preparation.

Tsai, J. L., & Levenson, R. W. (1997). Cultural influences of emotional responding: Chinese American and European American dating couples during interpersonal conflict. *Journal of Cross-Cultural Psychology, 28*, 600–625.

Tsai, J. L., Mortensen, H., Wong, Y., & Hess, D. (in press). What does "being American" mean? Differences between Asian American and European-American young adults. *Journal of Ethnic Minority and Cultural Diversity.*

Tsai, J. L., Ying, Y., & Lee, P. A. (2000). The meaning of "being Chinese" and "being American": Variation among Chinese American young adults. *Journal of Cross-Cultural Psychology, 31*, 302–322.

Tsai, J. L., Ying, Y., & Lee, P. A. (2001). Cultural predictors of self-esteem: A study of Chinese American female and male young adults. *Cultural Diversity and Ethnic Minority Psychology, 7*, 284–297.

U.S. Bureau of the Census. (1990). *Population profile of the United States.* Washington, DC: U.S. Government Printing Office.

Verkuyten, M., & Lay, C. (1998). Ethnic minority identity and psychological well-being: The mediating role of collective self-esteem. *Journal of Applied Social Psychology, 28*, 1969–1986.

Vollebergh, W. A. M., & Huiberts, A. M. (1997). Stress and ethnic identity in ethnic minority youth in the Netherlands. *Social Behavior and Personality, 25*, 249–258.

Ward, C., & Kennedy, A. (1994). Acculturation strategies, psychological adjustment, and sociocultural competence during cross-cultural transitions. *International Journal of Intercultural Relations, 18*, 329–343.

Westen, D., & Shedler, J. (1999). Revising and assessing Axis II, Part I: Developing a clinically and empirically valid assessment method. *American Journal of Psychiatry, 156*, 258–272.

Wolfe, M. M., Yang, P., Wong, E. C., & Atkinson, D. R. (2001). Design and development of the European American Values Scale for Asian Americans. *Cultural Diversity and Ethnic Minority Psychology, 7*, 274–283.

Yang, K. S., & Bond, M. H. (1980). Ethnic affirmation by Chinese bilinguals. *Journal of Cross-Cultural Psychology, 11*, 411–425.

Ying, Y. (1988). Depressive symptomatology among Chinese Americans as measured by the CES–D. *Journal of Clinical Psychology, 44*, 739–746.

Ying, Y. (1990). Explanatory models of major depression and implications for help-seeking among immigrant Chinese-American women. *Culture, Medicine, and Psychiatry, 14*, 393–408.

Ying, Y. (1995). Cultural orientation and psychological well-being in Chinese Americans. *American Journal of Community Psychology, 23*, 893–911.

Ying, Y. (1999). Strengthening intergenerational/intercultural ties in migrant families: A new intervention for parents. *Journal of Community Psychology, 27*, 89–96.

Ying, Y., & Chao, C. (1996). Intergenerational relationship in Iu Mien families. *Amerasia Journal, 22(3)*, 47–64.

Ying, Y., & Lee, P. A. (1999). The development of ethnic identity in Asian-American adolescents: Status and outcome. *American Journal of Orthopsychiatry, 69*, 194–208.

Ying, Y., Lee, P. A, & Tsai, J. L. (2000). Cultural orientation and racial discrimination: Predictors of coherence in Chinese American young adults. *Journal of Community Psychology, 28*, 427–442.

Ying, Y., Lee, P. A., Tsai, J. L., Yeh, Y., & Huang, J. S. (2000). The conception of depression in Chinese American college students. *Cultural Diversity and Ethnic Minority Psychology, 6*, 183–195.

3

PERSPECTIVES ON ASIAN AMERICAN DEVELOPMENT

LYNN OKAGAKI AND KATHRYN E. BOJCZYK

> My mother speaks pretty much only Japanese. I have learned a broken
> Japanese. As an adult, I have returned to it more, mostly to understand
> my mother better. And in a way, in studying the language . . . I've
> come to understand myself a lot more and how the Japanese language
> develops and molds the character of the people . . . I have found out
> the ways that I am Japanese and the ways I am American. (Schneider,
> Hieshima, Lee, & Plank, 1994, pp. 346–347)

Twenty years ago, Bronfenbrenner and Crouter (1982) observed that much of the existing work on contextual influences on development was limited to descriptions of differences between groups of children or families residing at different "social addresses" (e.g., racial or socioeconomic groups, two-parent vs. single-parent families). They exhorted developmental psychologists to go beyond these social address models to explore the processes that led to variations in child outcomes across social addresses. Following

We thank Sumie Okazaki, Gordon Nagayama Hall, Ruby Takanishi, Karen Diamond, and Susan Kontos for comments on earlier versions of this chapter.

their lead, we have attempted to identify underlying processes that make the development of Asian American children "Asian American."

For the most part, developmental psychologists have not examined normative development among ethnic and racial groups vis-à-vis physiological processes. Instead, most research has been based on what Bukowski and Sippola (1998) called a *local knowledge model*. According to this view, researchers have assumed that the basic processes of development are largely universal and that local culture provides the goals and the social constructs that lead to variations in developmental outcomes across cultural groups. In the studies we have reviewed, what makes Asian American development distinctive are (a) the processes that support the goals and social constructs that emerge from Asian American beliefs and values and (b) the experiences that derive from immigrating to a new culture and having minority status in the host culture. These factors emerged repeatedly throughout the research.

Readers of this chapter should keep in mind an important caveat: Although the term *Asian American* is used throughout the chapter, as has been emphasized in this book and elsewhere (e.g., Chan, 1991; Sue & Okazaki, 1990; Trueba, Cheng, & Ima, 1993; Uba, 1994), great diversity is reflected *across* Asian American groups and *within* these groups. Where the existing research allows distinctions among subgroups to be made, we have done so. In many cases, Asian Americans have been identified only as Asian Americans, and it was not possible to make finer distinctions.

SOCIAL DEVELOPMENT

The deeper the love, the greater the correction.

—Chinese proverb

In this section we have included illustrative studies related to parenting and parent–child relationships, development of autonomy, moral development, and peer relationships. Because other chapters in this volume examine ethnic identity, aggression, aging, and mental health issues, we have not addressed these topics, except to note a few developmental studies on ethnic identity and self-concept. It is unfortunate that developmental psychologists have conducted very little research on many areas of normative social development among Asian Americans, such as emotional development and regulation, empathy, perspective taking, or friendship relationships. Throughout this section, ways in which Asian American definitions of social constructs and goals are believed to result in differences in social relationships and social expectations and the effects of immigration, acculturation, and minority status on various aspects of social development are highlighted.

Parenting

Most research comparing Asian American and European American parents has been conducted within the framework of Western psychological constructs (e.g., parenting styles). One of the dominant models for understanding parenting in the United States has been the *parenting styles model*. Parenting style comprises behaviors that communicate to the child the parent's attitudes, emotions, and expectations about the child. Parenting style is assessed along two basic dimensions: (a) *parental demandingness*, which is the degree to which parents establish high expectations for their children's behaviors and monitor what their children actually do and (b) *parental responsiveness*, which is the degree to which parents are warm, nurturing, and sensitive to their children's cues (Baumrind, 1971; Maccoby & Martin, 1983). Crossing these two dimensions yields four types of parenting styles: authoritative, authoritarian, permissive, and indifferent. *Permissive* parenting involves being child oriented, responsive, and nurturing, and placing few demands on the child. Characteristics of *authoritarian* parenting include valuing obedience to and respect for authority, having high expectations for the child's behaviors, making decisions without considering the child's perspective, and not being warm and nurturing. *Authoritative* parents are responsive and nurturing while at the same time setting clear expectations, explaining the reasons behind their expectations, and considering the child's perspective in decision making. *Indifferent*, or *neglectful* parenting consists of low demands or expectations for the child coupled with low warmth and responsiveness to the child.

Several studies in which the parenting styles framework has been used have found that differences in parenting styles exist across ethnic groups (e.g., Dornbusch, Ritter, Leiderman, Roberts, & Fraleigh, 1987; Steinberg, Dornbusch, & Brown, 1992). In the majority of these studies Asian Americans are considered to be one group regardless of national background or generation status. In studies of adolescents, European American parents have generally been reported to be more authoritative than Asian American parents (e.g., Dornbusch et al., 1987; Steinberg, Mounts, Lamborn, & Dornbusch, 1991), whereas Asian American parents have been found to be more authoritarian (e.g., Chao, 2001; Dornbusch et al., 1987). Similar research has indicated that Asian American parents are more controlling and set higher expectations than European American parents (e.g., Huntsinger, Jose, & Larson, 1998; Lin & Fu, 1990).

One way to understand this work on Asian American parenting is to consider the beliefs and values that may shape Asian American family life. According to Ho (1982), Confucian ethics have provided a foundation for parent–child relationships in China, Japan, and Korea. This is a perspective that emphasizes obligation to others rather than individual rights and in parent–child relationships is epitomized by filial piety (Ho, 1994).

Among the filial precepts are: obeying and honoring one's parents, providing for the material and mental well-being of one's aged parents, performing the ceremonial duties of ancestral worship, taking care to avoid harm to one's body, ensuring the continuity of the family line, and in general conducting oneself so as to bring honor and not disgrace to the family name. (p. 287)

According to Bukowski and Sippola's (1998) local-knowledge model, these values may be reflected in parents' ideas about what it means to be a good parent and what constitutes a good or virtuous child. One interpretation of the research on Asian American parenting is that the emphasis on parental control and the high expectations emerge from the belief that good parents will expect their children to obey and gain honor for the family.

Given the distinctions between Asian American and European American parenting styles, natural questions to consider are whether these parenting styles are associated with differential child outcomes and whether parenting styles have the same impact in each ethnic-group context. Authoritative parenting has been touted as a better method of parenting because it has been associated with positive psychosocial and cognitive outcomes for children and adolescents (for reviews, see Baumrind, 1991a, 1991b; Maccoby & Martin, 1983). However, ethnic differences have been obtained in the relations between parenting styles and child outcomes—in particular, academic performance. For European American families, authoritarian and permissive parenting have been negatively related to school achievement, whereas authoritative parenting has been associated with higher school achievement and other positive aspects of psychosocial development (e.g., Dornbusch et al., 1987).

In contrast, a consistent finding is that differences in parenting styles have not explained very well the academic achievement of Asian American students (e.g., Chao, 2001; Steinberg et al., 1991, 1992). For example, Steinberg et al. (1991) examined the effects of ethnicity and social class on the relation between authoritative parenting and school achievement in a sample of about 10,000 high school students, approximately 14% of whom were Asian Americans. Among these adolescents the effect of authoritative parenting on school achievement was greater for European American students than for Asian American students. Similarly, Chao (2001) found that although European American adolescents from authoritative families reported higher grades than their peers from authoritarian families, there was no difference in scores of first- and second-generation Chinese American students from authoritative and authoritarian families.

In a study of elementary school children, degree of parental monitoring—a critical component of authoritative parenting—was positively correlated with school achievement for European American children, although no such relation was obtained for Asian American families (Okagaki &

Frensch, 1998). Similarly, an emphasis on obedience and conformity to external standards, a critical component of authoritarian parenting, was negatively related to school achievement in European American families but not related to school achievement for Asian American children (Okagaki & Frensch, 1998). One explanation is that Asian American children simply do not respond to authoritative and authoritarian parenting as European American children do because the overall family context in which these behaviors occur is different. It may be that the parenting styles construct does not adequately capture critical aspects of parenting in Asian American families. The lack of relation between parenting and child outcomes may reflect the lack of importance of these dimensions relative to other, more important characteristics of Asian American parenting.

Chao (1994, 2000) has argued that constructs developed from Asian perspectives would provide a better understanding of parenting in Asian American families. She has proffered the Chinese concept of training a child (*chiao shun*) as an example of an Asian parenting construct. Like parenting style, training is assessed by aspects of parental demandingness of and responsiveness to the child. A key feature of training is "a continuous monitoring and guidance of children" (Chao, 2000, p. 234). Unlike parenting style, the emphasis on demandingness in training a child does not include being restrictive or dominating the child. Similarly, the nurturing aspect of training is reflected in parental involvement and support (e.g., "A parent's most important concern involves taking care of the children" or "Children should be in the constant care of their mothers or other family members"; p. 239) but does not include overt demonstrations of the parent's affection for the child (e.g., praising or hugging the child).

In a study of immigrant Chinese American mothers and European American mothers of preschoolers, Chao (1994) examined the utility of applying the Chinese view of training a child to Chinese American mothers' beliefs about parenting. Chinese American mothers more strongly agreed with statements representing training; for example, "Mothers primarily express love by helping [their children] succeed, especially in school"; "A mother's sole interest is in taking care of her child"; and "Mothers must train [their children] to work very hard and be disciplined" (p. 1116). That is, the Chinese American mothers better fit the Chinese model of good parenting. In contrast, the European American parents better matched the Western model of parenting (i.e., higher scores on authoritative parenting, lower scores on authoritarian parenting, lower scores on parental control).

Ethnographic studies also provide insight into perspectives on parenting and family roles that would not have been identified through studies based on Western psychological theories. For example, according to informants in Smith-Hefner's (1999) study of Khmer Americans, the first task of the parent is to observe the child. A good parent is one who "knows his children before they know themselves" (p. 65). The parent closely watches the child, looking for clues to the child's past lives. Birthmarks or unusual physical traits may be signs of previous identities.

> Taouch Sok reported a similar experience. She knew her youngest son was the incarnation of a young man whose death she had witnessed during the Communist regime. She, too, had dreamed that the dead man's soul came to her, begging to be fed and cared for. She later bore a boy. The child, Taouch Sok said, had a scar on his lower back in the exact place where an ax had struck the dead man. (p. 67)

Smith-Hefner (1999) found that concern for the infant's spiritual and physical well-being required Khmer American parents to be with the infant all of the time. Through the first 2 years of life, infants typically slept with their mothers and were not left alone day or night. Families maintained certain rituals to protect their children from spirits. Even well-educated parents indicated that if their child became seriously ill, they would seek advice from the *krou khmae* (ritual specialist) as a precaution.

Smith-Hefner (1999) also found that belief in past lives appeared to set Khmer American parents in a tenuous position. They expressed feelings of insecurity. A child who remembered a past life might want to leave his or her present family to return to the family of a past life. In addition, stories were told of parents whose children had died later recognizing the soul of their dead child in a newborn infant. The parents of the infant then feared that the parents of the dead child might try to claim their infant.

Khmer American parenting of young children was described as permissive or indulgent (Smith-Hefner, 1999). Adults believed that young children did not yet know themselves—their place in society, their roles, and obligations—and were not accountable for their behavior. When a younger sibling was born, or by the time the child was 5 or 6 years old, parents began to discipline the child. Fathers became more emotionally distant from the child. The Khmer American fathers in Smith-Hefner's study believed that if they showed affection to their children then the children would be less inclined to obey them. Parents thought that praising, hugging, and kissing the child too much would spoil the child.

Smith-Hefner's (1999) study illustrates the local-knowledge model. Religious beliefs and beliefs about children's development influenced Khmer American parents' approach to child rearing. Furthermore, their implicit theories of child development and parenting might be completely missed in studies based on Western psychological theories.

Experiences accompanying immigration and acculturation may also shape child rearing (e.g., Jain & Belsky, 1997; Lin & Fu, 1990; Patel, Power, & Bhavnagri, 1996). For example, in their study of overseas Chinese, immigrant Chinese American, and European American parents, Lin and Fu (1990) observed that ratings of parental control were highest among overseas Chinese parents, followed by immigrant Chinese parents and then by European

American parents. They suggested that one indication of acculturation on the part of the immigrant Chinese American parents was that their ideas about parental control were becoming more like those of the European American parents.

Similar evidence of change in family life was garnered in a study of immigrant families from India. According to Jain and Belsky (1997), men in traditional societies such as India play a distant role in providing child care. Moving to a culture that encourages paternal involvement and presents different structural conditions for the immigrant family typically involves conflict, pressure, and adjustment for fathers. To examine patterns of father involvement and the influence of acculturation, Jain and Belsky studied two-parent Indian immigrant families with young children. The average length of residency in the United States of these families was 6.5 years. Jain and Belsky identified three types of fathering—engaged, caretaker, and disengaged—that were associated with their measure of acculturation. The fathers in the least acculturated families were disengaged from their children and had little direct interaction with the children. Engaged and caretaker fathers were more acculturated than the disengaged fathers with respect to traditional beliefs (e.g., regarding dating, education for daughters), feelings about India (e.g., missing family, friends, and cultural events), behaviors (e.g., language spoken at home, frequency of contact with people in India), and length of residence in the United States. The engaged fathers were involved in multiple aspects of child rearing, such as caretaking, playing, teaching, and disciplining their child. In contrast, the caretaker fathers had assumed some caretaking responsibilities but were not engaged in other kinds of activities with their child.

Taken together, these studies suggest that the ways in which Asian American adults approach the parental role may be influenced by their cultural beliefs and values and by experiences associated with immigration and acculturation to the United States. Chao's (1994, 2000) studies are excellent examples of how research on Asian American families is enriched by exploring Asian American definitions of social constructs.

Parent–Child Relationships

The parent–child relationship is arguably a child's most important social relationship. Several researchers have explored the hypothesis that immigration and the subsequent sociocultural changes that occur within the family may evoke new tensions and conflicts within the family—particularly with respect to parent–adolescent relationships. According to Edmonston and Passel (1994), for the next 50 years more than half of the Asian American population will comprise immigrants and their U.S.-born children. Acculturation has historically been considered a unidirectional process in which the acquisition of values and characteristics of the host culture occurs in conjunction with the loss of native culture. In contrast, current models emphasize the complexity of culture and the processes of immigration and acculturation. These models recognize the selective and multidimensional nature of the acculturation process. Some characteristics (e.g., clothing, language) may be acquired more quickly; others (e.g., socialization practices) may not ever be totally changed. Moreover, within a family, some members may acquire attitudes and behaviors of the host culture before other members do. This phenomenon may be the seed of conflict for immigrant Asian American families.

Nguyen and Williams (1989) hypothesized that conflict between generations may arise in immigrant families as the parent generation retains traditional values while the younger generation begins to adopt other beliefs and values. In their study of immigrant Vietnamese American adolescents and their parents, Nguyen and Williams examined attitudes toward traditional Vietnamese values (e.g., "The oldest girl in the family should help her parents take care of the house and the younger children whether she wants to or not" or "Parents always know what is best"). Vietnamese American parents supported traditional Vietnamese values more strongly than the adolescents did, and the difference between parents' and adolescents' beliefs was greater for daughters than for sons. In addition, the difference between parents' beliefs and adolescents' beliefs increased with time spent in the United States, particularly for girls. Although Vietnamese American parents continued to support traditional Vietnamese values, there was some indication of movement away from an entirely traditional Vietnamese view of family life. For example, there was no difference between Vietnamese American parents and adolescents in their support for granting autonomy to adolescents. Both groups agreed with statements about 16-year-old boys and girls being allowed to decide when and whom to date and 18-year-olds making decisions for themselves to move away from home for a job or college. According to Nguyen and Williams, the Vietnamese American parents were sending mixed messages to their children, and these mixed messages, coupled with the adolescents' movement away from traditional Vietnamese values, had the potential to increase conflict within Vietnamese families. Unfortunately, a measure of conflict was not included in this study.

However, a subsequent study (Dinh, Sarason, & Sarason, 1994) did explore conflict within Vietnamese American families. Believing that parents of foreign-born Vietnamese American college students would maintain more traditional Vietnamese values than their sons or daughters would, Dinh et al. hypothesized that the foreign-born Vietnamese American college students would experience more conflict in their relationships with their parents as compared to a mixed-ethnic sample of American-born college students, including students from European American, Asian American, and African American backgrounds. The foreign-born Vietnamese American students reported experiencing more conflict with their mothers; receiving less support, less care, and less acceptance from their mothers; and feeling more overprotected by their mothers. With respect to their fathers, foreign-born Vietnamese American students reported higher scores on conflict and overprotection and lower scores on acceptance and care.

Although the results of Dinh et al.'s (1994) study were consistent with the hypothesis that differences in traditional Vietnamese values are correlated with degree of intergenerational conflict, a direct test of the hypothesis was not possible, because they did not include a measure of Vietnamese values. They also did not directly measure the degree of acculturation of the students and their parents; neither did they indicate the number of years elapsed since the family immigrated to the United States. Because the parents had left Vietnam as political refugees under stressful conditions, there are also possible confounds because of the involuntary nature of the immigration. Nonetheless, this study, coupled with the one conducted by Nguyen and Williams (1989), illustrates a possible effect of acculturation on Asian American development.

In an ethnographic study of Vietnamese immigrants living in Philadelphia in the early 1980s (Kibria, 1993), both younger and older Vietnamese Americans reported that intergenerational conflict had increased as a result of immigration to the United States. Younger Vietnamese Americans were adopting the practices and speech of their mainstream American peers. From their parents' perspectives, the "Americanization" of their children resulted in a lack of respect for elders and more materialistic attitudes. Moreover, parents expressed helplessness in their ability to discipline their children, because some parenting strategies common in Vietnam (e.g., corporal punishment) were not accepted in the United States. When Vietnamese American children reported instances of physical punishment to school authorities or to the police, school or police intervention in the home undermined parental authority, while the underlying tensions between parents and children went unresolved. Parents were forced to give up traditional parenting strategies before learning alternative socialization practices. Because children often developed proficiency in English language skills more quickly than their parents, many children assumed the role of liaison between the family and the larger community. Because of this role, and because the Vietnamese American parents were not gaining new parenting strategies, the balance of power in families shifted.

> I have difficulty reading English, so Danny [twelve-year-old son] reads all of the letters that come to the house. He tells me how much to pay for the electric, the telephone. I give him the money and he takes it to the post office. I know Danny keeps money because he buys some things like this [points to a black leather jacket], and he doesn't work. I know it's not good. I asked him, why do you do like that? He doesn't say anything. If it was in Vietnam his father would beat him, but here it's different. We can't hit him because the police will come. (Kibria, 1993, p. 151)

As a group, the studies discussed in this section illustrate the ways in which experiences associated with immigration and acculturation play a role in Asian American parent–child relationships. For many parents, particularly fathers, the price of immigration included a profound loss in their parenting role and in their relationships with their children.

Development of Autonomy

Related to research on parent–adolescent relationships is work that more specifically targets development of autonomy during adolescence. In the United States, the transition from childhood to adolescence has typically been viewed as an important time in an individual's development. Adolescence is a time when the individual begins to make decisions for him- or herself. Researchers have reported that in European American families during this period the parent–child relationship undergoes a transformation such that the adolescent ultimately will have more freedom and autonomy. In a focus group study of Asian Indian American parents and adolescents, Segal (1991) observed that among Asian Indian American immigrant families, conflict emerged because parents and adolescents held different views about adolescence. Parents typically maintained traditional Indian conceptualizations of adolescence: that it is an extension of childhood in terms of role, status, and responsibility, not a transitional period in which the adolescent gained more autonomy. Parents expected their adolescent to listen to and agree with them. Because the norm for the parents had been arranged marriages, the parents did not want their adolescents to date. In particular, they wanted to limit contact with non-Asian Indians. In contrast, the adolescents expected more autonomy, saw their parents as prejudiced against non-Asian Indians, and wanted more two-way communication with their parents.

Fuligni (1998) saw the potential for adolescence to be a less conflictual period for Asian Americans. He hypothesized that, among cultural groups in which autonomy is de-emphasized, the transition from parent–child to parent–adolescent relationship might be different from the transition observed in European American families. His sample of 6th-, 8th-, and 10th-grade students included Chinese American, Filipino American, and European American families. With respect to generation status, the majority of the Filipino Americans (93%) and Chinese Americans (74%) were first or second generation. In contrast, the majority (80%) of the European American students were third generation or higher. In addition to measures of conflict and cohesion with parents, students responded to questions about their perceptions of how appropriate it was to disagree with parents, their beliefs about the legitimacy of parental authority, and their expectations for making autonomous decisions. Analyses of these data indicated that, relative to European American families, the Asian American families approached this transition period in a somewhat different manner. Compared to European American students, Filipino American students rated openly disagreeing with mothers or fathers as being less acceptable. Similarly, Chinese American students expected to be granted autonomy to make their own decisions at a later age than did the European American students.

Beliefs were also a function of generation status (Fuglini, 1998). Third-generation students indicated more willingness to openly disagree with their mothers or fathers and held earlier expectations for autonomy than did second-generation students. The beliefs of second- and third-generation students differed from the beliefs of first-generation students. Controlling for generation status eliminated the ethnic group differences in beliefs: There were no differences in reported conflict and cohesion with parents across groups. Fuligni (1998) suggested that

> within a single society, cultural variations in beliefs about autonomy and authority may play only a modest role in parent–adolescent relationships. If particular beliefs are not supported by the social settings within a society, then they may have little effect on relationships and will gradually change to more closely approximate the norms of the dominant group. (p. 790)

Alternatively, cultural differences in beliefs about relationships and development of autonomy (i.e., differences that would favor less conflict in the Asian American groups) may be offset by an increase in intergenerational differences between immigrant parents who are slower to adopt beliefs and practices of the mainstream culture than are their adolescents.

Because of the general Asian American cultural emphasis on filial piety, family, and respect for elders, Z.-Y. Chen (1999) proposed that development of emotional autonomy in Asian American adolescents might be correlated with adolescents' self-esteem. More individuated adolescents were hypothesized to have lower self-esteem, because achieving emotional autonomy from their parents would, in some sense, conflict with feelings related to filial piety. In Z.-Y. Chen's study, which included European American and Asian American high school students, individuation was negatively correlated with self-esteem for both Asian American and European American boys, but the relation was stronger for Asian Americans. Individuation was also negatively correlated with self-esteem for girls, but there was no difference between the two groups. These results suggest that there may be some differences between Asian American and European American boys in the impact of emotional autonomy on psychosocial well-being. Although there are limitations to this study (e.g., there were no measures of cultural values, such as filial piety, and the measure of emotional autonomy may have emphasized alienation from parents rather than development of healthy emotional autonomy), Z.-Y. Chen's study is an example of how exploiting differences in cultural values (or local knowledge) may yield interesting studies of various aspects of normative development.

Moral Development

Although developmental psychologists have attended to moral development and socialization of values in general (e.g., Gilligan, 1982; Grusec & Goodnow, 1994), interest in the socialization of values and moral development among Asian Americans has been limited. However, two recent ethnographic studies have included descriptions of socialization of moral beliefs and behaviors. These studies suggest ways in which Asian American understandings of moral behavior may differ from European American perspectives.

Smith-Hefner's (1999) ethnographic study of Khmer Americans focused on socialization and moral education. Adopting the moral values of one's social group requires the child not only to possess the knowledge of those values but also to identify with that group and desire to embrace those values. In a relatively homogeneous social environment, those values are reinforced by the child's family and by members of the greater community in a multitude of ways. In the U.S.'s pluralistic society, children are exposed to many different values, some of which may be antithetical to the values parents wish to develop in their children. This was the challenge faced by the Khmer Americans in Smith-Hefner's study.

Moral development in Khmer American families has been influenced by Khmer Buddhist traditions and by Brahmanic views on social relationships (Smith-Hefner, 1999). According to Khmer Buddhist beliefs, the infant enters the world with traits and abilities carried over from past lives. The task of the parent is to observe the infant carefully to identify and then encourage further development of interests and abilities from these preexisting lives. Thus, the infant is not a blank slate but rather an individual who is born with innate characteristics and personality, which the parent must understand. Juxtaposed to the Khmer Buddhist beliefs that focus on development of the individual are the Brahmanic traditions that emphasize social relationships and obligations. The child is a member of a family and is morally obligated to behave in ways that uphold the family's reputation, or "face." If a child misbehaves, it reflects poorly on the family's reputation. According to the Khmer Buddhist concept of *karma*, what an individual has done in previous lives, and the merit the individual has acquired, determines his or her present life. For the parent, this means that children are not randomly born to their parents. In essence, parents get the children they deserve on the basis of their previous lives. If a child misbehaves, it says something about the parents' morality and the entire family's collective karma. Thus, great importance is place on raising well-behaved children.

The underlying Khmer American socialization strategy is to develop the child's concern for his or her reputation and social status.

> Recognizing face and trying to maintain it are critical elements in becoming a Khmer adult. Knowing oneself means knowing how to behave properly according to one's status within the family and community; with self-knowledge, one would be aware of social obligations and would accept responsibility for one's actions. (Smith-Hefner, 1999, p. 94)

An important aspect of a child's understanding of social obligations is developing proper respect for superiors, especially parents. In fact, parents are considered to be the child's "first gods" or "gods within the house" (Smith-Hefner, 1999, p. 95). This means the child's primary moral obligation is to the parents, particularly to caring for the parents in their old age. Smith-Hefner (1999) elegantly described Khmer American social constructs related to conceptions of children, parents, development, and morality that are distinct from their traditional Western psychological counterparts and which may in turn affect development.

A second ethnographic study also provides insights into Asian American understandings of moral development. According to Kibria (1993), traditional Vietnamese beliefs about child development emphasize the role of the environment in shaping the child. Vietnamese proverbs eloquently articulate these beliefs: "If you live in a round thing you become round; if you live in a long thing you become long" or "If the straw is set near the fire, sooner or later it will catch fire" (Kibria, 1993, p. 146). For the immigrant Vietnamese American parents in Kibria's study, raising children in the United States meant their children were living in a new environment—and very near the fire. Her work gives voice to some Vietnamese American concerns about the moral development of their children.

> The biggest problem of living here is that it's difficult to teach your children how to be good and to have good behavior. The children learn how to be American from the schools, and then we don't understand them and they don't obey us. The customs here are so different from our culture. The children learn about sex from TV. Maybe American parents think that's okay, but for me that's not okay because I know the children will learn bad behavior from watching TV. (Vietnamese American mother; Kibria, 1993, p. 132)

Children's exposure to mainstream American culture through school, friends, and media, coupled with a diminution of parental authority, presented Vietnamese American parents with a great challenge in the socialization of their children.

> I have children and I can't educate them. The films and TV show bad things, things which are not suited for an Asian culture. On TV, they show love couples doing things, and I think that way it directly teaches

the children bad behavior. Books and magazines show naked pictures of women, and the children who don't know, they see it and try to find out about it. If one plays with the ink, one will get black. (Vietnamese American father of three; Kibria, 1993, p. 146)

Although moral development was not a primary focus of Kibria's study, comments from the parents indicated that it was an important issue for the parents. Moral development and socialization of values are currently understudied aspects of Asian American development. Because the moral values of some Asian American families may be different from values held by the larger U.S. society, examination of the socialization of these values could be particularly interesting.

Peer Relationships

To our knowledge, relatively little research has focused on the normative development of peer relationships among Asian American children and adolescents. Jordan (1984) suggested that Native Hawaiian youngsters struggled to adapt to formal school settings because of the nature of their peer relationships, which relied heavily on child-organized and child-initiated activities through sibling and friendship groups. Allowing children to work in small groups and encouraging peer assistance, rather than independent seat work, created a classroom social organization that achieved a closer match to children's outside-of-classroom social structure and facilitated children's adjustment to school (Jordan, 1984; Vogt, Jordan, & Tharp, 1993). Steinberg et al. (1992) hypothesized that peers may play an important role in supporting the academic achievement of Asian American adolescents. In a study of African American, Asian American, and European American adolescents, Hamm (2000) examined the similarity between friends' characteristics regarding academic orientation (self-reported grades, effort in schoolwork, and educational aspirations), ethnic identity (sense of belonging to and feelings about one's ethnic group), and substance use (frequency of use of various controlled substances). Academically oriented Asian American adolescents were more likely to have friends who were similar in their academic orientation than were Asian American adolescents with weaker academic orientations. Stronger similarity between friends with respect to substance use was associated with less frequent substance use. With respect to ethnic identity, Asian Americans were more similar in their ethnic orientation when ethnic identity was less important to them.

Asian American peer relationships have also been examined from the perspective of cross-racial relationships. In a study of college students attending a racially and ethnically diverse university, Ying et al. (2001) found that Asian American students who identified more cross-racial groups in their friendship network had a stronger sense of coherence; that is, they felt their lives were more meaningful, manageable, and comprehensible. In other studies, sense of coherence has been correlated with measures of psychological adjustment (e.g., Ying, Akutsu, Zhang, & Huang, 1999). Thus, examination of both in-group and out-group friendships may be important to understanding Asian American social development and psychosocial well-being.

T. E. Kim and Goto (2000) examined Asian American peer relationships vis-à-vis potential influences emerging from a collectivist orientation and the impact of acculturation on family relationships. They hypothesized that because adolescents may adopt mainstream European American values more quickly than their parents, some adolescents may perceive less parental social support. As a result, these Asian American adolescents may turn to peers for social support. In addition, they proposed that peer delinquency may have an even stronger influence on Asian American adolescents because of their collectivist beliefs. T. E. Kim and Goto's sample included Korean Americans, Japanese Americans, Chinese Americans, and other Asian Americans, including a few bi-ethnic adolescents. About 65% of the participants were second-generation Asian Americans; approximately 30% were first-generation Asian Americans, and 5% were third-generation Asian Americans. Parental support did not predict delinquent behaviors, but having a friend who engaged in delinquent behaviors did predict delinquency on the part of the target adolescent. Unfortunately, T. E. Kim and Goto did not include measures of acculturation or collectivism, so it is difficult to assess their effects on adolescent peer relationships.

Development of peer relationships has clearly been understudied among Asian American populations. The studies discussed in this section indicate how Asian American values and the experiences associated with acculturation might provide conceptual frameworks for the study of Asian American peer relationships.

Development of Ethnic Identity

Because an entire chapter of this volume is devoted to ethnic identity, we did not comprehensively review research addressing the development of ethnic identity and self-concept among Asian Americans, which is a critical dimension of Asian American social–cognitive development. In this section we simply note a few changes in the study of the development of ethnic identity. Behavioral scientists have progressed in understandings of ethnic identity, self-concept, cultural orientation, and bicultural development so that important nuances in the development of Asian American children and adolescents are beginning to emerge. For example, it is important to examine *multiple components of self-concept*. Whereas Asian American children feel positively about many dimensions of their self-concepts, there is evidence that Korean American children (Chang, 1975) and Japanese American children and young women (Arkoff & Weaver, 1966; Pang, Mizokawa, Morishima, & Olstad, 1985) have poorer body images than their non-Asian American counterparts. Similarly, *cultural orientation*—one's relation to one's ethnic culture and to the majority culture—is now considered to be multidimensional (Ying, Lee, & Tsai, 2000); that is, an individual's acceptance or rejection of ethnic and majority cultures may vary across domains. Yeh and Huang (1996) argued that to understand Asian American ethnic identity development, researchers need to consider the *impact of Asian American beliefs and values* (e.g., cultural emphasis on interdependence) on ethnic identity development. In Yeh and Huang's study of Asian American college students, social context, relationships, and avoiding shame were important themes in young adults' reports of their ethnic identity formation.

Generation status appears to affect some aspects of ethnic identity and cultural orientation more than others. In a comparison of foreign-born and U.S.-born Chinese American adolescents, Rosenthal and Feldman (1992) found that U.S.-born Chinese American adolescents were less likely than foreign-born adolescents to feel totally or mostly Chinese. However, there were differences neither in the degrees to which their school friends and nonschool friends comprised Chinese American and non-Chinese American friends nor in their preference for marrying someone who was of Chinese descent. Although the foreign-born Chinese American adolescents scored higher in their participation in culturally related behaviors (e.g., engaging in Chinese worship, speaking a Chinese language), there were no differences between groups in ratings of the importance of their ethnic identity, their attitudes toward their Chinese backgrounds, and in their orientation toward individualism versus collectivism.

Research on *ethnic socialization* of Asian American children is important to understanding the development and experiences of Asian American children. Phinney and Chavira (1995) observed that, relative to African American and Mexican American parents, Japanese American parents were less likely to report talking about discrimination with their adolescents, teaching their adolescents how to get along in mainstream American society, or preparing their adolescents for living in a culturally diverse society. However, the three groups of parents were equally likely to report teaching their sons or daughters about their cultural heritage. African American and Japanese American parents were more likely to emphasize adaptation to society than Mexican American parents were. In general, relatively little is known about Asian American ethnic socialization. What influences the development of children's ethnic identity and cultural orientation? What supports, and what inhibits, bicultural development among children from different Asian American subgroups? These are among the questions about ethnic identity socialization and bicultural development to which there are very few answers.

Limitations to Current Knowledge on Asian American Social Development

Three major limitations exist in researchers' understanding of Asian American social development. First, many aspects of normative social development have been ignored. For example, very little is known about development of Asian American sibling, peer, and friendship relationships; social cognitive development; perspective taking; emotional development and regulation; and social problem solving. Second, much of the research has been based on Western psychological theories that do not necessarily provide an adequate framework for understanding Asian American social development. Chao's (1994, 2000) research on Chinese American parenting in which she has used the concept of training is an excellent example of how Asian American social constructs can inform and enrich an understanding of Asian American development. Third, research covering multiple Asian American subgroups is scarce. Large-scale studies have primarily included Chinese Americans and Japanese Americans. Less is known about Cambodian Americans, Korean Americans, Filipino Americans, Asian Indian Americans, and Vietnamese Americans. More normative data are needed about development of children in these Asian American subgroups.

COGNITIVE DEVELOPMENT

> The sea of learning knows no bounds; only through diligence may its shore be reached.
>
> —Chinese proverb

Overview: Intellectual Achievement and Underachievement

As a group, Asian American students have done well in American schools (E. S. Lee & Rong, 1988; Tsang, 1988; see Sue & Okazaki, 1990). According to the 1990 census, 37% of Asian Americans had completed at least a bachelor's degree, whereas only 20% of the total population had graduated from college (U.S. Bureau of the Census, 1993a). Among high school seniors, 7% of Asian American students performed at the advanced level on the National Assessment of Educational Progress mathematics assessment (National Center for Education Statistics, 1997), as compared to 2% of European American students. About 33% of Asian American 12th grade students were at or above the proficient level in mathematics, whereas 20% of European American students were at or above the proficient level.

Despite the overall high performance of Asian American students, great diversity in school performance exists across Asian American subgroups (Tsang, 1988; Wong, 1990; see also Hsia & Peng, 1998). Overall, higher rates of college completion (30% or more) have occurred among Chinese American, Filipino American, Japanese American, Asian Indian American, and Korean American adults (U.S. Bureau of the Census, 1993b). Some of the more recent immigrant groups (e.g., Cambodian, Hmong, and Laotian) are not as well educated (U.S. Bureau of the Census, 1993a). In 1990, about 80% of the Vietnamese, Laotian, and Cambodian populations living in the United States were foreign born; 65% of the Hmong population was foreign born. Less than 10% of Cambodian American, Hmong American, and Laotian American men aged 25 years and older held college degrees. Less than 4% of the women in these groups were college graduates. Although 22% of the Vietnamese American men had bachelor's degrees, only 12% of the women were college graduates (U.S. Bureau of the Census, 1993b).

Because in the United States income is closely tied to education, the less educated Asian American subgroups were more likely to experience poverty. In 1989, about 10% of all American families were at or below the poverty level. In contrast, 62% of Hmong American families and 42% of Cambodian American families were living in poverty (U.S. Bureau of the Census, 1993b).

Underachievement also exists among younger Asian American students (Hsia & Peng, 1998). In the National Education Longitudinal Study of 8th graders in 1988 (NELS 1988), the mean standard reading scores of Southeast Asian American children were below the national average standard score. Moreover, these comparisons excluded students with limited English proficiency (Hsia & Peng, 1998). In a study of Southeast Asian American students in San Diego, the 11th- and 12th-grade reading test average scores of Southeast Asian American students were below those of all other groups except Samoan American students. Their math scores were also below those of European American students, even though the students with limited English proficiency were excluded from the study (Hsia & Peng, 1998).

A major limitation to an understanding of Asian American educational achievement is the lack of research on Asian Americans who underachieve in the U.S. school system. In this section we discuss the data that currently exist and, consequently, focus primarily on the success of Asian American students. In general, Asian Indian American, Chinese American, Filipino American, Japanese American, and Korean American students have fared well in U.S. schools (Hsia & Peng, 1998; U.S. Bureau of the Census, 1993a). In many of the studies we review, Asian Americans were considered to be one group, with specific national background or generation status not identified. We have noted those distinctions whenever possible.

Parental Expectations for Achievement

One explanation for Asian Americans' higher achievement is that Asian American parents have higher expectations for their children's schoolwork (e.g., C. Chen & Stevenson, 1995; Okagaki & Frensch, 1998). In a study of Asian American, Latino American, and European American families with fourth- and fifth-grade children, Asian American parents reported higher ideal expectations, higher expected educational attainment, and higher minimum expectations for their child's education than either European American or Latino American parents expressed (Okagaki & Frensch, 1998). The Asian American parents ideally wanted their child to obtain a graduate or professional degree. In contrast, European American and Latino American parents ideally hoped that their child would graduate from college. The Asian American parents expected their child to graduate from college; the other parents expected their child to obtain some college education. Asian American parents set the lower boundary for their child's education at college graduation. In comparison, European American parents had a minimum expectation of high school graduation, whereas Latino American parents set the lower boundary at some college education. Relative to other parents, the Asian American parents also expressed higher expectations for the grades their child earned on schoolwork. They were less satisfied with grades of B's and C's than the other parents were.

Consistent with the finding that Asian American parents set high expectations for their child's school achievement is the observation that parents take responsibility for their child's school achievement. In Asian American families the emphasis on educational success is directed not only to the student but also to the parent. Chao (1994) reported that one of the primary goals of immigrant Chinese American parents was to help their children succeed in school. A good parent is one whose children do well in school. Similarly, Hieshima and Schneider (1994) observed that third-generation Japanese American parents' high academic expectations for their children were held in conjunction with parents' views about the parenting role—that parents are their children's primary teachers and that parents are responsible for their children's development and achievement.

Do parents' aspirations for their children's education relate to their children's expectations for educational achievement? In his analysis of Chinese American, Japanese American, and Filipino American high school seniors in the *High School and Beyond* data, Wong (1990) found that both fathers' and mothers' expectations for their adolescent's educational attainment were related to the adolescent's educational expectations. In addition, Chinese American, Japanese American, and Filipino American high school seniors were more likely than European American students to indicate that they planned to go to college and expected to graduate from college.

Underlying Beliefs About Intellectual Performance

Asian American parents' beliefs about intelligence incorporate a broader set of abilities than those typically identified in traditional Western psychological theories. In a study of immigrant parents from Cambodia, Mexico, the Philippines, and Vietnam, and U.S.-born Mexican American and European Americans parents, Okagaki and Sternberg (1993) found that motivation was an important component of the Asian American parents' understanding of intelligence. A child who is intelligent is one who tries hard to get good grades. In contrast, European American parents' ideas about intelligence were consistent with traditional Western psychological theories that describe intelligence in terms of cognitive abilities; first- and later generation Mexican American parents included social skills in their conceptions of intelligence. These findings illustrate differences in social constructs across ethnic groups.

In an ethnographic study of immigrant Punjabi (Indian) American and non-Punjabi American adolescents in California, Gibson (1987) noted that both the Punjabi American students and their parents believed that effort was the determining factor in educational achievement. On the basis of interviews with Japanese American high school students who were primarily third generation, Matute-Bianchi (1986) reported that "belief in diligence, persistence, and hard work—as opposed to inherent ability—as the keys to academic success is the single most commonly shared perception among the Japanese-descent students" (p. 247). In their study of Southeast Asian American immigrants, Caplan, Whitmore, and Choy (1989) suggested that three common values—an emphasis on education and achievement, belief in the importance of maintaining a cohesive family, and belief in the efficacy and importance of hard work—served as the foundation for Southeast Asian American children's academic achievement. Almost all of the Southeast Asian American parents (97%) and children (93%) attributed academic success to hard work; in contrast, 86% of the parents and 67% of the children identified intellectual ability as causally related to academic achievement. In a comparison of several Asian American subgroups (Chinese, Filipino, Japanese, Korean, Vietnamese, and other Southeast Asian), Mizokawa and Ryckman (1990) found that, overall, Asian American students (including elementary, junior high, and high school students) were more likely to attribute academic success and failure to effort than to ability. Across subgroups, Korean American students placed the most emphasis on effort as a causal factor in academic achievement. C. Chen and Stevenson (1995) observed that, relative to European American students, Asian American high school students were more likely to indicate that doing well in math was the result of studying hard.

Socialization for Intellectual Achievement

Analyses of national data sets have revealed that Asian American students report spending more time working on schoolwork and are more likely to engage in extracurricular classes than are other students. For example, analyses of the *High School and Beyond* data indicated that Asian American students were more likely than European American students to take academic courses (English, math, science, social studies, foreign language, and computer science; Tsang, 1988), to take college preparatory courses (Wong, 1990), and to spend 5 or more hours each week on homework (Tsang, 1988; Wong, 1990) and were less likely to be absent from school (Wong, 1990). Similarly, analysis of NELS 1988 data revealed that Asian American students spent more time working on their homework than other students, participated in more extracurricular classes (e.g., music, language, art) than other minority students, and engaged in more educational activities outside of school (e.g., going to libraries and museums) than other minority students (Peng & Wright, 1994). These studies suggest that, as a group, Asian American students may take a more serious approach to schoolwork. What role do Asian American parents play in their children's approach to education?

Among several Asian American groups emphasis is placed on parents' support of their children's educational achievement. As one Vietnamese proverb indicates, "If one has children and does not educate them, it's better to spend one's time rearing pigs for their tripes" (Kibria, 1993, p. 149). The importance of the parents' role in children's education has been observed among Chinese American parents (Chao, 1994), Japanese American parents (Hieshima & Schneider, 1994), and Vietnamese American parents (Caplan, Choy, & Whitmore, 1992; Kibria, 1993). However, the way in which Asian American parents provide support for their children's schoolwork is not necessarily the same as the way European American parents help their children.

Using the parents' data from the NELS 1988 study, Peng and Wright (1994) found that Asian American parents did not report spending more time directly helping their children with homework or explicitly talking about school with their children than other parents did. Similarly, Wong's (1990) comparison of Chinese American, Filipino American, Japanese American, and European American students in the *High School and Beyond* data set indicated that, relative to European American parents, only the parents of Chinese American students were reported to engage in more monitoring of their adolescent's schoolwork. If, for the most part, Asian American parents are not providing more direct monitoring of their child's school progress, what are they doing to encourage school achievement?

Several researchers have observed that Asian American parents use indirect strategies to encourage their children's school achievement, such as structuring the home environment to facilitate children's learning, rather than directly helping the children with schoolwork (e.g., Caplan et al., 1992; Chao, 2000; Schneider & Lee, 1990). For example, parents may set aside a specific time for the children to do homework and restrict the amount of time the children spend watching television (e.g., Schneider & Lee, 1990). Parents may not want or allow their adolescents to work after school because they believe that an adolescent's "job" is to study for school (e.g., Gibson, 1987). On the basis of an ethnographic study of third- and fourth-generation Japanese Americans, Hieshima and Schneider (1994) noted that even native-born parents' encouragement of schoolwork was indirect. The third-generation Japanese American parents did not directly tell their child what to do; instead, they made indirect comments, such as "You sure finished with your homework fast" or "Not much homework tonight?" (p. 322). Schneider and Lee (1990) found that Asian American parents were more likely than European American parents to encourage their children to take private classes in music, language, and computer science and that their children spent more time practicing for their lessons than did European American children.

Compared with their European American counterparts, Chinese American immigrant parents of primary grade students reported engaging in more *"structural parental involvement in school"* (Chao, 2000, p. 240; e.g., setting rules for how the children spent time after school and buying extra workbooks or materials to give the children more practice on school tasks) than European American parents. Conversely, European American parents had higher scores on what was called *"managerial* parental involvement in school" (Chao, 2000, p. 240)—activities such as checking homework and attending school functions. It appears that in Asian American homes an important aspect of socialization for academic achievement is the creation of an overall environment in which discipline, studying, and practice are integral elements of the child's role in multiple contexts. This indirect—rather than instrumental—support apparently is the vehicle through which parents are able to facilitate their children's school achievement.

Finally, Japanese Americans provide an interesting opportunity to examine changes in cultural values, because emigration of Japanese families to the United States has been extremely limited since World War II. The vast majority of Japanese American families in the United States today originally came to the United States prior to World War II. Moreover, many family ties to Japan were broken during the war. To what degree, then, do fourth-generation Japanese American children differ from European Americans?

In a comparison of Chinese Americans, European Americans, Japanese Americans, and Korean Americans who participated in the NELS 1988 data collection, Schneider et al. (1994) observed that Japanese American students at times are more like their European American counterparts and at other times are more like their Asian American peers. Whereas approximately 60% of the Chinese American and Korean American students were in the upper quartile of grades, about one third of the Japanese American and European American students were in the upper quartile. However, on test scores, the Japanese Americans appeared to fit more closely to their Asian American peers. Slightly less than one third of European Americans were in the upper quartile on test scores. Among Asian American students, about half of the Chinese American and Japanese American students were in the upper quartile for test scores, and just over 60% of the Korean American students were in the top quartile. (The difference between European Americans and Japanese Americans was not statistically significant, whereas the differences between the European Americans and the other two groups were significant.) Students' expectations for their educational attainment followed a similar pattern, with 22% of European American, 44% of Japanese American, 48% of Chinese American, and 61% of Korean American students indicating that they planned to attend graduate school. The Japanese American students were as likely as the Chinese American and Korean American students to be taking algebra classes in eighth grade. The Asian American students were all more likely to be taking algebra than were the European American students. Japanese Americans were similar to Chinese Americans and Korean Americans in their participation in music lessons and language school but more like European Americans in their participation in sports activities. Although the Japanese American children were becoming more like European American children in terms of grades and other behavioral outcomes, interviews with Japanese American parents and children suggested that the families continued to adhere to some Japanese values, such as commitment to education for its intrinsic value, obligation to family, and respect for authority.

Underachievement Among Asian Americans

As noted earlier, not all Asian Americans have succeeded in school (Hsia & Peng, 1998; Tsang, 1988; Wong, 1990). In a 1988–1989 ethnographic study of Asian American high school students in Philadelphia, S. J. Lee (1994) described different types of underachieving Asian American students. One group of low-achieving students consisted of studious, hardworking students who struggled with schoolwork because of their poor English language skills. Although these Asian American students believed that obtaining a good education was critical for their futures, they did not seek help. These students believed that calling attention to their poor performance and asking for help would bring shame to their families. In contrast, another group of underachievers comprised Asian American students who actively distanced themselves from the Asian American stereotype of model students. In contrast to other Asian American students, who were concerned with how their families viewed them, these students were peer oriented; they wanted to be "cool." In their eyes, good students were nerds who were not accepted by non-Asian American students. Distancing themselves from the Asian American model student stereotype was a way to gain acceptance by non-Asian American peers. These underachievers cut classes, did not do their schoolwork, and did the least amount of work possible to pass.

In an ethnographic study conducted in the mid-1980s, Trueba, Jacobs, and Kirton (1990) described the challenges of Hmong American children in a small California community. As a group, these children were not doing well in school. Most of the parents were unfamiliar with American public education and had little knowledge of what their children did in school. Because their own educational experiences in Laos were quite different from their children's schooling, the parents had little understanding of what their children were learning and what teachers expected of them. Communication with school personnel was inhibited, because parents' English skills were quite limited, and translators were not readily available. Limited knowledge of the mainstream society also made it difficult for parents to develop clear goals for their children. "One mother said, 'I feel my children can be anything they want, I just don't know what there is to be'" (field notes, Jacobs, 1986, quoted in Trueba et al., 1990, p. 71).

The Hmong American children, in turn, struggled to cope with the demands of living in two very different worlds. In their elementary school of 600 children, about half of the children spoke English as a second language. Within the school, 25 languages were represented. Limited English language skills coupled with limited knowledge of mainstream culture appeared to inhibit children's participation in class activities. Children were frequently passive and disengaged. When children interpreted information from their cultural perspective, teachers often mistakenly inferred that the children did not understand the material. Many of the Hmong American children were viewed as having some type of learning disability. When given individual or small-group support from the resource teacher, the Hmong American children with so-called learning disabilities improved much more quickly than did mainstream students with learning disabilities. Although the rapid improvement was acknowledged as being atypical for children with learning disabilities, teachers and staff continued to see the Hmong American children as learning disabled because they were unable to cope with the demands of the regular classroom.

In their study of Southeast Asian refugees in San Diego, California, Rumbaut and Ima (1988) included field observations and interviews with Southeast Asian refugees and quantitative data from schools and the county probation department. Their work highlighted the great diversity in academic achievement among Asian American students and directed attention to problems associated with immigration and refugee experiences. Although some Southeast Asian Americans had grades that were above those of European Americans, Khmer American and Laotian American students' grades were below the average grades of European Americans. As a group, Southeast Asian students had scores above the national average on standardized math tests but below-average scores on verbal tests.

Many factors were associated with school performance. In general, length of stay in the United States was positively correlated with academic performance. Age was also a factor: Younger refugees did better in school than older refugee students. Refugees who had arrived in the United States as adolescents, and those with little prior education, had great difficulty adjusting to an age-based high school placement system. Academic achievement was also related to the educational level of the students' parents and to parents' general well-being. For example, mothers with high levels of depression were more likely to have children who were having difficulties in school. It is not surprising that rates of clinically significant levels of psychological distress among refugees were much higher than rates found in the general population of American adults. Rumbaut and Ima also noted discrepancies in performance, such as Hmong American students having high grade-point averages but low standardized test scores on reading comprehension and vocabulary. Similarly, even though the Hmong American students in this study earned higher grades than European American students, were the least likely to drop out of school, and had good attendance rates, very few Hmong American students sought postsecondary education. According to Rumbaut and Ima, lack of knowledge about potential careers, lack of role models, and economic constraints limited the achievement of educational goals, especially among Hmong American and Khmer American students.

According to Walker-Moffat (1995), there are many flaws in the academic writing about Asian Americans. She argued that the "Asian American success story" appears to be a new form of racism.

> The perception of Asian American academic success is now so widespread that Asian Americans are not considered minorities in need of affirmative action. Asian Americans are not regarded as "at risk" students, regardless of the reality of their situations. (Walker-Moffat, 1995, p. 21)

Because of the pervasiveness of this belief in the success of Asian American students, Walker-Moffat reported that many schools have failed to notice the academic problems of Asian American students, such as discrepancies between high grade-point averages and low standardized test scores or high dropout rates among female Hmong Americans. She suggested that the difference between what is perceived as academic success and real academic achievement is related to the fact that grades are a subjective measure and that neatness, effort, attentiveness, and good behavior pay off when teachers are determining grades. Teachers pointed out that the Southeast Asian refugee students were model pupils. "They are quieter, more polite and respectful than other minority students. They do their homework and are eager learners" (p. 14). Sociocultural theorists have argued that a collectivist orientation may interfere with learning in typical mainstream American classrooms (e.g., Jordan, 1984; Tharp, 1989; Vogt et al., 1993). As Walker-Moffat noted, "Hmong students have learned to work with others rather than as individuals. The idea of sitting down at a desk and writing answers on a piece of paper without discussing the problem is un-Hmong" (p. 100).

These studies represent the beginnings of research on underachievement among Asian American children. They call into question the stereotype of Asian American students as the model minority and highlight the needs of ethnic minority students whose difficulties in school go beyond their limited ability in English language.

Pressure to Succeed and Psychological Maladjustment

Concern has been raised relative to the psychosocial adjustment of Asian American students whose parents have high expectations for their academic achievement. To test whether the high expectations of Asian American parents have resulted in negative psychosocial outcomes for their adolescents, C. Chen and Stevenson (1995) explored indicators of academic orientation (e.g., achievement attitudes, aspirations, math test scores) and of possible maladjustment related to a high level of achievement (e.g., depression, stress, academic anxiety, and psychosomatic symptoms) in a sample of 304 Asian American and 1,958 European American 11th graders. Asian American students had higher math test scores and higher expectations for their own school performance than European American students did. Their perceptions of their parents' expectations for their school performance and their perceptions of the importance their parents place on getting good grades and going to college were higher than the perceptions of the European American students. In addition, Asian American students reported spending more time each week studying outside of class than their European American counterparts. Asian American students were less likely to hold part-time jobs and spent less time socializing each week. The data were thus consistent with the hypothesis that among Asian American families there were higher expectations and more emphasis on doing well in school.

In contrast, there were no differences between groups in reports of stress, depression, aggressive feelings, or somatic complaints. In general, higher math scores were negatively correlated with indexes of psychological maladjustment. For Asian American students the only positive correlation was a low but significant correlation between math scores and stress ($r = .17$). Thus, there was very little evidence that emphasis on academic achievement was associated with poor psychosocial outcomes for Asian American students.

Very little research has focused on young Asian American children. Huntsinger et al. (1998) recently conducted a longitudinal study of young European American and second-generation Chinese American children and their parents' child-rearing strategies. In both the initial assessment, when the children were in preschool or kindergarten, and 2 years later, the Chinese American parents were more controlling and had used a more systematic, formal approach to teaching their child (e.g., having their child write book reports every week, using math flash cards to help the child memorize math facts). The young Chinese American children had daily homework routines to follow. Compared with their European American counterparts, the Chinese American children spent more time working on homework, music lessons, and Chinese lessons; had less free time; and spent less time engaged in sports activities.

At Huntsinger et al.'s (1998) initial assessment in preschool or kindergarten there were no differences in teacher ratings of children's social behaviors. Two years later, teacher ratings of Chinese American and European American children's positive social adjustment (including politeness, negativism, and extroversion) did not differ. The only observed difference on teacher ratings of negative social adjustment indicated that European American children were perceived by their teachers to be more anxious and depressed than were the Chinese American children. Although 2 years does not provide long-term evidence, in this study Chinese American children did not incur negative social effects from their parents' emphasis on academic achievement.

In contrast to these two quantitative studies, qualitative studies of Asian American students suggest that the emphasis on academic achievement has had negative psychosocial consequences. In P. A. Lee and Ying's (2001) analysis of Asian American adolescents' essays on being Asian American, 13% of the adolescents reported only negative attitudes toward academic achievement, 43% indicated only positive feelings about academic achievement, and 44% revealed both positive and negative attitudes. An overwhelming majority of adolescents reported that they worked hard at schoolwork (83%), 1% rejected schoolwork (e.g., would not study, skipped classes, did not intend to go to college), and 16% reported a mixture of accepting and rejecting behaviors. Thus, although most of these Asian American adolescents engaged in positive academic behaviors, 57% expressed at least some negative attitudes toward school. As the authors noted, an essay competition is likely to elicit submissions from students who are more academically oriented and not attract those who do not write well or have little interest in school. Consequently, their data may underestimate the proportion of Asian American adolescents who have negative feelings about school. On the other hand, what is not clear is the extent to which the expressed negative attitudes reflected actual psychological maladjustment or the degree to which these attitudes reflected normative attitudes of adolescents toward school.

Limitations to Current Knowledge on Asian American Cognitive Development

First, it is obvious that research on Asian American cognitive development has been narrowly focused on school achievement. Other aspects of cognitive development have yet to be addressed. Second, the research on school achievement has endorsed the stereotype of the Asian American model student with little consideration of those who are not doing well in school.

Although examination of cross-ethnic research indicates that, as a group, Asian American students are doing well in school compared with other groups, this is not the entire story. Subgroups of Asian American children, such as Hmong, Cambodian, and Thai children, have not done well in school. It appears that these children are underachieving, at least in part, because of difficulties associated with limited English language skills, limited knowledge about the mainstream culture, and a lack of familiarity with formal school systems. Relatively little research has addressed the needs of Asian American children who are underachieving in school. Third, the degree to which emphasis on academic achievement in Asian American families is associated with increased stress and psychological maladjustment among Asian American children and adolescents is not clear. Findings from qualitative and quantitative studies on this problem have yielded conflicting results. More attention should be given to research in this area.

LESSONS LEARNED

In this chapter we have highlighted the ways in which development of Asian Americans may be influenced by Asian American beliefs and values and by the experiences associated with immigration and acculturation to a new culture. We now turn to a few general observations about current knowledge of Asian American development and some suggestions for future research. First, a major shortfall of the existing research is that researchers have primarily identified differences on some belief or behavior by ethnicity and then hypothesized that these differences are the result of differences in cultural values (a > c) without assessing the relations between ethnicity and the specific cultural value (a > b) or the relation between the cultural value and the belief or behavioral outcome (b > c)—that is, researchers rarely check their hypothesis that a difference in a specific cultural value mediates observed differences in behaviors or beliefs. This type of research harkens back to Bronfenbrenner and Crouter's (1982) exhortation about the problems of social address studies. Researchers need to test the hypothesis that cultural beliefs and values mediate the relation between ethnicity and observed differences in behavioral outcomes.

Second, a major limitation to current knowledge is that research on Asian Americans has primarily been conducted from Western psychological theoretical perspectives. Researchers have, for the most part, ignored Asian developmental concepts and then are at a loss for an explanation when Western constructs do not adequately explain Asian American development. Future research would benefit from following Chao's (1994, 2000) example of using Asian psychological constructs as a framework for studying Asian American and non-Asian American development. Asian psychological theories—both explicit and implicit—may provide useful models for examining and understanding human behavior.

While encouraging the use of Asian psychological constructs, we note that one of the striking themes that emerged in the studies we reviewed related to ideas about collectivism. Asian cultures have generally been identified as collectivist in orientation, emphasizing interdependence and the priority of social obligations and duties over individual desires (e.g., Ho, 1994; U. Kim & Choi, 1994; Triandis, Bontempo, Villareal, Asai, & Lucca, 1988). Recent discussions of individualist and collectivist perspectives have elaborated these constructs to recognize multiple forms of individualism and collectivism (e.g., U. Kim & Choi, 1994; Triandis et al., 1988). Theorists acknowledge that although the general orientation of a society may be, for example, collectivist in orientation, members of the society may also hold some beliefs that are decidedly individualistic (e.g., Ho, 1994). Lin and Fu's (1990) study of parenting provides an example of the complexity of these constructs. They hypothesized that overseas Chinese and Chinese American immigrant parents would place less importance on encouraging independence in their child relative to European American parents based on the collectivist orientation of the traditional Chinese culture. Quite unexpectedly, however, overseas Chinese and Chinese American immigrant parents rated encouragement of independence as more important than European American parents. Thus, independent behaviors and achievement were not being discouraged within their collectivist orientation. More sophisticated definitions of Asian American beliefs and values may yield a better understanding of the impact of these beliefs and values on development.

Third, very few studies have examined differences across Asian American subgroups even though the national histories, cultural backgrounds, and immigration histories of these subgroups may drastically differ. In addition, the effects of continued immigration and a "renewal" of cultural values on the part of some groups versus the discontinuation of immigration and the distancing of exposure to original cultures are rarely discussed. However, as researchers begin to focus on specific subgroups of Asian Americans they must remember that findings from multi-ethnic group studies make important contributions to an overall understanding of Asian American development. Drawing conclusions from single-ethnic studies can lead researchers to draw conclusions that might ignore alternative explanations. For example, previously described research on Vietnamese immigrant families suggested that adolescents were embracing attitudes and behaviors of the dominant culture more quickly than their parents were (e.g., Kibria, 1993; Nguyen & Williams, 1989) and that this difference led to increased parent–child conflict during adolescence. In Fuligni's (1998) study of parent–adolescent conflict in multiple groups, however, there was no difference between the European American students' reports of parent–adolescent conflict and the reports of students of Filipino and Chinese descent. Approximately 25% of the Chinese-descent students and 40% of the Filipino-descent students were first generation; about half of the students in each of these groups were second generation.

It is possible that the parent–adolescent conflict observed in Asian American immigrant families is quite similar to the conflict observed in non-immigrant European American families, which is hypothesized to result from the differences between the adolescent peer culture and the adult culture in U.S. society. If researchers focus only on single-group studies they lose the perspective that can be gained from multi-ethnic group studies. Similarly, as Takanishi (1994) noted, "The Asian diaspora provides a rich laboratory for exploring continuities and discontinuities in child socialization" (p. 358). Researchers' understanding of Asian American development would benefit from comparison of the development of individuals of Asian descent across countries.

Fourth, a major theme in this review is that very little research has been conducted systematically on Asian American children in many areas of developmental psychology (e.g., emotional development, social cognition, peer relationships, personality development). Examination of developmental domains beyond academic achievement and parent–child relationships could be extremely productive. For example, a potentially fascinating area is the development of self-concept or self-awareness. Hsu (1971) described the Western construct of personality as a Ptolemaic view of human beings, a view in which one's social relationships revolve around oneself. He argued that the Asian view, in contrast, was more consistent with a Galilean view of social life. He offered the Chinese term *jen* (personage):

> *Jen* contrasts sharply with the concept of personality. The concept of personality puts the emphasis on what goes on in the individual's psyche including his deep core of complexes and anxieties. . . . But the concept of *jen* puts the emphasis on interpersonal transactions. . . . it sees the nature of the individual's external behavior in terms of how it fits or fails to fit the interpersonal standards of the society and culture. (p. 29)

Others (e.g., Kondo, 1992; Lebra, 1992; Rosenberger, 1992) have described Japanese understandings of the self in terms distinct from Western perspectives of the self and provide alternative frameworks for exploring Asian American conceptions of the self.

One of the most interesting new avenues of research is at the intersection of cognitive processing and social identity research. Recent work by Steele (e.g., Spencer, Steele, & Quinn, 1999; Steele & Aronson, 1995) suggests that there may be a particular way in which social identities, such as ethnic or gender identity, interact with and bring about a conflict that inhibits student achievement. Steele has argued that students who strongly identify with academic achievement and are members of groups that have not traditionally done well in school face an additional barrier when they try to achieve in school: that of stereotype threat. *Stereotype threat* is defined as

> the event of a negative stereotype about a group to which one belongs becoming self-relevant, usually as a plausible interpretation of something one is doing, for an experience one is having, or for a situation one is in, that has relevance to one's self-definition. (Steele, 1997, p. 616)

Evoking negative stereotypes in experimental settings has been shown to lower math performances of women (Spencer et al., 1999), to lower verbal scores of African American college students (Steele & Aronson, 1995), and to lower math scores of European American male college students (for whom the negative stereotype was a comparison with Asian students; Aronson et al., 1999). Stereotypes can also facilitate performance. In a study of Asian American female undergraduates, priming participants on gender identity resulted in lower math scores than the scores of a no-priming control group, whereas priming participants on ethnic identity produced higher math scores than the scores of the control group (Shih, Pittinsky, & Ambady, 1999).

The impact of social identity and cultural knowledge on cognitive processing becomes even more evocative when one considers bicultural development. Hong, Morris, Chiu, and Benet-Martínez (2000) showed that in bicultural individuals priming one cultural identity produced responses on a separate task that are consistent with the cultural content of the primed culture. Westernized Hong Kong Chinese college and high school students were presented with Chinese cultural icons (e.g., a picture of the Great Wall), American cultural icons (e.g., a picture of the American flag), or neutral symbols (e.g., a picture of a physical landscape) and asked to write descriptions of the pictures. Participants then completed a separate causal attribution task, which participants could interpret through a Western cultural lens or a Chinese cultural lens. Responses on the causal attribution task varied according to the cultural perspective that had been evoked. For example, college students were presented with a realistic picture of a single fish swimming in front of a small group of fish. They rated how confidently they believed that the single fish was swimming in front of the other fish because the fish was being chased by the other fish (an external cause) and how confidently they believed that the single fish was leading the other fish (an internal cause). Students who had been primed with American icons were more confident that the fish was leading the other fish (the internal cause) than those who had been primed with Chinese icons. The ratings of participants in the control condition, who had been primed with neutral symbols, fell between the two other scores. The opposite result was obtained with respect to the external, or social cause. Hong et al. described this phenomenon as *frame switching*, the idea that a bicultural individual can process information from one cultural perspective or the other, depending on which cultural framework has been activated. Research along these lines could open up new understandings of what it means to be Asian American.

In general, relatively little is known about the socialization of cultural values. As we have shown, not much attention has been given to examinations of the similarities and differences across generations of Asian Americans. Previously described research indicated that third- and later generation adolescents of Chinese and Filipino descent are similar to their peers with European backgrounds in some aspects of parent–adolescent relationships (Fuligni, 1998) and that the grades of fourth-generation Japanese American students were more like grades of European American children than those of Chinese or Korean American students (Schneider et al., 1994). It seems, however, that third- and fourth-generation Japanese Americans retain certain cultural values and that some aspects of Japanese culture may be retained in parent–child relationships (Hieshima & Schneider, 1994; Schneider et al., 1994). Being a visible ethnic minority and facing continued racial discrimination may help Japanese Americans retain their ethnic identity and values.

> Ironically, continued racial discrimination and being made to feel somehow different from mainstream society play an important role in the retention of a collective orientation, ethnic community involvement, the tenacity of the cultural construct of empathy, and the ability to convey understandings tacitly among Sansei and Yonsei. (Hieshima & Schneider, 1994, p. 326)

As Hieshima and Schneider (1994) suggested, Asian Americans cannot assume that they will be completely assimilated into the mainstream culture—neither is assimilation necessarily a goal for Asian American parents. Consequently, Asian American development is fundamentally the product of bicultural socialization and the interaction between two dynamic cultures. "Mainstream" culture in the United States is continuously changing as it is influenced by immigration from individuals representing a variety of cultures and by technological, economic, and political developments. Asian American cultures are also influenced by the influx of new immigrants (or lack of new immigrants) and by the social, economic, and political forces in the United States. Each generation creates new Asian American identities. Examining the process of bicultural socialization and studying Asian American identity as a dynamic, evolving identity will enhance an understanding of Asian American development.

FUTURE RESEARCH DIRECTIONS

Future research should focus on the following areas:

- Going beyond social address models to examine the relations between general cultural values (e.g., collectivist orientation, traditional beliefs) and specific belief or behavior outcomes.
- Exploring Asian psychological constructs as frameworks for understanding Asian American development.
- Observing the distinctions among subgroups of Asian Americans.
- Examining the impact of minority status on Asian American development.
- Going beyond the existing emphasis on parent–child relationships and academic achievement to consider other aspects of social and cognitive development.

REFERENCES

Arkoff, A., & Weaver, H. B. (1966). Body image and body dissatisfaction in Japanese-Americans. *Journal of Social Psychology, 68*, 323–330.

Aronson, J., Lustina, M. J., Good, C., Keough, K., Steele, C. M., & Brown, J. (1999). When White men can't do math: Necessary and sufficient factors in stereotype threat. *Journal of Experimental Social Psychology, 35*, 29–46.

Baumrind, D. (1971). Current patterns of parental authority. *Developmental Psychology Monograph, 4*(1, Part 2).

Baumrind, D. (1991a). The influence of parenting style on adolescent competence and substance use. *Journal of Early Adolescence, 11*, 56–95.

Baumrind, D. (1991b). Parenting styles and adolescent development. In J. Brooks-Gunn, R. Lerner, & A. C. Petersen (Eds.), *The encyclopedia of adolescence* (pp. 746–758). New York: Garland.

Bronfenbrenner, U., & Crouter, A. C. (1982). Work and family through time and space. In S. Kamerman & C. Hayes (Eds.), *Families that work: Children in a changing world* (pp. 39–83). Washington, DC: National Academy Press.

Bukowski, W. M., & Sippola, L. K. (1998). Diversity and the social mind: Goals, constructs, culture and development. *Developmental Psychology, 34*, 742–746.

Caplan, N., Choy, M. H., & Whitmore, J. K. (1992, February). Indochinese refugee families and academic achievement. *Scientific American*, 36–42.

Caplan, N., Whitmore, J. K., & Choy, M. H. (1989). *The Boat People and achievement in America: A study of family life, hard work, and cultural values*. Ann Arbor: University of Michigan Press.

Chan, S. (1991). *Asian Americans: An interpretive history*. Boston: Twayne.

Chang, T. S. (1975). The self-concept of children in ethnic groups: Black American and Korean American. *Elementary School Journal, 76*, 52–58.

Chao, R. K. (1994). Beyond parental control and authoritarian parenting style: Understanding Chinese parenting through the cultural notion of training. *Child Development, 65*, 1111–1119.

Chao, R. K. (2000). The parenting of immigrant Chinese and European American mothers: Relations between parenting styles, socialization goals, and parental practices. *Journal of Applied Developmental Psychology, 21,* 233–248.

Chao, R. K. (2001). Extending research on the consequences of parenting style for Chinese Americans and European Americans. *Child Development, 72,* 1832–1843.

Chen, C., & Stevenson, H. W. (1995). Motivation and mathematics achievement: A comparative study of Asian-American, Caucasian-American, and East Asian high school students. *Child Development, 66,* 1215–1234.

Chen, Z.-Y. (1999). Ethnic similarities and differences in the association of emotional autonomy and adolescent outcomes: Comparing Euro-American and Asian-American adolescents. *Psychological Reports, 84,* 501–516.

Dinh, K. T., Sarason, B. R., & Sarason, I. G. (1994). Parent–child relationships in Vietnamese immigrant families. *Journal of Family Psychology, 8,* 471–488.

Dornbusch, S. M., Ritter, P. L., Leiderman, P. H., Roberts, D. F., & Fraleigh, M. J. (1987). The relation of parenting style to adolescent school performance. *Child Development, 58,* 1244–1257.

Edmonston, B., & Passel, J. S. (1994). The future immigrant population of the United States. In B. Edmonston & J. S. Passel (Eds.), *Immigration and ethnicity* (pp. 317–353). Washington, DC: Uran Institute.

Fuligni, A. J. (1998). Authority, autonomy, and parent–adolescent conflict and cohesion: A study of adolescents from Mexican, Chinese, Filipino, and European backgrounds. *Developmental Psychology, 34,* 782–792.

Gibson, M. A. (1987). The school performance of immigrant minorities: A comparative view. *Anthropology and Education Quarterly, 18,* 262–275.

Gilligan, C. F. (1982). *In a different voice.* Cambridge, MA: Harvard University Press.

Grusec, J. E., & Goodnow, J. J. (1994). Impact of parental discipline methods on the child's internalization of values: A reconceptualization of current points of view. *Developmental Psychology, 30,* 4–19.

Hamm, J. V. (2000). Do birds of a feather flock together? The variable bases for African American, Asian American, and European American adolescents' selection of similar friends. *Developmental Psychology, 36,* 209–219.

Hieshima, J. A., & Schneider, B. (1994). Intergenerational effects on the cultural and cognitive socialization of third- and fourth-generation Japanese Americans. *Journal of Applied Developmental Psychology, 15,* 319–327.

Ho, D. Y. F. (1982). Asian concepts in behavioral science. *Psychologia, 25,* 228–235.

Ho, D. Y. F. (1994). Cognitive socialization in Confucian heritage cultures. In P. M. Greenfield & R. R. Cocking (Eds.), *Cross-cultural roots of minority child development* (pp. 285–313). Hillsdale, NJ: Erlbaum.

Hong, Y.-y., Morris, M. W., Chiu, C.-y., & Benet-Martínez, V. (2000). Multicultural minds: A dynamic constructivist approach to culture and cognition. *American Psychologist, 55,* 709–720.

Hsia, J., & Peng, S. S. (1998). Academic achievement and performance. In L. C. Lee & N. W. S. Zane (Eds.), *Handbook of Asian American psychology* (pp. 325–357). Thousand Oaks, CA: Sage.

Hsu, F. L. K. (1971). Psychosocial homeostasis and *jen*: Conceptual tools for advancing psychological anthropology. *American Anthropologist, 73*, 23–44.

Huntsinger, C. S., Jose, P. E., & Larson, S. L. (1998). Do parent practices to encourage academic competence influence the social adjustment of young European American and Chinese American children? *Developmental Psychology, 34*, 747–756.

Jain, A., & Belsky, J. (1997). Fathering and acculturation: Immigrant Indian families with young children. *Journal of Marriage and the Family, 59*, 873–883.

Jordan, C. (1984). Cultural compatibility and the education of Hawaiian children: Implications for mainland educators. *Educational Research Quarterly, 8*(4), 59–71.

Kibria, N. (1993). *Family tightrope: The changing lives of Vietnamese Americans.* Princeton, NJ: Princeton University Press.

Kim, T. E., & Goto, S. G. (2000). Peer delinquency and parental social support as predictors of Asian American adolescent delinquency. *Deviant Behavior: An Interdisciplinary Journal, 21*, 331–347.

Kim, U., & Choi, S.-H. (1994). Individualism, collectivism, and child development: A Korean perspective. In P. M. Greenfield & R. R. Cocking (Eds.), *Cross-cultural roots of minority child development* (pp. 227–257). Hillsdale, NJ: Erlbaum.

Kondo, D. (1992). Multiple selves: The aesthetics and politics of artisanal identities. In N. R. Rosenberger (Ed.), *Japanese sense of self* (pp. 40–66). New York: Cambridge University Press.

Lebra, T. S. (1992). Self in Japanese culture. In N. R. Rosenberger (Ed.), *Japanese sense of self* (pp. 105–120). New York: Cambridge University Press.

Lee, E. S., & Rong, X. (1988). The educational and economic achievement of Asian-Americans. *Elementary School Journal, 88*, 545–560.

Lee, P. A., & Ying, Y. (2001). Asian American adolescents' academic achievement: A look behind the model minority image. *Journal of Human Behavior in the Social Environment, 3*, 35–48.

Lee, S. J. (1994). Behind the model-minority stereotype: Voices of high- and low-achieving Asian American students. *Anthropology and Education Quarterly, 25*, 413–429.

Lin, C. C., & Fu, V. R. (1990). A comparison of child-rearing practices among Chinese, immigrant Chinese, and Caucasian-American parents. *Child Development, 61*, 429–433.

Maccoby, E. E., & Martin, J. A. (1983). Socialization in the context of the family: Parent–child interaction. In P. H. Mussen (Series Ed.) & E. M. Hetherington (Vol. Ed.), *Handbook of child psychology: Vol. 4. Socialization, personality, and social development* (4th ed., pp. 1–101). New York: Wiley.

Matute-Bianchi, M. E. (1986). Ethnic identities and patterns of school success and failure among Mexican-descent and Japanese-American students in a California high school: An ethnographic analysis. *American Journal of Education, 95,* 233–255.

Mizokawa, D. T., & Ryckman, D. B. (1990). Attributions of academic success and failure: A comparison of six Asian-American ethnic groups. *Journal of Cross-Cultural Psychology, 21,* 434–451.

National Center for Education Statistics. (1997). *NAEP 1996 mathematics report card for the nation and the states: Findings from the National Assessment of Educational Progress.* Washington, DC: Office of Educational Research and Improvement, U.S. Department of Education.

Nguyen, N. A., & Williams, H. L. (1989). Transition from East to West: Vietnamese adolescents and their parents. *American Academy of Child and Adolescent Psychiatry, 28,* 505–515.

Okagaki, L., & Frensch, P. A. (1998). Parenting and children's school achievement: A multi-ethnic perspective. *American Educational Research Journal, 35,* 123–144.

Okagaki, L., & Sternberg, R. J. (1993). Parental beliefs and children's early school performance. *Child Development, 64,* 36–56.

Pang, V. O., Mizokawa, D. T., Morishima, J. K., & Olstad, R. G. (1985). Self-concepts of Japanese-American children. *Journal of Cross-Cultural Psychology, 16,* 99–109.

Patel, N., Power, T. G., & Bhavnagri, N. P. (1996). Socialization values and practices of Indian immigrant parents: Correlates of modernity and acculturation. *Child Development, 67,* 302–313.

Peng, S. S., & Wright, D. (1994). Explanation of academic achievement of Asian American students. *Journal of Educational Research, 87,* 346–352.

Phinney, J. S., & Chavira, V. (1995). Parental ethnic socialization and adolescent coping with problems related to ethnicity. *Journal of Research on Adolescence, 5,* 31–53.

Rosenberger, N. R. (1992). Tree in summer, tree in winter: Movement of self in Japan. In N. R. Rosenberger (Ed.), *Japanese sense of self* (pp. 67–92). New York: Cambridge University Press.

Rosenthal, D. A., & Feldman, S. S. (1992). The relationships between parenting behaviour and ethnic identity in Chinese-American and Chinese-Australian adolescents. *International Journal of Psychology, 27,* 19–31.

Rumbaut, R. G., & Ima, K. (1988). *The adaptation of Southeast Asian refugee youth: A comparative study* (Final report to the Office of Refugee Resettlement). San Diego, CA: San Diego State University. (ERIC Document Reproduction Service No. ED299372)

Schneider, B., Hieshima, J. A., Lee, S., & Plank, S. (1994). East-Asian academic success in the United States: Family, school, and community explanations. In P. M. Greenfield & R. R. Cocking (Eds.), *Cross-cultural roots of minority child development* (pp. 323–350). Hillsdale, NJ: Erlbaum.

Schneider, B., & Lee, Y. (1990). A model for academic success: The school and home environment of East Asian students. *Anthropology and Education Quarterly, 21*, 358–377.

Segal, U. A. (1991). Cultural variables in Asian Indian families. *Families in Society: The Journal of Contemporary Human Services, 72*, 233–241.

Shih, M., Pittinsky, T. L., & Ambady, N. (1999). Stereotype susceptibility: Identity salience and shifts in quantitative performance. *Psychological Science, 10*, 80–83.

Smith-Hefner, N. J. (1999). *Khmer American: Identity and moral education in a diasporic community.* Berkeley: University of California Press.

Spencer, S. J., Steele, C. M., & Quinn, D. M. (1999). Stereotype threat and women's math performance. *Journal of Experimental Social Psychology, 35*, 4–28.

Steele, C. M. (1997). A threat in the air: How stereotypes shape intellectual identity and performance. *American Psychologist, 52*, 613–629.

Steele, C. M., & Aronson, J. (1995). Stereotype threat and the intellectual test performance of African Americans. *Journal of Personality and Social Psychology, 69*, 797–811.

Steinberg, L., Dornbusch, S. M., & Brown, B. B. (1992). Ethnic differences in adolescent achievement: An ecological perspective. *American Psychologist, 47*, 723–729.

Steinberg, L., Mounts, N., Lamborn, S., & Dornbusch, S. (1991). Authoritative parenting and adolescent adjustment across various ecological niches. *Journal of Research on Adolescence, 1*, 19–36.

Sue, S., & Okazaki, S. (1990). Asian-American educational achievements: A phenomenon in search of an explanation. *American Psychologist, 45*, 913–920.

Takanishi, R. (1994). Continuities and discontinuities in the cognitive socialization of Asian-originated children: The case of Japanese Americans. In P. M. Greenfield & R. R. Cocking (Eds.), *Cross-cultural roots of minority child development* (pp. 351–362). Hillsdale, NJ: Erlbaum.

Tharp, R. G. (1989). Psychocultural variables and constants: Effects on teaching and learning in school. *American Psychologist, 44*, 349–359.

Triandis, H. C., Bontempo, R., Villareal, M. J., Asai, M., & Lucca, N. (1988). Individualism and collectivism: Cross-cultural perspectives on self–ingroup relationships. *Journal of Personality and Social Psychology, 54*, 323–338.

Trueba, H. T., Cheng, L., & Ima, K. (1993). *Myth or reality: Adaptive strategies of Asian Americans in California.* Washington, DC: Falmer Press.

Trueba, H. T., Jacobs, L., & Kirton, E. (1990). *Cultural conflict and adaptation: The case of Hmong children in American society.* New York: Falmer Press.

Tsang, S.-L. (1988). The mathematics achievement characteristics of Asian-American students. In R. R. Cocking & J. P. Mestre (Eds.), *Linguistic and cultural influences on learning mathematics* (pp. 123–136). Hillsdale, NJ: Erlbaum.

Uba, L. (1994). *Asian Americans: Personality patterns, identity, and mental health.* New York: Guilford Press.

U.S. Bureau of the Census. (1993a). *We the Americans: Asians* (WE-3). Washington, DC: U.S. Department of Commerce.

U.S. Bureau of the Census. (1993b). *We the Americans: Our education* (WE-11). Washington, DC: U.S. Department of Commerce.

Vogt, L. A., Jordan, C., & Tharp, R. G. (1993). Explaining school failure, producing school success: Two cases. In E. Jacob & C. Jordan (Eds.), *Minority education: Anthropological perspectives* (pp. 53–65). Norwood, NJ: Ablex.

Walker-Moffat, W. (1995). *The other side of the Asian American success story.* San Francisco: Jossey-Bass.

Wong, M. G. (1990). The education of White, Chinese, Filipino, and Japanese students: A look at "High School and Beyond." *Sociological Perspectives, 33,* 353–374.

Yeh, C. J., & Huang, K. (1996). The collectivistic nature of ethnic identity development among Asian-American college students. *Adolescence, 31,* 645–661.

Ying, Y., Akutsu, P. D., Zhang, X., & Huang, L. N. (1999). Psychological dysfunction in Southeast Asian refugees as mediated by sense of coherence. *American Journal of Community Psychology, 25,* 839–859.

Ying, Y., Lee, P. A., & Tsai, J. L. (2000). Cultural orientation and racial discrimination: Predictors of coherence in Chinese American young adults. *Journal of Community Psychology, 28,* 427–442.

Ying, Y., Lee, P. A., Tsai, J. L., Hung, Y., Lin, M., & Wan, C. T. (2001). Asian American college students as model minorities: An examination of their overall competence. *Cultural Diversity and Ethnic Minority Psychology, 7,* 59–74.

4

AGING AND ASIAN AMERICANS: DEVELOPING CULTURALLY APPROPRIATE RESEARCH METHODOLOGY

GAYLE Y. IWAMASA AND KRISTEN H. SOROCCO

Given the rapid growth of the Asian American population in the United States, it is of no surprise that the population of Asian American older adults is increasing as well. According to the American Association of Retired Persons and the Administration on Aging (1999), of the major U.S. ethnic groups of older adults (ages 65 and older), the Asian American population is projected to increase by 323% by 2030, second only to Latino Americans, whose older adult population is expected to increase by 341%. This is likely based in part on census projections that in 2020 the median age of Asian Americans will be 34.5 years, and the mean age will be 36.0 years (U.S. Bureau of the Census, 2000a). In addition, according to the 2000 census, older adults comprised 7.8% of the Asian American population (U.S. Bureau of the Census, 2001a) and 5.2% of the Native Hawaiian and other Pacific Islander population (U.S. Bureau of the Census, 2001b). Census projections indicate that these percentages will jump to 12.6% by 2025 and to 14.5% by 2045 (n.b., Asian Americans and Pacific Islanders were combined in population projections; U.S. Bureau of the Census, 2000b). Thus, it is essential that researchers in the field of Asian American psychology explore and understand the unique issues and diverse experiences facing this group.

Researchers have acknowledged that although there is some, very sparse, literature on the mental and physical health of a number of older ethnic minorities, such as African Americans and Latino Americans, there are little comparable data on older Asian Americans. As a result, health care practitioners currently have few resources to assist them in the assessment and treatment of older Asian American adults who may be experiencing psychological distress. Indeed, many clinicians probably rely on assumptions that Asian Americans tend to somaticize their psychological distress, a belief that has not received much empirical attention beyond studies conducted in the 1970s on Asian American college students. Somatization of distress is a complex issue for Asian American older adults, because older adults tend to experience more somatic complaints as a result of the aging process in general. Thus, in assessing an Asian American older adult, distinguishing between physical complaints as a result of the aging process or as an expression of psychological distress is quite challenging.

In addition, there is some evidence that ethnic group differences exist among Asian Americans concerning the reporting of somatic symptoms during psychological distress (e.g., Enright & Jaeckle, 1963; Marsella, Kinzie, & Gordon, 1973; Marsella, Sanborn, Kameoka, Shizuru, & Brennan, 1975; Zheng et al., 1997). However, much of this work has not focused on Asian American older adults. Furthermore, a majority of this research has been conducted on Chinese and Chinese American populations, so less is known regarding the reporting of somatic symptoms during psychological distress among other Asian American groups, such as Japanese and Korean Americans. Research examining the somatization of psychological distress among Asian American older adults is greatly needed so that researchers can begin to tease apart cultural variables from the developmental variables of aging and physical decline.

Popular issues and topics that psychologists have examined among White older adults have not yet been examined among Asian American older adults. For example, there are no data on the experience of retirement among Asian American older adults. There is no information on the experiences of widowhood among Asian American older adult women, or on gender differences in Asian American elders' risk for developing psychological or cognitive disorders. There are no data on the relationships of Asian American grandparents and their grandchildren. The concept of "successful aging" has become increasingly popular yet has not been examined among Asian American older adults. There is a small, albeit growing, literature on cognitive decline, dementia, caregiving, and information processing among Asian American older adults; however, it is clear that Asian American older adults have largely been ignored in the psychological literature devoted to older adult issues. Because there has been so little attention paid to the mental health of Asian American older adults, researchers have yet to discern which aspects of aging among this population are culture specific versus culture general.

It is interesting that popular issues that have been examined in the Asian American psychology literature also have neglected older adults. For example, concepts and topics examined with younger and middle-adult Asian American groups, such as generational status, acculturation, ethnic identity, women's issues, psychological assessment, gender and sex roles, and biracial and multiracial relationships, have not yet been examined among Asian American older adults.

Some of the life experiences of Asian Americans, such as the internment of Japanese Americans during World War II, the immigration experiences of the Vietnamese boat people, and the attacks on Korean American store owners in Los Angeles during the riots that followed the Rodney King trial verdict, are clear examples of specific factors that may influence the development of distress among certain Asian American groups. Less clear, and more difficult to define, are the consequences of subtle racism and discrimination faced by many Asian Americans, which also may lead to the development of depression and anxiety. These experiences, in conjunction with traditional Asian cultural values of not expressing emotions, saving face (i.e., maintaining one's public image), and interpersonal cooperation and harmony, may lead to differences in the experience and expression of symptoms of depression and anxiety. This is particularly true for older Asian Americans, who are more likely to maintain traditional values and beliefs compared with younger Asian Americans, who are likely to be more acculturated and thus more likely to follow Western values and beliefs.

In addition to facing potential discrimination as an older person, the older Asian American adult faces possible discrimination based on ethnicity. Sue, Chun, and Gee (1995) referred to this as *minority group status* and suggested that, as a result of their ethnicity, ethnic minorities such as Asian Americans have a history of being the targets of prejudiced attitudes and discrimination. Thus, just by virtue of being an ethnic minority, older Asian American adults are more likely to have more frequent stressful and negative experiences in their interactions with others, perhaps even from other older adults who may maintain beliefs that some Asian Americans are not as good as other Americans. For example, many older World War II veterans may perceive Japanese Americans as equivalent to the Japanese and thus hold negative prejudicial attitudes about them, which may result in discriminatory behavior. A specific example is Sen. Daniel Inouye of Hawaii, who, on returning to the United States from a tour of duty as a highly decorated soldier in uniform, was refused service by a barber in San Francisco because he "did not serve Japs."

Although some racist incidents based on one's ethnicity may have happened a long time ago, some older Asian Americans may still clearly remember being the recipients of racism and discrimination. The impact of such events and the effects of minority status on the mental health of older Asian American adults have yet to be examined. However, one can hypothesize that such experiences influence the manifestation and expression of psychological distress of older Asian American adults and, as a result, may differ from the manifestation and expression of distress in older adults of other ethnic groups.

Given the preceding brief review, the potential to learn from studying Asian American older adults is clear. For example, Asian American older adults' lifestyles, methods of coping with aging, coping with prolonged racism and discrimination, and social support may have major implications regarding the concept of successful aging for elders from other ethnic groups. Acculturation and ethnic and racial identity, as well as general developmental issues associated with aging, may also provide researchers with important and helpful information, such as identifying protective factors related to psychological distress. Researchers have much to learn about the role of culture in the aging process for Asian American older adults, and such information may lead to reformulation of hypotheses about adult and older adult development.

HETEROGENEITY OF ASIAN AMERICAN OLDER ADULTS

The population of older Asian Americans is just as heterogeneous as the general Asian American population, if not more so. Many of the major within-group differences that are applicable to the general Asian American population, such as ethnicity, generational and immigration status, socioeconomic status (SES), language(s) used regularly (both spoken and written), educational and occupational status, acculturation and ethnic identity, and community environment, are also applicable to older Asian Americans. Among older adult Asian Americans there exist additional ethnic group differences in some of these variables. For example, older Asian Americans who belong to ethnic groups having a longer history in the United States (e.g., Japanese Americans and Chinese Americans) are more likely to be of higher generational status (e.g., second and third) as compared to "newer" Asian American elders (e.g., from Southeast Asia, Korea, and Vietnam), who are likely to be first-generation immigrants. Asian American older adults with high generational status are likely to speak English as their first language, have some of their own ethnic American traditions (e.g., Nisei Week, which celebrates second-generation Japanese Americans), and are likely to have higher levels of acculturation. This is in contrast to newer Asian American older adult immigrants, who may not speak English, maintain more traditions from their home country, and have lower levels of acculturation.

Ethnic group differences also are found among older adult Asian Americans in educational level, SES, and work experience. Cambodian American immigrant elders are believed to be at higher risk for depression, anxiety and posttraumatic stress disorder. There are numerous dialects of the Chinese language among Chinese American older adults. The motivation to immigrate to the United States, and personal immigration experiences, differ greatly among immigrant Asian American elders. For example, some Asian American older adults are in the United States not by choice but because they were forced to leave their countries for fear of political persecution, torture, and perhaps death, whereas others immigrated to the United States because they wanted to. These and other between-group differences that highlight the heterogeneity among Asian Americans have been summarized by Iwamasa (1997) and Lee (1997). Such culture-specific experiences and issues must be examined among older adult Asian Americans.

Older Asian Americans also have unique experiences that differentiate them from their younger counterparts. For example, the living situation of older adults is increasingly changing. When parents would become infirm or otherwise unable to care for themselves, or when one parent passed away, the surviving parent traditionally would live with a particular child's family, often the family of the firstborn son. However, recent research with Japanese American older adults has indicated that they would prefer to remain in their own homes as long as possible, even if a partner dies. In addition, among couples with one ill partner, many research participants have reported that they would prefer to make substantial efforts to care for the ill partner in their own homes. The existence of senior citizen's day program facilities also have enabled many Asian American older adults to obtain certain services, such as regular health care checkups, minor health care services, financial services, meals, and exercise programs in convenient locations. Such facilities also provide these seniors with additional social support, which likely reduces reliance on immediate family for these needs as the individual ages. Many of these facilities also provide members with a large array of social activities, such as art classes, educational programs, and leisure trips. The role of factors such as acculturation and generational status, which may influence an Asian American older adult's desire to live on his or her own, attend a senior citizen's program, and to participate in social activities, has not yet been investigated. Again, examining these culture-specific qualities of Asian American elders may result in information that could benefit older adults of other ethnic groups.

An additional important within-group difference among older adult Asian Americans is the concept of age cohorts. In the general older adult psychology literature, researchers have begun to distinguish among age cohorts among older adults. Specifically, young-old, mid-old, and old-old subgroups have been identified (Knight, 1986). The need to specify age cohorts among older adults is important given the possibility that one older adult (e.g., age 60 years) could likely be the child of another older adult (e.g., age 84 years). Given their increasing life expectancy, identification of age cohorts among Asian American older adults is important.

Finally, gender issues among older adult Asian Americans must be examined. For example, are life expectancies for Asian American women and men similar to those of other U.S. ethnic groups? Although not delineated along gender lines, the psychological literature on older adults does tend to differentiate some issues—widowhood, for example—by gender. In addition, other topics, such as reactions to retirement and caregiving, tend to focus on one gender. Such issues must also be examined among older Asian Americans, particularly given that some of them may adhere to more traditional Asian sex roles. It is also highly likely that, because of vast heterogeneity, there exist significant ethnic group differences among Asian American older adults in terms of sex roles and gender issues.

TOWARD DEVELOPING A THEORETICAL FRAMEWORK FOR ASIAN AMERICAN AGING

Most frameworks or models of aging do not incorporate ethnic or cultural background and thus do not provide researchers with directions in terms of how being Asian American would influence one's aging experience. For example, Rowe and Kahn's (1997) model of successful aging comprises three components: (a) avoiding disease and disability, (b) engagement with life, and (c) high cognitive and physical function. However, much of their model is based on biological data and includes some potentially culturally biased interpretations of what are considered to be integral components of the model, such as productive activities, self-efficacy, and response to stress.

In terms of considering ethnicity and culture in aging, much of the literature focuses on specific issues in aging within specific ethnic groups and has not provided a cohesive framework in which to consider the influence of ethnicity. For example, Sokolovsky's (1997) edited volume contains very interesting and informative chapters on specific issues in specific cultural groups and does not focus solely on ethnic minority groups in the United States. In addition, Tsai and Carstensen (1996) discussed the influence of ethnicity on the aging process, such as attitudes toward aging, ethnic identity, and intergenerational support. However, their review is a general discussion pertaining to ethnic minorities and is within the context of mental health treatment. Issues specific to Asian Americans were not discussed.

The field of Asian American psychology clearly would benefit from a comprehensive model of aging among Asian Americans that would incorporate specific cultural variables. We currently are developing such a framework from which researchers may begin to examine the aging process among Asian Americans. Such a model would provide researchers with a programmatic method of examining the multitude of experiences faced by Asian American older adults.

METHODOLOGICAL ISSUES IN RESEARCH WITH ASIAN AMERICAN OLDER ADULTS

On behalf of the Asian American Psychological Association, Sue and Sue (2000) summarized the important components of conducting research with Asian American individuals. Much of what they included incorporates both the etic (universal) and emic (culture specific) aspects of conducting research with culturally diverse populations. Triandis (1994) summarized the importance of conducting research with culturally diverse populations from an emic perspective. This is even more important in considering research with Asian American older adults, because not only are ethnically related variables important, but so too are age-related issues.

As indicated earlier, when studying Asian American older adults many additional emic demographic characteristics must be considered. For example, Kim (1983) emphasized that older Asian Americans may have differing needs, such as health care needs, income needs, social service needs, nutritional needs, and issues related to "postfigurative role loss." According to Kim, *postfigurative culture* is based in transgenerational communication of cultural variables, by which children learn about their culture from their parents. Kim noted that, given the technologically based society of the United States, this role is increasingly being lost. In addition, the generation gap, which includes differences not only in behaviors and values but also in language ability, may also contribute to a decrease in transgenerational communication of cultural values and concepts. Kim also noted that as the generation gap increases, older adults become more susceptible to deteriorating physical and mental health conditions as they lose their role of being wise elders.

Another important methodological aspect about conducting research with older Asian Americans is assessment. Hayes (1996) suggested using a framework termed *ADRESSING* with older ethnic minority clients in treatment; however, its components can also be applied to the development of research projects with Asian American older adults. The ADRESSING framework includes (a) Age and generation-specific influences, (b) Disability, (c) Religion, (d) Ethnicity, (e) Social status, (f) Sexual orientation, (g) Indigenous heritage, (h) National origin, and (i) Gender. Hayes recommended using this framework to assist with developing rapport and understanding the individual's cultural identity and heritage and to assess the individual's current context, needs, and strengths. Again, each of these areas is applicable to the research situation and may be used as a guide for researchers in beginning projects with Asian American older adults.

Recruiting and retaining older adult ethnic minorities in psychological research is a challenge. Arean and Gallagher-Thompson (1996) provided recommendations for researchers interested in conducting mental health research with ethnic minority older adults. Techniques they considered to be successful included the following.

- Developing a strong, positive relationship with the community to alleviate fear and distrust of the researchers.
- Conducting research within the communities in which the participants live, or providing them with transportation.
- Educating potential participants of the relevance and importance of the study to them.
- Demonstrating that you understand cultural issues and reducing barriers by conducting the project in the community and staffing it with bilingual and bicultural individuals who are familiar with and sensitive to cultural values of the participants.
- Providing feedback to the community and participants about the results of the study.
- Being flexible about data collection procedures when health-related issues may arise.
- Providing participants with incentives to participate (such as a convenient location and monetary payments).

These recommendations provide an excellent example of how researchers can tailor their projects specifically to the needs of Asian American older adults.

A final general issue to consider is the role of the researcher as seen by the potential Asian American older adult research participants. What is the researcher's motivation for doing the research? Why is he or she studying this particular group of Asian American older adults? Why should the participants take part in the project? How will it be of benefit to them and other Asian American older adults? How much does the researcher know about the particular Asian American older adult population of interest? Issues such as these have implications for whether the study will have adequate internal and external validity (Sue, 1999; Sue & Sue, 2000).

Traditional Asian values include emphasis on a group over an individual orientation, interpersonal relationships, well-defined roles and status based on age (respect for elders), and interpersonal harmony and cooperation (Iwamasa, 1997). Given that the researcher is likely to be younger than the potential participants, these values clearly have implications for the researcher in terms of credibility. Is the researcher able to identify such traditional Asian values and consider how they may affect participants' perceptions of the researcher? Will the researcher be able to take appropriate preparation steps in the development of the project? Will the researcher be able to develop and implement a research project that is consistent with these Asian values? The answers to these questions will likely influence whether a researcher will be able to effectively conduct research with Asian American older adults.

CHOOSING A RESEARCH DESIGN: WHAT HAS BEEN DONE WITH ASIAN AMERICAN OLDER ADULTS?

Culturally Appropriate and Effective Research Designs

Given the numerous methodological issues involved in conducting research with Asian American older adults, developing a culturally appropriate and effective research methodology with them in mind may be challenging. Culturally appropriate research designs take into consideration the population one is investigating (Flick, 1998; Sue & Sue, 2000). For example, emically based research designs with Asian American older adults consider cultural beliefs, accessibility to the population, participants' potential concerns about being involved in research, and so on. Effective research designs involve methodologies that best answer the researcher's questions in a manner that is culturally compatible with the population being studied. Given that research on Asian American older adults is in its infancy, both qualitative and quantitative designs are useful. Quantitative research methodologies are effective for answering "why" questions, whereas qualitative research methodologies are effective for answering "how" or "what" questions (Creswell, 1998).

To date, no published research studies have examined the cultural appropriateness or effectiveness of particular research methodologies with ethnic minority older adults. As Sue (1999) pointed out, the emphasis on internal validity has jeopardized the external validity of psychological research with ethnic minority populations. Given the previous review of the methodological considerations for conducting research with Asian American older adults, concerns about external validity in the development of a research project with such populations are particularly important.

Participants' input regarding their involvement in particular research methods would be helpful in the design of research projects for several reasons. First, the reliability and validity of measures would be improved. For example, over a period of several years and numerous research projects with Japanese American older adults, we have observed that data are more complete (and, at times, more accurate) when researchers conduct interviews or use a focus group format. Researchers often rely on survey questionnaires to measure outcomes. However, when cultural factors, such as age and English as a second language are considered, interviews and focus groups appear to facilitate the research design for all involved. Second, if participants enjoy being involved in the research project, then recruitment is enhanced, because they tell their friends about it. This is particularly important when working with Asian Americans and other ethnic minority older adults because of potential reservations they may have about participating in psychological research. We actually ask our potential research participants ahead of time what formats of projects they would prefer. We then use the methodologies they prefer. This indicates to the participants that we value their opinions, respect them, and take them seriously. That, in turn, increases our participant recruitment and their enjoyment in our projects.

We believe that researchers who use an interview or focus group methodology enhance both the cultural appropriateness and the effectiveness of a research design. Cultural appropriateness is enhanced in that specific factors, such as language and respect for elders, are considered, and the effectiveness of the research design is thus enhanced, because additional steps were taken to ensure that the data were complete and clinically relevant.

We clearly believe that developing a solid research program with Asian American older adults requires a commitment to the actual community— actually joining the community, and collaborating with community members on projects rather than using traditional scientific research methods in which participants are seen as data points. This may seem like a challenging task; however, we believe it is doable. In terms of moving the research on Asian American older adults forward, it may be necessary for researchers to think beyond traditional methods, such as a strictly quantitative study or a strictly qualitative study. Combining quantitative and qualitative research methodologies (e.g., structured interviews, reading a self-report measure with the participant) when working with Asian American older adults might be the best way to ensure both cultural appropriateness and effectiveness. However, in addition to combining research methodologies, it is important for future research to examine which research methodologies are the most culturally appropriate and effective when working with Asian American older adults.

Determining what research methodologies are most culturally appropriate, effective, and enjoyable for Asian American older adults can be done with minimal effort. This information can be obtained simply by adding a few questions to one's research instruments.

Focus Groups

For example, Iwamasa and Hilliard (1998) were interested in determining whether the focus group methodology was effective with Japanese American older adults. Participants were 32 Japanese American older adults (18 women and 14 men) recruited from two senior centers in Los Angeles. Participants volunteered to take part in a focus group on the topic of successful aging. Participants completed both a demographic questionnaire and a follow-up survey (postgroup and at 3 months over the telephone); in addition, the group discussion was audiotaped.

The follow-up survey consisted of a rating scale that ranged from 1 to 5 (1 = *not at all comfortable or enjoyable*, 3 = *somewhat comfortable or enjoyable*, and 5 = *extremely comfortable or enjoyable*). The questions and means for participants are as follows: (a) How comfortable did you feel in signing up for the group? (M = 4.31), (b) How comfortable were you being a part of the group? (M = 4.42, (c) How comfortable were you voicing your opinions and perceptions in the group? (M = 4.19), (d) How much did you enjoy participating in the group? (M = 4.65), and (d) How comfortable do you think you will be in seeing the other group members outside of the group? (M = 3.97). On average, participants felt comfortable taking part in focus groups on successful aging and reported enjoying their participation in the project both immediately following the group and at the 3-month follow-up. Overall, focus groups appear to be effective in (a) allowing researchers to collect data in a manner consistent with traditional Asian values (e.g., the researcher asks the participants to share their expertise and emphasizes cooperation and interpersonal harmony), (b) collecting in-depth data on which hypotheses and research questions may be based, (c) assessing how valuable or important the research topic is to Asian American older adults, and (d) demonstrating the researcher's interest in participants as real people. Given the lack of descriptive data on Asian American older adults, such a research format is culturally appropriate for this population. It is interesting to note that a search of the empirical literature revealed that no other research project with Asian American older adults has used the focus group format.

Inclusion of a few additional questions assessing participants' perceptions of outcome measures would provide researchers with a better idea of what methodologies are the most culturally appropriate and effective when conducting research with Asian American older adults. As discussed earlier, one explanation for the lack of usage of focus groups is that traditional scientific methods have tended to focus on quantitative rather than qualitative and descriptive methods and on internal over external validity (Sue, 1999). This has been particularly problematic for research on ethnic minority populations, for whom there exists little descriptive information in the psychological literature; what information is provided is frequently offered in comparison to White samples.

Interview Studies

Like focus groups, interview studies are qualitative in nature, but each participant is questioned individually. In the general psychological literature, interviews have been used more in research than have focus groups; however, they have not been used very much with Asian American populations. The interview format is particularly useful when one is researching a topic that has not received much attention, because often the results lead to new research questions. Furthermore, the interview format provides researchers with a solid foundation on which to base their research, rather than relying on findings from research with older adults from other ethnic groups. Areas of research in which an interview format has most frequently been used with Asian American older adults include family and social support, caregiving, abuse, and conceptualizations of mental illness.

Several interview studies that focus on Asian American older adults have examined the role of family and social support as one ages. A majority of the studies focusing on support have been conducted with Korean older adults. In particular, family appears to be a main source of support for Korean older adults (Kaugh, 1997, 1999; Sung, 1991). In addition, a study conducted by Moon (1996) suggested that health, intimacy with children, education, and preference between Korea and the United States as a place to live predict morale among Korean older adults.

Caregiving and Asian American older adults has also begun to receive attention in the empirical literature. Interview studies have examined the experiences of Japanese caregivers (Freed, 1990; Kobayashi, Masaki, & Noguchi, 1993; Yamamoto & Wallhagen, 1997) and the decision-making process of Chinese American caregivers throughout the course of caregiving. Hicks and Lam (1999) conducted an interview study with Chinese American caregivers to develop a more realistic decision-making model regarding chronic illness and culture. The model they developed takes a systems perspective to examine the relationships among all individuals who are part of the decision-making process. In addition, Gallagher-Thompson et al. (2000) summarized caregiver issues among culturally diverse caregiving populations, including Asian American older adults, and discussed caregiving issues related to specific Asian American subgroups.

Related to the stresses of caregiving, some interview studies have been conducted on elder abuse among Japanese and Korean older adults. Tomita (1999) found that female Japanese elders were at greater risk for abuse because of group and male primacy and the stigma of bringing shame to the family by reporting the abuse. Similar findings were found with Korean older adult women in that they were less likely to perceive a situation as abusive as compared to women from other ethnic groups (Moon & Williams, 1993). These interview data were part of a cross-cultural study that examined African American and European American elderly women in addition to Korean elderly women.

Iwamasa, Hilliard, and Osato (1998) conducted an interview study to determine how Japanese American older adults conceptualized depression and anxiety. Twenty-nine older adults from a senior center were interviewed using open-ended questions directed at defining anxiety and depression. Most participants conceptualized anxiety and depression similarly to mental health professionals; however, some participants defined anxiety and depression by using symptoms from the other disorder. For example, in defining anxiety, some participants used symptoms associated with depression and vice versa.

Using an interview methodology to understand how Asian American older adults conceptualize various mental and physical problems would help researchers to better understand potential confounds. For example, Asians' cultural beliefs might possibly exacerbate somatization of both physical and mental distress (National Institutes of Health, 1976). Asian American older adults could be interviewed about their perceptions of somatic and physical complaints across their life spans as well as their perceptions of the etiology of those symptoms. Qualitative methods are necessary to determine the specific factors involved in the issues of reporting somatic problems. Even though qualitative methodologies such as interviews and focus groups cannot be used to answer all research questions, they provide researchers studying a neglected population with a solid foundation of data from which to work. Once descriptive data have been obtain using qualitative methodologies, theories can be developed, and then relationships and cause and effect can be studied with quantitative measures (Creswell, 1998).

The above-mentioned studies clearly indicate the utility of interview formats for research projects with Asian American older adults. Interviews provide research participants with a more personalized interaction with the researcher, enabling the researcher to actively demonstrate interest in, respect for, and attention to each participant. An interview allows the researcher to be flexible in how he or she obtains the desired information and allows for clarification of responses, which is not possible with surveys, the next type of methodology we review.

Potential concerns about interviews and focus groups include social desirability and generalizability of the data to individuals beyond the research participants. In terms of social desirability, it is unknown whether these methods increase the likelihood of a more acquiescent response set over written surveys. Individuals who agree to participate in an interview or a focus group (or both) typically are those who are willing to verbally share their perspectives. Unlike written instruments, in these methods the researcher can more readily emphasize that he or she is not looking for particular answers but wants to honestly know participants' experiences and perspectives. Regarding generalizability, as with any research project, individuals who participate in psychological research may differ from others, and thus their responses may not generalize to the population at large. Until researchers can develop methods to gain the participation of those Asian American older adults who choose not to participate in psychological research, this issue will not be resolved.

Survey Studies

Most studies of older adults incorporate surveys or questionnaires as part of their outcome measures. This is not surprising given that questionnaires are very useful in obtaining concrete data, such as demographic information and assessment screening information, such as that provided by the Geriatric Depression Scale (Yesavage et al., 1983). In using written surveys with older adults, researchers must consider issues such as the print size of the instruments used, which has implications for the length of a survey. A related issue is that of fatigue, both physical and psychological, for older adults who are asked to complete written surveys. When using surveys with Asian American or other ethnic minority older adults, additional factors need to be taken into consideration. For example, participants' understanding of both written and spoken language, familiarity with the language of the instruments, visual acuity, and the researcher's operational definition of the variables being measured should be considered when using written surveys. Failure to consider these factors may affect the reliability and validity of the data obtained.

In terms of selecting items for written instruments, there are a number of different formats researchers may use. We ourselves have used checklists, multiple-choice items, fill-in-the-blank items, and rating scale formats with Japanese American older adults. The type of survey format depends on the research question as well as the population of interest. For example, Hilliard and Iwamasa (2001) were interested in determining how Japanese American older adults conceptualize anxiety. Because this area had not received any attention in the empirical literature, they used a checklist format. The checklist contained items from the *Diagnostic and Statistical Manual of Mental Disorders* (4th ed.; American Psychiatric Association, 1994) for generalized anxiety disorder and major depression, as well as symptoms participants had identified in an interview study that examined how Japanese American older adults defined depression and anxiety (Iwamasa, Hilliard, & Osato, 1998). Participants were asked to simply check off the symptoms that a Japanese American older adult experiencing anxiety would be experiencing. This emically derived checklist survey format was successful in Hilliard and Iwamasa's (2001) study.

Other survey formats include fill-in-the-blank items and rating scales. Hilliard and Iwamasa (2000) recently used both of these survey formats in a research project that examined the effectiveness of a workshop for Japanese American older adults on becoming a health-active older adult. Participants were asked to complete the Multidimensional Health Locus of Control Scale (Wallston, Wallston, & Devillis, 1978), which assesses beliefs that health is or is not determined by one's own behavior. Participants rate their beliefs on a scale that ranges from 1 (*strongly disagree*) to 6 (*strongly agree*). Most participants did not have difficulty with this format, but they did have some difficulty understanding why they had to fill the rating scale out three times (pre, post, and follow-up), even after the researchers explained the research process. In addition, participants were asked to use a fill-in-the-blank survey format to answer questions regarding information that they learned during the workshop on how to become a health-active older adult. For example, they were asked to write out responses to questions such as what steps to take to prepare for a physician's visit and what types of health-related information they should be sure to provide their physician. Hilliard and Iwamasa's (2000) observations, similar to other researchers who have used the fill-in-the-blank survey format, were that such items were difficult for the Japanese American older adult participants to complete and yielded less useful data compared with other survey formats. When asked some of the fill-in-the-blank questions orally, Japanese American older adult participants were able to generate more, and more complete, responses than when they were asked to write the answers by hand. This observation could have been due to English being a second language; preference for one-on-one conversation over an individualized activity; differences in cognitive styles; lack of clarity of the instructions, the items on the written surveys, or both; and communication patterns, such as a preference for verbal communication over written communication.

Another survey format often used with older adults is multiple choice. We typically use a multiple-choice format when obtaining demographic information, because it appears to facilitate survey completion. The demographic information usually is complete, and participants are able to complete such items in a shorter amount of time compared with open-ended or fill-in-the-blank items.

Another consideration in using written surveys is that many university institutional review boards and federal funding agencies, such as the National Institutes of Health, require extensive and detailed informed-consent documents. Although clearly implemented and emphasized in order to protect the research participants, explanations and reviews of increasingly lengthy informed-consent forms take a considerable amount of time. Researchers must incorporate the amount of time required for explaining the informed-consent form and procedures of the study into the overall amount of time required of participants for the research project. Such procedures must be factored in when considering issues such as fatigue and attention span of participants in the use of written instruments.

In general, surveys can be a useful research measure for Asian American older adults, but a few issues must be considered. First, surveys that are quick and simple appear to be completed more successfully by Asian American older adults. Second, surveys with a rating scale format may be successful, but researchers need to be aware of such issues as length of the survey, print size, and language ability when working with Asian American older adults. Third, the fill-in-the-blank format should be avoided if at all possible. Answers to rating scales will be more useful if they are used in an interview format. Fourth, when using survey formats it is very important for researchers to establish adequate reliability and validity of a scale with their population of interest. We discuss in a later section the validity of measures for Asian American older adults.

Intervention Studies

A search of the literature found no intervention studies examining the effectiveness of a psychological intervention for Asian American older adults.

This is not surprising, given that little psychological research has been conducted with Asian American older adults, which is vital to the development of appropriate interventions for this population. We currently can say only that a little is known about a few of the Asian American subgroups, with the most information known about Japanese American older adults. Much work still needs to be done for researchers to better understand which psychological principles and concepts currently being examined among Asian Americans also generalize to Asian American older adults. In addition, issues and concepts specific to older Asian Americans must be identified and described. We hope that someday enough research will have been conducted to direct the research on Asian American older adults toward the design of intervention studies. Until then, intervention research on Asian American older adults using traditional scientific intervention methods, such as repeated measures designs, may be based on an etic, and perhaps culturally inappropriate, set of hypotheses, measures, and assumptions about the population of interest.

As Sue (1999) discussed, psychology's emphasis on internal over external validity has hampered emic and culturally appropriate research designs with ethnically diverse populations.

Choosing Culturally Appropriate Measures

A major step in conducting culturally appropriate research with Asian American older adults is choosing culturally appropriate research measures. It is unfortunate that very little research has examined the reliability and validity of psychological measures with Asian American older adults. The lack of research in this area is of concern, because most psychological measures have been normed on a Western, predominantly European American sample, and therefore one cannot be certain they are useful with Asian American older adults.

The largest amount of research on the reliability and validity of psychological measures with Asian American older adults has examined depression measures. Iwamasa, Hilliard, and Kost (1998) examined the utility of the Geriatric Depression Scale (GDS; Yesavage et al., 1983) with Japanese American older adults. Eighty-six Japanese American older adults from a senior center in Los Angeles completed the GDS. Overall, psychometric analyses indicated the GDS had fairly high internal consistency and reliability with this sample. Results were comparable to the internal consistency and reliability coefficients found with the original normative sample. Furthermore, GDS scores were low and did not significantly differ between men and women, indicating that the sample was relatively healthy and nondepressed. Despite these promising results, however, the authors stated that further research should be done with a larger sample of Japanese American older adults before any conclusive results can be stated.

The reliability and the validity of the 10-item short form of the Center for Epidemiologic Studies Depression Scale (CESD–10; Radloff, 1997) has also been examined with a sample of Chinese elderly participants (Boey, 1999). The CESD–10 was administered to 554 elderly individuals in the general community, 30 elderly individuals from a community center, and 31 elderly individuals with depressive symptoms ages 70 years and older. Boey (1999) examined the internal consistency of the CESD–10 over a 3-year period. The short-term the internal consistency of the CESD–10 was found to be satisfactory, and moderate consistency was found over a 3-year period. The CESD–10 was also found to differentiate between groups of normal and clinically depressed Chinese elderly people. Overall content and temporal reliability, as well as construct and concurrent validity, were established. Boey reported that the CESD–10 was appropriate for use with Chinese elderly individuals.

Park, Upshaw, and Koh (1988) examined the effectiveness of the Minnesota Multiphasic Personality Inventory (Hathaway & McKinley, 1943) with elderly Korean, Japanese, and European Americans. Written responses were compared with 15 Minnesota Multiphasic Personality Inventory items answered in an interview format. Differences between groups were found in the self-report data rather than the interview data. Park et al. discussed the hypothesis that the differences were the result of an interaction between different workings of test items and cultural background. The results from this study emphasize (a) that anticipated social desirability effects did not occur with the interview format and (b) the interethnic differences among Asian American older adults.

For researchers interested in conducting research on Asian American older adults for whom English is not their first language, some work has been done on non-American populations in Asia, in which measures developed on European American older adults were used with Asian older adults. In their review of the literature on depression and anxiety among Asian American older adults, given the lack of examination of Asian American older adults, Iwamasa and Hilliard (1999) discussed studies on these non-American populations because of their potential relevance for non-English-speaking Asian American older adults. Iwamasa and Hilliard discussed studies in which the GDS was translated into Chinese, the Diagnostic Interview Schedule–III (DIS–III; Robins, Helzer, Croughan, & Ratcliff, 1981) was translated into Korean, and both the CES–D and the Zung Self-Rating Depression Scale (Zung, 1967) were translated into Japanese. Readers are encouraged to review Iwamasa and Hilliard's (1999) review for more specific information about these studies.

Another area of research that has begun to examine the usefulness psychological measures with Asian American older adults is caregiving. Trockman et al. (1997) examined the usefulness of 12 different measures that assessed caregiver burden and quality of life. Participants were 195 Japanese American female caregivers living in Hawaii. Specifically, the authors examined five characteristics of these measures: (a) content and semantic equivalence, (b) technical equivalence, (c) criterion equivalence, (d) conceptual equivalence, and (e) response format. Trockman et al. found that, overall, an interview format may be more useful with this population and suggested that researchers give interviewees a dichotomous choice to answer a question and then proceed to open-ended questions to obtain further information. They indicated that a reason for the success of this research methodology is that some research has suggested that Central American and Vietnamese participants were found to have difficulty with Likert-type scales and preferred a yes–no format (Flaskerud, 1988). They suggested that the preference for a yes–no format is cultural in nature. Trockman et al.'s study highlights the challenges of adapting measurements for cross-cultural research and the need for researchers to pilot test measures while focusing on equivalence and formatting issues.

CONDUCTING RESEARCH WITH ASIAN AMERICAN AND PACIFIC ISLANDER OLDER ADULTS: A CASE EXAMPLE

Conducting research that focuses on Asian American older adults is apt to be time consuming, expensive, and require additional considerations. However, we believe that these challenges may be overcome if researchers follow culturally appropriate procedures in the development of their projects. To illustrate some of the suggestions highlighted in this chapter, we would like to share our firsthand experience working with the Seinan Senior Citizens' Center, a senior center for Japanese American older adults in Los Angeles. In addition to projects planned and in progress, we have conducted five research projects at the Seinan Center over the past 6 years. We believe that what has made our collaborative relationship with the Seinan Center most successful is the inclusion of culturally appropriate considerations into our research designs.

The first step in conducting culturally appropriate research with older adults is to identify a community-based organization (CBO) and potential resources available to the population of interest. Most cities have listings of CBOs for particular services and populations of interest. Researchers might also become aware of these organizations through another colleague or a research article. In some instances it might be necessary for researchers to travel to other geographic regions to recruit an adequate sample of participants, as the population of Asian American older adults may be inadequate in one's own location.

Once a potential CBO has been identified it is important for the principal investigators to develop a collaborative relationship with the CBO and its staff. To develop such a relationship it is necessary that the researchers understand how the organization works. This information will ensure that the study design will work within the organizational framework of the CBO as well as make it easier to recruit staff to serve as research assistants. For example, the Seinan Center is a nonprofit organization that relies heavily on city and state funding, donations, and volunteers. Understanding the organizational framework helped us to assess staff members' level of interest in our projects, which influenced how much help we would receive from them. In addition, our assessment of the center's activities and schedule enabled us to assess the time members had available to participate in our research projects. Also, familiarizing ourselves with the roles and functions of the organization allowed us to find out what other projects researchers had conducted at the center as well as how those researchers approached their research design.

Understanding the organizational framework also helps in the participant recruitment process, particularly with Asian American older adults, because it helps to identify a *gatekeeper*—an individual who can provide entrance to a research site and is often used in qualitative research designs (Creswell, 1998). A gatekeeper is necessary when conducting research with Asian American older adults, because they often rely solely on services offered within the Asian American community (Uba, 1994). A gatekeeper can also provide the researcher with valuable information regarding the population of interest. For example, we work closely with a staff member at the Seinan Center who provides us with the overall demographics of the members. Knowing the demographics of the population, such as generational status, gender and age distribution, and income level, as well as the scheduling of the center's activities, allowed us to consider what research methods might work best. For example, when collecting data, we consider which activities are scheduled and collect our data on specific days and times that would maximize participation. Understanding the demographics of the population also helps researchers learn the customs of the population with which they are working. For example, first-generation Chinese older adults who follow traditional beliefs might continue to view touch and eye contact as disrespectful. Knowing the subtle verbal and nonverbal interactional styles of one's population of interest can greatly enhance the participant recruitment process.

Investigators should also provide a rationale as to why the CBO could benefit from allowing the research project to be conducted at the facility. One benefit that may be offered is how the information gained from the study may potentially help the population of interest as well as the CBO itself. In our case, one research project examined how Japanese American older adults conceptualized anxiety, an area that had not been previously researched. We included in our surveys questions such as how often participants attended the CBO and what activities they attended while at the center. In addition to being useful and interesting questions from a research standpoint, this type of information also was useful for the center, because it was used in annual reports and grant proposals to demonstrate the effectiveness of the center, its staff, and its activities.

After a collaborative relationship has been established with a CBO, it is also important to determine the most appropriate way to conduct the research in a way that will help to develop a good rapport not only with the CBO staff but also with the participants. Therefore, it is important for researchers to have an understanding of the culture. For example, in the Japanese culture, the concept of *omiyage*—giving of a gift to extend appreciation when one visits someone else's home—is very important. Thus, we have brought gifts such as plants, flowers, and art and photography supplies to members and staff on multiple occasions. We also have sent thank you notes and gifts to staff for assisting us with our projects. This also is consistent with traditional Asian values that emphasize interpersonal relationships over individual self-fulfillment.

In conducting our projects, we have used the following steps. First, it was important to develop a relationship with the participants so they understood that we were interested in and cared about them and their CBO. To do this, we have personally visited the center on a number of occasions to get to know the participants and by joining in on community center activities. For example, we have attended dance classes, visited art classes, purchased items made by center members, and have eaten many meals with members (and of course, helped with kitchen duty afterward!). We knew that participants felt comfortable with us when they remembered our names and the projects that we had previously conducted. During these visits we explained to members that we were psychologists, and we shared with them the kinds of topics and issues in which we were interested. We then asked members about which, if any, of those topics they were interested in learning more. This allowed participants to know that they were involved with the development of the research design.

Prior to data collection, we provide fliers to announce the upcoming research projects. These are either included in the center's newsletter, posted around the center, or both. Furthermore, when possible, we personally collect the data at the center rather than conducting data collection by means of mail or CBO staff. We have found that this greatly increases participation.

We have also learned to attempt to collect pilot data to ensure cultural appropriateness of our measures and questions. Pilot data will provide researchers with information necessary to develop culturally appropriate and relevant research questions and hypotheses, and thus any adjustments or revisions may be made before actual data collection begins.

Next, we incorporate culturally appropriate incentives for participating in our studies. For example, in one of our research projects, for every survey that was completed a $10 donation was made to the CBO; in another project, participants received enrollment in an educational program in which they had previously expressed an interest, such as classes on holiday blues, Alzheimer's disease, or successful aging.

Finally, at the conclusion of every project we return to the center and present the results of the research in both oral and written form, and we provide the center with reprints of any published articles. Again, these products are very useful to the members and staff. In our published articles we thank the staff and participants for their participation. It is interesting that, at this particular CBO, we were informed that we were the first of numerous researchers who actually came back to the center and provided members with results of our projects. This generated much goodwill and communicated to members that we were interested in them as people and not just as data points. We believe this has contributed to our ability to maintain a good working relationship with the center and its members, thus providing us with a stable group of research participants. This also demonstrates that few previous researchers have considered Japanese American culture in the design and implementation of their research at this center and that the researchers were more interested in completing their own projects than in their participants.

The positive collaborative relationship that we have experienced working with the Seinan Center might be due in part to the fact that members themselves are healthy Japanese American older adults who could be considered to be aging successfully. Our research has indicated that the members of the Seinan Center attend the center on a regular basis and have normal levels of depression and anxiety (Iwamasa, Hilliard, & Kost, 1998). We hypothesize that Japanese American older adults who attend non-ethnic-focused centers, or those who do not attend a senior day center at all, would be different from the members of the Seinan Center, but no research has yet been conducted to either confirm or disconfirm this hypothesis. Also, the setting of the organization also should be considered in one's research design. For example, if one were recruiting Asian Americans from a mental health agency, then collaboration with the health care workers would be crucial, because levels of stigma and shame might affect recruitment and compliance.

Overall, there are three main factors that have contributed to our successful collaborative relationship with the Seinan Center. First, we assessed the role and functions of the staff and members and learned about how the organization functioned. Next, we established a collaborative process by visiting the center before, during, and after data collection. Finally, we incorporated cultural considerations throughout the development and design of each project. In a sense, because we are regular visitors to the Seinan Center, we have become part of its community. Although our experiences are specific to Japanese American older adults, we believe that researchers using a similar process of collaboration with other Asian American older adults also will be able to develop a successful program of research.

CONCLUSION

In this chapter we summarized the research methodologies used with Asian American older adults. We discussed some modifications and considerations related to conducting research with older adults in general (such as increasing the font size of written instruments). We also summarized issues specific to conducting research with Asian American older adults.

Asian American older adults have been largely neglected in both the older adult and Asian American psychological literature. Given that the population of Asian American older adults is growing rapidly, researchers in the field of psychology must begin to turn their attention to their life experiences, as researchers have much to learn from them that will be of benefit not only to them but also to older adults in general. Researchers must incorporate cultural considerations into the development of their studies, from participant recruitment, to the development of instruments, to data collection procedures, to providing participants with a summary of the results.

As yet, researchers have little or no knowledge on the following life experiences and issues among Asian American older adults: retirement, widowhood, relationships with children and grandchildren, cognitive decline, dementia, caregiving, and health care. In addition, researchers must begin to examine the following culturally influenced issues as well: generational status, ethnic identity and acculturation, women's issues, psychological assessment, gender and sex roles, biracial and multiracial relationships, and sexuality, among others.

Although conducting successful research with Asian American elders is more challenging than conducting research with other older adult groups and other Asian Americans, we have outlined steps researchers may take in the development of a research program. This work requires a commitment to culturally appropriate scientific research and, of course, to the Asian American older adult group being studied. Although difficult at times, it has been our experience that this research program with Asian American older adults has been very enjoyable and immensely rewarding, and we look forward to the increased number of colleagues who also will demonstrate a commitment to this group as it continues to grow and need attention.

FUTURE RESEARCH DIRECTIONS

- There is a paucity of psychological research on Asian American older adults.
- The population of Asian American older adults will continue to increase over time, and thus the need for more researchers interested in aging Asian Americans is imperative.
- A model of Asian American aging would help guide researchers in conducting programmatic research on Asian American elders.

- Research methods with Asian American older adults need to be not only ethnically consistent but also age consistent.
- Investigators conducting research with Asian American elders must be able to articulate and demonstrate their commitment to their participants and their motivation for conducting the research, and they should consider the role of their own age and ethnicity in the conduct of their research.
- Research projects with Asian American elders must be beneficial to them.
- A variety of research methods may be used successfully with Asian American elders; however, researchers must carefully consider the questions being asked in developing the methodology.
- Qualitative designs such as focus groups and interviews are particularly useful when no previous data exist and when the investigator is conducting exploratory research.
- In using surveys, researchers must attend to age-related issues such as font size, fatigue, primary language of participants, and appropriateness of measures for the participants.
- Researchers should factor in the time required for review and explanation of informed-consent documents and study procedures and how they will affect participant fatigue and attention.
- Researchers should explain the choice of measures used in their studies with older adults, particularly when measures developed and normed on other ethnic groups are being used.

REFERENCES

American Association of Retired Persons & Administration on Aging. (1999). A profile of older Americans [Brochure]. Washington, DC: Author.

American Psychiatric Association. (1994). Diagnostic and statistical manual of mental disorders (4th ed.). Washington, DC: Author.

Arean, P. A., & Gallagher-Thompson, D. (1996). Issues and recommendations for the recruitment and retention of older ethnic minority adults into clinical research. Journal of Consulting and Clinical Psychology, 64, 875–880.

Boey, K. W. (1999). Cross-validation of a short form of the CES–D in Chinese elderly. International Journal of Geriatric Psychiatry, 14, 608–617.

Creswell, J. W. (1998). Qualitative inquiry and research design: Choosing among five traditions. London: Sage.

Enright, J. B., & Jaeckle, W. R. (1963). Psychiatric symptoms and diagnosis in two subcultures. International Journal of Social Psychiatry, 9, 12–17.

Flaskerud, J. H. (1988). Is the Likert scale culturally biased? *Nursing Research, 37*, 185–186.

Flick, U. (1998). *An introduction to qualitative research.* London: Sage.

Freed, A. (1990). How Japanese families cope with fragile elderly. *Journal of Gerontological Social Work, 15*(1–2), 39–56.

Gallagher-Thompson, D., Arean, P., Coon, D., Menendez, A., Takagi, K., Haley, W. E., Arguelles, T., Rubert, M., Lowenstein, D., & Szapocznik, J. (2000). Development and implementation of intervention strategies for culturally diverse caregiving populations. In R. Schulz (Ed.), *Handbook on dementia caregiving: Evidence-based interventions for family caregivers* (pp. 151–185). New York: Springer.

Hathaway, S. R., & McKinley, J. C. (1943). *The Minnesota Multiphasic Personality Inventory.* New York: Psychological Corp.

Hayes, P. A. (1996). Culturally responsive assessment with diverse older clients. *Professional Psychology: Research and Practice, 27*, 188–193.

Hicks, M. H., & Lam, M. S. (1999). Decision-making within the social course of dementia: Accounts by Chinese-American caregivers. *Culture, Medicine and Psychiatry, 23*, 415–452.

Hilliard, K. M., & Iwamasa, G. Y. (2000). *Becoming a health-active older adult: The effects of a workshop for Japanese American older adults.* Manuscript in preparation.

Hilliard, K. M., & Iwamasa, G. Y. (2001). Japanese American older adults' conceptualization of anxiety. *Journal of Clinical Geropsychology, 7*, 53–65.

Iwamasa, G. Y. (1997). Asian Americans. In S. Friedman (Ed.), *Cultural issues in the treatment of anxiety* (pp. 99–129). New York: Guilford Press.

Iwamasa, G. Y., & Hilliard, K. M. (1998). *Are focus groups effective with Japanese American older adults?* Poster presented at the annual meeting of the Association for the Advancement of Behavior Therapy, Washington, DC.

Iwamasa, G. Y., & Hilliard, K. M. (1999). Depression and anxiety among Asian American elders: A review of the literature. *Clinical Psychology Review, 19*, 343–357.

Iwamasa, G. Y., Hilliard, K., & Kost, C. (1998). The Geriatric Depression Scale and Japanese American older adults. *The Clinical Gerontologist, 19*(3), 13–24.

Iwamasa, G. Y., Hilliard, K. M., & Osato, S. (1998). Conceptualizing anxiety and depression: The Japanese American older adult perspective. *The Clinical Gerontologist, 1*, 77–93.

Kaugh, T. (1997). Intergenerational relations: Older Korean-Americans' experiences. *Journal of Cross-Cultural Gerontology, 12*, 245–271.

Kaugh, T. (1999). Changing status and roles of older Korean immigrants in the United States. *International Journal of Aging and Human Development, 49*, 213–229.

Kim, P. K. H. (1983). Demography of the Asian-Pacific elderly: Selected problems and implications. In R. L. McNeely & J. L. Cohen (Eds.), *Aging in minority groups* (pp. 29–41). Beverly Hills, CA: Sage.

Knight, B. (1986). *Psychotherapy with older adults*. Newbury Park, CA: Sage.

Kobayashi, S., Masaki, H., & Noguchi, M. (1993). Developmental process: Family caregivers of demented Japanese. *Journal of Gerontological Nursing, 19*(10), 7–12.

Lee, E. (1997). *Working with Asian Americans: A guide for clinicians*. New York: Guilford Press.

Marsella, A. J., Kinzie, D., & Gordon, P. (1973). Ethnocultural variations in the expression of depression. *Journal of Cross-Cultural Psychology, 4*, 435–458.

Marsella, A. J., Sanborn, K., Kameoka, V., Shizuru, L., & Brennan, J. (1975). Cross-validation of self-report measures of depression among normal populations of Japanese, Chinese, and Caucasian ancestry. *Journal of Clinical Psychology, 31*, 281–287.

Moon, A. (1996). Predictors of morale among Korean immigrant elderly in the USA. *Journal of Cross-Cultural Gerontology, 11*, 351–367.

Moon, A., & Williams, O. (1993). Perceptions of elder abuse and help-seeking patterns among African-American, Caucasian American, and Korean-American elderly women. *The Gerontologist, 33*, 386–395.

National Institutes of Health. (1976). *Medicine in Chinese cultures* (DHEW Publication No. NIH 75-653). Washington, DC: U.S. Government Printing Office.

Park, K. B., Upshaw, H. S., & Koh, S. D. (1988). East Asians' responses to Western health items. *Journal of Cross-Cultural Psychology, 19*, 51–64.

Radloff, L. S. (1997). The Center of Epidemiological Studies Depression Scale. *Applied Psychological Measurement, 1*, 385–401.

Robins, L. N., Helzer, J. E., Croughan, J. & Ratcliff, K. (1981). National Institute of Mental Health Diagnostic Interview Schedule: Its history, characteristics, and validity. *Archives of General Psychiatry, 38*, 381–389.

Rowe, J. W., & Kahn, R. L. (1997). Successful aging. *The Gerontologist, 37*, 433–440.

Sokolovsky, J. (1997). *The cultural context of aging: Worldwide perspectives* (2nd ed.). Westport, CT: Bergin & Garvey.

Sue, S. (1999). Science, ethnicity, and bias: Where have we gone wrong? *American Psychologist, 54*, 1070–1077.

Sue, S., Chun, C., & Gee, K. (1995). Ethnic minority intervention and treatment research. In J. F. Ponte, R. Y. Rivers, & J. Wohl (Eds.), *Psychological interventions and cultural diversity* (pp. 266–282). Needham Heights, MA: Allyn & Bacon.

Sue, S., & Sue, D. W. (2000). Conducting psychological research with the Asian American/Pacific Islander population. In Council of National Psychological Associations for the Advancement of Ethnic Minority Interests (Ed.), *Guidelines for research with ethnic minority communities* (pp. 2–4). Washington, DC: American Psychological Association.

Sung, K. (1991). Family-centered informal support networks of Korean elderly: The resistance of cultural traditions. *Journal of Cross-Cultural Gerontology, 6*, 431–447.

Tomita, S. K. (1999). Exploration of elder mistreatment among the Japanese. In T. Tatara (Ed.), *Understanding elder abuse in minority populations* (pp. 119–139). Philadelphia: Brunner/Mazel.

Triandis, H. C. (1994). *Culture and social behavior.* New York: McGraw-Hill.

Trockman, C., Murdaugh, C., Kadohiro, J., Petrovitch, H., Curb, D., & White, L. (1997). Adapting instruments for caregiver research in elderly Japanese American women. *Journal of Cross-Cultural Gerontology, 12,* 109–120.

Tsai, J. L., & Carstensen, L. L. (1996). Clinical intervention with ethnic minority elders. In L. L. Carstensen, B. A. Edelstein, & L. Dornbrand (Eds.), *The practical handbook of clinical gerontology* (pp. 76–106). Thousand Oaks, CA: Sage.

Uba, L. (1994). *Asian Americans: Personality patterns, identity, and mental health.* New York: Guilford Press.

U.S. Bureau of the Census. (2000a). *Projections of the total resident population by 5-year age groups, race, and Hispanic origin with special age categories: Middle series, 2016-2020.* [NP-T4-E]. Retrieved October 26, 2001 from http:/www.census.gov/population/projections/nation/summary/np-t4-e.txt

U.S. Bureau of the Census. (2000b). *Projections of the total resident population by 5-year age groups, race, and Hispanic origin with special age categories: Middle series, 2025-2045.* [NP-T4-F]. Retrieved October 26, 2001 from http:/www.census.gov/population/projections/nation/summary/np-t4-f.txt

U.S. Bureau of the Census (2001a). *Table 4. General demographic characteristics for the Asian population.* [PHC-T-15]. Available from U.S. Bureau of the Census Web site, http://factfinder.census.gov/servlet/ProductBrowserServlet?id=101797&product=PHC-T-15.%20General%20Demographic%20Characteristics%20by%20Race%20for%20the%20United%20States%3A%202000&_lang=en

U.S. Bureau of the Census. (2001b). *Table 5. General demographic characteristics for the Native Hawaiian and other Pacifica Islander population.* [PHC-T-15]. Available from U.S. Bureau of the Census Web site, http://factfinder.census.gov/servlet/ProductBrowserServlet?id=101797&product=PHC-T-15.%20General%20Demographic%20Characteristics%20by%20Race%20for%20the%20United%20States%3A%202000&_lang=en

Wallston, K. A., Wallston, B. S., & Devillis, R. (1978). Development of the Multidimensional Health Locus of Control (MHLC) Scales. *Health Education Monographs, 6,* 160–170.

Yamamoto, N., & Wallhagen, M. (1997). The continuation of family caregiving in Japan. *Journal of Health and Social Behavior, 38,* 164–176.

Yesavage, J. A., Brink, T. L., Rose, T. L., Lum, O., Huang, V., Adey, M., & Leirer, V. O. (1983). Development and validation of a geriatric depression screening scale: A preliminary report. *Journal of Psychiatric Research, 17,* 37–49.

Zheng, Y., Lin, M., Takeuchi, D., Kurasaki, K., Wang, Y., & Cheung, F. (1997). An epidemiological study of neurasthenia in Chinese Americans in Los Angeles. *Comprehensive Psychiatry, 38,* 249–259.

Zung, W. W. K. (1967). Depression in the normal aged. *Psychosomatics, 8,* 287–297.

5

CAREER PSYCHOLOGY OF ASIAN AMERICANS: CULTURAL VALIDITY AND CULTURAL SPECIFICITY

FREDERICK LEONG AND ERIN HARDIN

The growing recognition of the increasing cultural diversity of the U.S. population and workforce has resulted in a steady growth of attention to the career psychology of culturally different populations (Leong, 1997). Much of the research that has emerged in this area has taken an etic approach, examining the extent to which existing theories of career psychology apply across cultural groups. With this approach, some support has been found for the etic dimension; that is, that some aspects of these theories do seem to be valid across the various cultural groups. This research has also found some interesting cultural differences, which suggest that certain emic, or culture-specific, elements may be at work. However, the authors of these early studies generally have not taken the next step of suggesting what these culture-specific elements might be. As the study of the career psychology of minorities has advanced, so has an understanding of the importance of considering both the cultural validity and culture-specificity dimensions (etic vs. emic) in cross-cultural research (Leong & Brown, 1995).

Leong and Brown (1995) argued that cultural validity and cultural specificity are two dimensions that can serve as components of a unifying theoretical framework for cross-cultural career development research. According to Leong and Brown, *cultural validity* is concerned with the validity of theories and models across other cultures in terms of the construct, concurrent, and predictive validities of these models for culturally different individuals. For example, do the relevant constructs have the same meaning across cultures? Are the predicted consequences of certain behaviors or cognitions the same for Asian Americans as for European Americans? As a more specific example, Lent, Brown, and Hackett (1994) argued that self-efficacy mediates the relationship between career interest and choice; is the same true for Asian Americans? *Cultural specificity*, on the other hand, is concerned with concepts, constructs, and models that are specific to certain cultural groups in terms of their role in explaining and predicting behavior (e.g., what effect does filial piety have on career choices of Asian Americans?).

Such culture-specific variables can serve two functions. First, they can be useful in filling in the cultural gaps in Western-based models of career psychology. Under this condition, these culture-specific constructs are believed to provide incremental validity to the understanding and prediction of vocational behavior among culturally different populations. Second, culture-specific variables, independent of Western models, can be useful variables for understanding the career psychology of Asian Americans without necessarily being linked to existing models. Under this condition, these culture-specific variables can serve as competing explanatory models to the Western-based models that are currently dominant.

It is the integration of cultural validity and these cultural specificity approaches that will best advance researchers' knowledge of the career psychology of Asian Americans. The basic premise of Leong and Brown's (1995) framework is that research that emphasizes cultural validity at the expense of cultural specificity addresses only half of the problem. Conversely, relying solely on cultural specificity studies would be to assume—without empirical research—that Western-oriented career theories and models would not work for Asian Americans.

In this chapter we therefore present a critical review of the literature on the career psychology of Asian Americans by using the twin concepts of cultural validity and cultural specificity. Given the relatively recent attention to these issues in the domain of career psychology, research in some areas has been quite limited, leading to certain necessary limitations within this chapter. First, the section on cultural validity is limited to only three major theories of vocational development. Furthermore, given the disproportionate attention paid to these theories in the literature, the discussions of two of the theories are necessarily more limited than that of the third. Second, work on culture-specific factors in the career psychology of Asian Americans has emerged even more recently. Virtually all of the existing research in this area has examined what might more accurately be called *minority-specific factors*—factors that are not specific to Asian American culture per se but that apply to multiple minority groups, such as acculturation, effects of minority status, and self-construal. However, given that these factors appear to be able to fill gaps in existing theories and have the potential to be useful explanatory factors independent of current theories, we discuss them in the context of culture-specific variables that are useful in understanding the specific career psychology of Asian Americans. We also briefly discuss the possible roles of Asian American culture-specific variables, such as loss of face.

CULTURAL VALIDITY

As noted earlier, cultural validity is an etic question: To what extent do current theories of career development reflect universally valid phenomena? Given the limited amount of research that has examined the cultural validity of these theories with Asian Americans, in this section we review recent research on three theories: Holland's (1985) person–environment match theory, Super's (1957) life span developmental model, and Lent et al.'s (1994) social cognitive theory.

Holland's Theory

Holland (1985) hypothesized six vocational personality types and work environments: Realistic (R), Investigative (I), Artistic (A), Social (S), Enterprising (E), and Conventional (C). The theory predicts that individuals attempt to match their personality styles to characteristics of work environments and that the more successful this match is, the more satisfied the individual will be with his or her career choice. The six personality–work environment types were hypothesized to form the points on an equilateral hexagon (in the order RIASEC), with the distance between points indicating the similarity or dissimilarity between types. So, for example, investigative occupations (e.g., psychologist) are perceived as quite similar to artistic occupations (e.g., writer), somewhat similar to social occupations (e.g., teacher), and quite dissimilar to enterprising occupations (e.g., salesperson). Holland hypothesized not only that adjacent interest types (e.g., Realistic and Investigative) are more similar than alternate interest types (e.g., Realistic and Artistic), which are more similar than opposite types (e.g., Realistic and Social; a circular model) but also that distances between types are equal (a circumplex or hexagonal model).

Internal Validity

An important question regarding the cultural validity of Holland's (1985) theory is whether this structure of interests holds for Asian Americans. Given the evidence that cultural differences affect such basic psychological processes as cognition and emotion (see Markus & Kitayama, 1991, for a discussion), it is not inconceivable that they would also affect one's perceptions of the relationships between activities and interests. If so, the fundamental predictions of Holland's model may not be valid for Asian Americans.

Research on this question has yielded mixed results. Early research suggested that the structure of vocational interests is in fact different for overseas Asians (Farh, Leong, & Law, 1998) and Asian Americans (Haverkamp, Collins, & Hansen, 1994; Rounds & Tracey, 1996) than for European Americans. Given that broad cultural factors relevant to both overseas Asians and Asian Americans (e.g., self-construal), rather than more specific factors relevant only to Asian Americans (e.g., minority status), would be expected to affect this underlying structure of interests, we consider in the following discussion research on both overseas Asians and Asian Americans.

For example, Haverkamp et al. (1994) used multidimensional scaling analysis to investigate the validity of the hypothesized hexagonal structure of Holland types among Asian American and European American men and women. Although a circumplex structure was obtained for all four groups, the Asian American groups in particular did not exhibit a good hexagonal shape. In addition, although the structure of interests for the European American sample did exhibit the hypothesized order (i.e., RIASEC), the interest structures of the Asian American samples were different. Asian American women showed a reversal of the Conventional and Enterprising types (RIASCE), and the interests of the Asian American men were in the order RISCEA. Distances between the interest types also were not uniform.

However, other evidence better supports the fit of Holland's (1985) model with overseas Asians and Asian Americans. For example, the hypothesized order of interests (i.e., RIASEC) was supported in a large sample of employed adults from four different racial–ethnic groups (including Asian Americans) in the United States, although the circumplex (hexagonal) structure was not supported (Fouad, Harmon, & Borgen, 1997). However, the hypothesized hexagonal model was found to fit the interest structure in a sample of 172 employed adults in India (Leong, Austin, Sekaran, & Komarraju, 1998).

It has recently been suggested that these mixed findings may be due to methodological artifacts from small, nonrepresentative, less motivated samples used in many previous studies (Day & Rounds, 1998; Day, Rounds, & Swaney, 1998). To investigate this possibility, the authors used data from the American College Test (ACT) Assessment program. These data came from extremely large, national samples of 11th- and 12th-grade college-bound high school students who completed the Unisex Edition of the ACT Interest Inventory (UNIACT; Swaney, 1995). The UNIACT is a 90-item interest inventory, with 15 items reflecting each of the six Holland types. It was argued that these students were likely to be highly motivated to complete the

UNIACT accurately, given that all had voluntarily registered for the assessment program (Day & Rounds, 1998).

Using multidimensional scaling, these studies (Day, Rounds, & Swaney, 1998) found that the structure of interests obtained for the Asian American students was nearly identical to that obtained for European American students. There were 1,959 Asian Americans and 2,454 European Americans in the first sample (Day et al., 1998) and 6,523 Asian Americans and 16,106 European Americans in the second sample (Day & Rounds, 1998). Day and Rounds also examined data from 10th-grade students who were part of the 1992 UNIACT norm sample and found the same structure of interests, indicating that the fit of the model is not limited to college-bound students. "[These] findings suggest that large, motivated, cross-sectional samples (in this case, thousands of college-bound students throughout the United States) may be the key to finding good fits to Holland's model" (Day et al., 1998, p. 43).

Predictive Validity

There are still other important questions about the predictive validity of Holland's (1985) theory. "One might argue that even given a similar structure of interests, the upshot, choice of career, might be different for a person from an ethnic or racial minority group than for a White-majority member" (Day & Rounds, 1998, pp. 733–734). Holland's theory predicts that people in different occupations should evidence different patterns of interest, that career interests should predict career choice, and that factors such as congruence should predict job satisfaction and tenure. Although there is some evidence for the first prediction, little evidence has been found for the remaining two.

Supporting the validity of the first prediction, Day and Rounds (1998) reported that when researchers at ACT examined the interests of students who were "very sure" of their career choice, "they found that students who chose the same occupations landed in similar hexagon locations, no matter what their racial or ethnic group" (p. 734). Farh et al. (1998) also found that Hong Kong Chinese students who preferred Realistic jobs evidenced higher Realistic interests than students not interested in Realistic jobs. Similar results were found for students interested in Investigative, Enterprising, and Conventional jobs.

Despite this apparent support for the first prediction, there is evidence disputing the validity of the other predictions. For example, Tang, Fouad, and Smith (1999) found that, contrary to the predictions of Holland's (1985) model, career interests were not a significant predictor of career choice. This seems to contradict the findings that Asian Americans in different occupations do evidence different patterns of interest. Perhaps although interest does not affect career choice, career choice subsequently affects interest. Regarding the third prediction, Leong et al. (1998) found that neither congruence (match between interests and work type), nor consistency (among an individual's top three interest types), nor differentiation (distance between an individual's highest and lowest interest) was a significant predictor of job satisfaction.

The results just discussed seem consistent with what is known about Asian American career development. Given the strong influence of family on the career choices of Asian Americans, the importance of prestige and careers in which success is perceived as likely (see the following discussion under "Minority Status" in the Cultural Specificity section), it is not surprising that career interests would be much less predictive of career choice for Asian Americans than for European Americans. Furthermore, the apparently different relationship of congruence, consistency, differentiation, and job satisfaction for Asian Americans and European Americans also seems logical. Given that

> career choice and career advancement may be seen more as a means of providing for one's own family, helping one's siblings, and fulfilling one's responsibility to care for parents in their old age than as ways of implementing self attributes, (Leong & Chou, 1994, p. 140)

it seems likely that the factors that contribute to job satisfaction may be very different for Asian Americans than for European Americans. As we discuss later, acculturation is likely to moderate these relationships. Finally, Osipow (1975) also noted that Holland's (1985) theory fails to take into account the reality that many occupational environments may not be equally accessible to minorities.

An important methodological note is raised by these points, and addressed by Day et al. (1998), who noted that many interest inventories use as stimuli occupational titles, which are likely to elicit respondents' perceptions of prestige and availability; this may influence their ratings of interest in these occupations. However, the UNIACT uses activity names (e.g., "explore a science museum,") which are likely to be free from these influences.

Super's Theory

Super's (1957) theory of vocational development is unique, because it was among the first to focus not on the content but on the process of career choice. Super posited that career choice is one event in a lifelong developmental process. For Super, career choice ideally represented the implementation of one's self-concept, and thus his theory emphasized exploring and discovering one's personal interests and abilities as crucial tasks in this developmental process. Super outlined several specific stages and developmental tasks for each stage, arguing that all individuals progress through the same stages, in the same order, and that successful mastery of the tasks in each stage is critical for successful career development. The degree to which one has mastered the tasks appropriate to his or her stage of career development is known as *career maturity*. For example, in adolescence, when individuals are expected to be crystallizing their career choices, more career-mature individuals are those who are actively acquiring information about possible careers and who are basing their career choices on factors such as personal interests, not the advice of parents.

The primary criticism of Super's (1957) theory when applied to Asian Americans is its emphasis on individual choice and implementation of self-concept. First, in asserting that individuals are able to freely choose careers, the theory does not adequately address the impact of discrimination and limited opportunity experienced by minorities (Leong & Brown, 1995). Second, several authors have argued that this emphasis on individual choice is incongruent with traditional Asian values and leaves no room for the important role of the family for Asian Americans (Hardin, Leong, & Osipow, 2001; Leong & Serafica, 1995; Leong & Tata, 1990).

For example, an early study found that Asian American college students exhibited a more dependent decision-making style and lower career maturity than European American students (Leong, 1991). However, a recent study suggests that the definition and measurement of career maturity may be less valid for Asian Americans because they fail to accurately distinguish among independence, interdependence, and dependence (Hardin et al., 2001). Thus Asian Americans, who tend to be more interdependent than European Americans, are considered dependent (not interdependent) and therefore erroneously considered less career mature. In addition, although Leong (1991) found the Asian Americans to have lower career maturity than European Americans, the two groups did not differ in terms of vocational identity. These results suggest that Asian Americans may approach the career decision-making process differently than European Americans but arrive at similarly crystallized vocational identities.

These studies clearly cast doubt on the cultural validity of Super's (1957) theory for Asian Americans. They suggest that Asian Americans do not approach the process of making a career choice in the same way as European Americans. Little research has explicitly examined this process. Important questions are whether Asian Americans progress through some, but not all, of the stages hypothesized by Super and whether Asian Americans progress through these stages at a reliably different rate or in a different order. We discuss more fully the importance of interdependence in the career behavior of Asian Americans later.

Social Cognitive Theory

Based on social learning theory, social cognitive theory (Lent et al., 1994) posits that an individual's learning history interacts with his or her inherent abilities to influence interests, self-concept, and career behavior. A key feature of this model is *self-efficacy* (Bandura, 1986), or one's belief in one's ability to be successful in a particular domain. Self-efficacy is important because it is hypothesized to mediate the relationship between variables such as interest and persistence in activities. This theory seems to have useful implications for Asian Americans and other minorities because of its explicit focus on how environmental factors such as discrimination may affect self-efficacy and hence one's choice of or persistence in certain careers.

Tang et al. (1999) directly examined the validity of this theory with Asian Americans. They collected data from 187 Asian American adults to examine several hypotheses. Four of these hypotheses were derived directly from social cognitive theory: that (a) acculturation and (b) family socioeconomic status (SES) directly influence self-efficacy and career interests, (c) family involvement affects self-efficacy and choice, and (d) self-efficacy influences career interests and choice. Tang et al. further hypothesized that, contrary to the predictions of social cognitive theory, interests would be weakly related to career choice among Asian Americans, for the reasons discussed earlier.

The results revealed support for all of these hypotheses except the one regarding SES; family SES was not found to be a significant predictor of self-efficacy, interest, or career choice. Acculturation, which we discuss in greater detail later, was found to directly predict self-efficacy, interest, and career choice, whereas family involvement was a significant predictor of career choice. Although acculturation and self-efficacy were found to be significant predictors of interest, interest was not a significant predictor of choice. Only acculturation, self-efficacy, and family involvement were found to predict career choice.

Summary of Cultural Validity Studies

As is obvious in the preceding discussions, significantly more attention has been paid to the cultural validity of Holland's (1985) theory than to either Super's (1957) theory or to social cognitive theory (Lent et al., 1994). Social cognitive theory has probably received less attention because it is relatively new, whereas Super's theory may have received less attention because it is older; although Super's developmental theory remains one of the more important ones in understanding vocational development, research directly testing this theory has waned in recent years. In addition, the cultural validity of Super's theory may be more difficult to assess because of the lack of developed measures for certain aspects of the theory. For example, whereas several instruments exist for assessing mastery of tasks important during the adolescent Exploration stage, instruments for assessing tasks of earlier and later stages are either few or nonexistent.

Furthermore, as demonstrated by Hardin et al. (2001), some of the measures that do exist may be culturally biased. Given the limitations in existing quantitative measures, more qualitative methods may prove useful in investigating the cultural validity of Super's (1957) theory. It would also be valuable to replicate Super's longitudinal career pattern study with Asian Americans to determine which aspects of career development yield cultural-general dimensions and which reveal culture-specific patterns. Such a study would enable researchers to conduct in-depth interviews with Asian American youth to determine specific developmental markers that may differentiate them from Super's White European American youth.

CULTURAL SPECIFICITY

The research just discussed suggests that aspects of these theories do seem to be culturally valid for Asian Americans while also suggesting limitations or gaps in these theories that limit their validity when applied to Asian Americans. In the context of Leong and Brown's (1995) framework, these gaps suggest culture-specific variables that are missing from these existing theories. Understanding minority status, acculturation, filial piety, and self-construal may fill in these gaps, suggest alternative explanations for the career development of Asian Americans, or both.

Minority Status

Research has shown that being a racial or ethnic minority member has certain associated psychological costs and consequences. This relationship between minority status and various negative experiences also applies to the vocational or work domain. For example, prior research has shown that Asian Americans tend to be underrepresented in some occupations (e.g., sales, production, and labor-related occupations) and overrepresented in others (e.g., professional, technical, and service-related occupations; Hsia, 1988; Leong & Serafica, 1995). Asian Americans' reactions to their minority status may be one possible explanation for their pattern of occupational segregation.

Given that Asian Americans are a minority in the United States, they are likely to experience barriers to success due to racism and discrimination, both real and perceived. Data from different studies have also found that Asian Americans experience barriers to advancement in organizations similar to the "glass-ceiling" effect found for women (e.g., see Woo, 2000). Thus, it has been suggested that Asian Americans select occupations high in prestige as a means of ensuring success in the U.S. social system (e.g., Leung, Ivey, & Suzuki, 1994). This hypothesis also assumes that Asian American parents push their children toward high-prestige jobs in which Asian Americans have traditionally been successful and in which there is less possibility of experiencing discrimination and racism (see Leong & Serafica, 1995).

Sue and Okazaki (1990) offered a similar explanation for the higher average academic achievement of Asian American students. They argued that Asian Americans experience and perceive limited mobility in many areas, especially those in which success does not rely heavily on education, such as sports, politics, and entertainment. Asian Americans thus see education as the only route to success; they perceive racial discrimination as limiting their opportunities, they perceive more opportunities for success in education-dependent math- and science-related fields, and therefore they work harder in school, and a disproportionate number of them enter education-dependent occupations.

As discussed earlier, some theories of career development, such as Super's (1957), may be limited in their cultural validity because they fail to take into account the culture-specific factor of minority status. Such theories assume equal opportunity and choice for all individuals, which is simply not the case for many members of minority groups. Minority status may influence career interests by affecting activities and occupations to which individuals are exposed. In addition to examining how real barriers to career opportunities are related to overt categories of minority membership, it is just as important, if not more important, to examine how perceptions of one's minority status affect one's perceptions of career opportunities. These perceptions for Asian Americans are likely to be linked to their level of acculturation.

Acculturation

In addressing the cultural specificity dimension in career psychology research, acculturation has proven to be a consistent and long-standing variable of relevance to Asian Americans. In his review of the literature, Leong (1985) pointed out the salience of acculturation as a moderator variable specific to Asian Americans in the early studies of career interest patterns conducted by Derald Sue. Indeed, Leong and Chou (1994) provided a systematic set of formulations regarding the career problems likely to be encountered by Asian Americans based on their acculturation status.

First, Leong and Chou (1994) argued that ethnic identity and acculturation are highly related constructs for Asian Americans. They proposed an integrated framework for combining racial–ethnic identity models and acculturation models. Using Berry's (1980) model as the foundation, Leong and Chou (1994) proposed that the question of racial and ethnic identity is essentially a two-dimensional problem; namely, how do members of a racial or ethnic minority group view their own culture, and how do they view their dominant host culture?

Although it is called an *acculturation* model, Berry's (1980) model deals more directly with cultural identity. Leong and Chou (1994) pointed out that Berry's (1980) model maintains that individuals who hold positive views of both their own culture and the host culture are Integrationists. These individuals attempt to have the best that both cultures have to offer. This group is similar, if not identical to, Sue and Sue's (1973) Asian American; Suinn, Rickard-Figueroa, Lew, and Vigil's (1987) Bicultural persons; and Cross's (1971) Internalization group (see Helms, 1993). According to Cross (1971), African Americans who have achieved *Internalization* are those who have come to value their African American culture but also find things of value in the European American culture. All four models view this as the ideal outcome.

Individuals who have achieved *assimilation*, the second possible acculturation outcome, hold a positive view of the host culture but a negative view of their own culture (Berry, 1980). This group parallels Sue and Sue's (1973) Marginal Man; Suinn et al.'s (1987) Western- or American-Oriented group; and Cross's (1971) Pre-Encounter individual, who holds pro-White and anti-Black attitudes (Helms, 1993).

Individuals who view their host culture negatively and their own culture positively compose the group that has achieved the third possible acculturation outcome; they are called *Separationists* (Berry, 1980), *Traditionalists* (Sue & Sue, 1973), or *Asian oriented* (Suinn et al., 1987). Two of Cross's (1971) Black racial identity groups fall into this category: the Encounter and Immersion/Emmersion groups (Helms, 1993). Both of these groups hold negative views of European American culture and increasingly positive views of their own African American culture. Finally, Berry's (1980) model includes a group that is not recognized by the other models: A *Marginal* person holds a negative view of both the host culture and his or her own culture.

This integrated model of racial and ethnic identity reveals a considerable amount of convergence in the racial–ethnic identity literature, regardless of whether one studies the acculturation of Cree Indians in Canada (Berry, 1976), Asian American clients struggling with ethnic identity issues at the University of California's counseling center (Sue & Sue, 1973), or African American college students' racial identity (Parham & Helms, 1985a, 1985b). Berry's (1980) two-dimensional model of acculturation provides an organizational scheme for examining racial and ethnic identity development, identifies areas of divergence in need of further research, and points to areas of confusion that need further clarification.

Leong and Chou (1994) went on to hypothesize specific career outcomes for Asian Americans, given these different acculturation statuses. For example, they hypothesized that Asian Americans with a Separationist identity, compared with those with Integrationist or Assimilationist identities, are more susceptible to occupational segregation, stereotyping, and discrimination. They also proposed that, because of the predominantly Eurocentric work environments in most organizations and institutions, Asian Americans with a Separationist identity are most at risk for negative career outcomes, including lower levels of job satisfaction and upward mobility and higher levels of job stress. On the other hand, Asian Americans with Integrationist or Assimilationist identities are hypothesized to be less susceptible to occupational segregation, stereotyping, and discrimination because of the greater cultural congruence between themselves and the managers and supervisors in organizations. They are also hypothesized to exhibit higher levels of job satisfaction and lower levels of job stress than Asian Americans with a Separationist identity.

Leong and Chou (1994) thus speculated that Assimilationist and Integrationist Asian Americans are likely to have advantages over Separationist Asian Americans in terms of various career outcomes. However, this may be true only when considering Asian Americans working in the context of predominantly European American or multicultural organizations. Given the higher likelihood of occupational segregation and stereotyping, Separationist Asian Americans may be less likely to work in these environments and more likely to work in settings composed primarily of other Asian Americans or Asian immigrants. In these cases, Separationist Asian Americans may experience more positive career outcomes than Integrationist or Assimilationist Asian Americans. Thus, outcome variables such as job satisfaction are likely affected by an interaction between acculturation status and the culture of work environments.

Although no empirical research to date has investigated this interaction between acculturation and work environment with respect to outcome variables, several previous studies have demonstrated the value of using acculturation as a culture-specific variable in predicting other variables among Asian Americans. For example, Leong and Tata (1990) examined the relation between Chinese American children's level of acculturation and work values. Sex differences in work values among Chinese American children were studied as well. Leong and Tata administered to 177 Chinese American fifth- and sixth-graders in a Los Angeles inner-city elementary school the Ohio Work Values Inventory (Hales & Fenner, 1973, 1974) and the Suinn–Lew Asian Self-Identity Acculturation Scale (Suinn et al., 1987). The Ohio Work Values Inventory yields scores on 11 scales. The two most important values for Chinese American children were money and task satisfaction. Object orientation and solitude appeared to be of considerably lower importance. Boys valued object orientation, self-realization, and ideas–data more than did girls. Girls valued altruism more than did boys. These sex differences may have represented non-culture-specific sex differences in work values.

The Chinese American children were also divided into three groups— a low-acculturation group, a medium-acculturation group, and a high-acculturation group—according to their scores on the Suinn–Lew Asian Self-Identity Acculturation Scale. Significant acculturation differences were found for self-realization; highly acculturated Chinese American children valued self-realization more than low-acculturated Chinese American children did. Self-realization seems to be more a part of European American culture than of Chinese American culture. Leong and Tata (1990) concluded that knowledge of this pattern of occupational values among Chinese American children can serve as an advance organizer for counselors who help this group of minority children with their career planning. The challenge lies in broadening the occupational options for Chinese American children while still respecting their cultural values, which may underlie their occupational values.

In a study we reviewed earlier, Tang et al. (1999) investigated the role of career self-efficacy in career choice behaviors among Asian Americans. They found that the highest levels of self-efficacy for Asian Americans were in Social, Conventional, and Investigative types of occupations. In addition, they found that the effects of self-efficacy on the career choice of Asian Americans was mediated by acculturation. In the conclusion to their article, Tang et al. noted that

> the main theme of Lent et al.'s model is the mediating role of self-efficacy in career choice performance. The results of this study support this proposition . . . [and] Lent et al.'s theoretical model that individuals tend to choose [a] career they feel confident in. (p. 152)

Thus, Tang et al.'s research suggests that the prediction that self-efficacy has a strong influence on career choice is culturally valid and that there are culture-specific factors, such as acculturation, that predict self-efficacy for Asian Americans.

Taken together, the conceptual and empirical articles we have discussed thus far suggest that acculturation continues to be an important culture-specific variable in researchers' understanding of the career psychology of Asian Americans. The existing research suggests that Asian Americans can be consistently differentiated along an acculturation continuum, with highly acculturated Asian Americans being more similar to European Americans. To the extent that the acculturation variable serves as a significant moderator variable for the career and vocational behaviors of Asian Americans, it will be an important culture-specific variable for an understanding of the career psychology of Asian Americans. Future research should further the explore the extent to which acculturation can both fill gaps in existing theories of career development and provide alternative explanations for the career behavior of Asian Americans. Tang et al.'s (1999) research provided a crucial first step in the former approach by demonstrating that adding acculturation to the existing social cognitive model increases its predictive utility with Asian Americans. Adding an understanding of the effects of acculturation on work values, interests, and perceived opportunities may similarly increase the predictive utility of both Holland's (1985) and Super's (1957) theories of vocational development. Research examining the interaction between acculturation status and work environment may alternatively provide additional theories to explain career outcomes. For example, perhaps the degree of match between an individual's cultural values and the dominant values of his or her work environment is an important predictor of job satisfaction, independent of one's career interests or abilities.

Self-Construal

Another prominent culture-specific variable for the understanding of the career psychology of Asian Americans is concerned with the value dimension of individualism–collectivism. Following the pioneering work of Geert Hofstede (1980) and the systematic program of research conducted by Harry Triandis (Triandis, Bontempo, Villareal, Asai, & Lucca, 1988), this value dimension has become a dominant construct in cross-cultural psychological research during the past 20 years. The concept has also been applied to the career psychology of racial and ethnic minorities. For example, Leong and Tata (1990) observed that Asian Americans in general and Chinese Americans in particular tend to be more collectivistic in their value orientation than European Americans do. They went on to note that Super's (1957) theory that one's career choice is an implementation of one's self-concept may not apply readily to Asian Americans, especially those who have more collectivistic value orientations. Incidentally, they also found that Chinese American children's work values were moderated by their acculturation level, with more acculturated children exhibiting a greater endorsement of individualistic values such as self-realization.

There has been some controversy regarding whether individualism–collectivism, which was originally conceptualized as a culture-level phenomenon, can be adequately measured at the individual level. By referring to people with individualistic value orientations as *idiocentric* and those with collectivistic value orientation as *allocentric*, Triandis had argued that the value dimension can be assessed at both levels (i.e., the cultural level and the individual level; Triandis, Leung, Villareal, & Clack, 1985). For example, even though the United States, as measured in Hofstede's study, is a highly individualistic culture, there are likely to be some members of the U.S. culture who are allocentric even though the majority are likely to be idiocentric. An alternative model for examining this issue of individualism–collectivism as an individual-difference variable was proposed by Markus and Kitayama (1991), who framed value differences within the rubric of self psychology.

According to Markus and Kitayama (1991), Asian Americans, who have more collectivistic values, may conceive of the self as interdependent, whereas people from individualistic cultures may view the self as independent. According to this model, the independent self has a core need to strategically express or assert the internal attributes of the self, whereas the interdependent construal formulates the self in relation to others (Markus & Kitayama, 1991). Being unique is critical for the independent self, and fitting in is critical for interdependent self. The basis of self-esteem for the independent self is the ability to express the self and to validate internal attributes. For the interdependent self the basis of self-esteem is the ability to adjust, restrain the self, and maintain harmony with the social context (Markus & Kitayama, 1991). Such differences in self-conception may make career decision making a much more interpersonal process for collectivists than for individualists. For the latter, career decision making may be an individual matter based mainly on personal interests, values, and aspirations, whereas for the former, career decision making may be a familial matter based on group interests, values, and needs.

In their review of the literature, Leong and Serafica (1995) argued that this concept of self-construal should be helpful in understanding the vocational behavior of Asian Americans in work settings. For example, Asian Americans are often passed up for promotion or tenure because of a perceived lack of managerial skills, a persistent problem that needs further investigation. One possible explanation for this problem may be because the self-construal of Asian Americans leads them to behave differently from what is expected in the typical method of evaluating job performance (i.e., one has to present and express oneself to let others know that one has done excellent work). Because the majority of U.S. employers and supervisors are European Americans who are likely to have independent self-construals, Asian Americans' quietness, modesty, and deference to the group may often be mistakenly viewed as lack of confidence or ability.

Some research has already begun to demonstrate the value of self-construal as a culture-specific variable in the analysis of the career psychology of Asian Americans. In a research project examining ethnic differences in career maturity between Asian Americans and European Americans, Leong (1991) found that although Asian Americans showed less mature career-choice attitudes that than their European American counterparts, as measured by Crites's (1978) Career Maturity Inventory, the two groups did not differ in terms of vocational identity, as measured by Holland, Daiger, and Power's (1980) My Vocational Situation. Leong (1991) concluded that these results indicated that Asian Americans and European Americans approached the career decision-making process differently yet still arrived at similarly crystallized vocational identities. On the basis of these results, Leong (1991) introduced the concept of *cultural relativity* in the construct of career maturity. He suggested that, rather than automatically assuming that Asian Americans actually have lower career maturity, researchers and counselors needed to carefully investigate possible ways in which cultural differences moderate the meaning of career maturity.

One such cultural difference may be the concept of independence. Crites's (1965) theory of career maturity, based on Super's (1957) theory of vocational development and the basis of Crites's (1978) measure of career maturity, includes Independence in career decision making as a crucial component of career-mature attitudes, along with Compromise, Decisiveness, Involvement, and Orientation. *Compromise* is the extent to which one is willing to compromise wishes and reality. *Decisiveness* refers to how certain one is about a career choice. *Involvement* is the degree to which an individual is actively participating in the career-choice process. *Orientation* is "the extent to which an individual is familiar with and relates self to the decisional process" (M. L. Savickas, Northeastern Ohio University College of Medicine, personal communication, February 21, 2000). *Independence* in career decision making is defined as the "extent to which [an] individual relies upon others in the choice of an occupation" (Crites & Savickas, 1995, p. 9). More decisiveness, involvement, and independence in career decision making; a greater self-orientation; and more willingness to compromise one's desires with reality are all considered characteristics of a more career-mature individual.

However, this emphasis on independence, to the exclusion of other alternatives, such as interdependence, may underlie the cultural differences between Asian Americans and European Americans in their approaches to the career decision-making process discussed earlier. To investigate this possibility, Hardin et al. (2001) administered several instruments, including the Crites Career Maturity Inventory (Crites, 1978) and the Self-Construal Scale (Singelis, 1994), to 235 self-identified non-Hispanic European American and 182 self-identified Asian American college students. Consistent with previous research (Leong, 1991; Luzzo, 1992), the Asian American participants exhibited less mature career-choice attitudes, as measured by the Career Maturity Inventory, than their European American counterparts.

Hardin et al.'s (2001) results were moderated, however, by self-construal. Specifically, participants who had high interdependent self-construals, regardless of the level of their independent self-construals, had less mature career-choice attitudes than participants who had lower interdependent self-construals. No differences in maturity of career-choice attitudes were observed on the basis of level of independence. Furthermore, the three subscales on which the Asian Americans were found to exhibit less mature career-choice attitudes than the European Americans (Compromise, Independence, and Involvement) were also the three subscales most related to an interdependent self-construal. Specifically, participants who had a higher interdependent self-construal had lower scores on these subscales than participants who had a lower interdependent self-construal.

It is important to remember that independence and interdependence are conceptualized as separate dimensions, and therefore the presence of interdependence does not imply the absence of independence. Therefore, the results of Hardin et al.'s (2001) study suggest that Asian Americans may appear to exhibit less mature career-choice attitudes because their greater interdependent self-construal is misconstrued as a lack of independence. Although more research is needed on the role of self-construal in the career psychology of Asian Americans, these results do provide strong initial evidence that self-construal is an important culture-specific variable that affects both the career psychology of Asian Americans and the cultural validity of theories of career development.

Both the value orientation of individualism–collectivism and the concept of self-construal appear to be promising culture-specific variables for continued research into the career psychology of Asian Americans. Cross-cultural psychologists have long observed that values are an important dimension for analyzing cross-cultural differences, and early research with these constructs has certainly supported this contention.

CONCLUSIONS

In applying the theoretical framework proposed by Leong and Brown (1995) to the case of Asian Americans, the basic premise of this chapter has been that the integrated and combined used of etic and emic approaches to examine the cultural validity and cultural specificity of career theories and models would be the most fruitful strategy for advancing researchers' knowledge of the career psychology of Asian Americans. As Leong (1997) pointed out, studies that examine the cultural validity of Western-based models of career development tend to be able to answer only the question of whether these models and theories work for racial and ethnic minority groups and not why they do or do not work.

The two studies by Fouad et al. (1997) and Tracey, Watanabe, and Schnieder (1997) reviewed by Leong (1997) are good examples not only of the value of the cultural validity approach but also of its limitations. When cultural validity studies find that Western-based models do not fit exactly for racial and ethnic minority groups, then it is up to culture-specific studies to provide possible answers as to why these models are not readily transferable. Culture-specific studies provide concepts such as acculturation or self-construal as possible moderator or additional explanatory variables for enhancing researchers' understanding of the career psychology of racial and ethnic minority groups such as Asian Americans. Therefore, the logical recommendation of this analysis of research strategies is that both cultural validity (etic) and cultural specificity (emic) studies are needed to advance researchers' understanding of the career psychology of Asian Americans (Leong, 1997; Leong & Brown, 1995).

In terms of future directions, a first step is to broaden researchers' understanding of which culture-specific variables are most relevant to which groups. The discussion of culture-specific variables in this chapter was based largely on literature regarding East Asian cultures; future research will need to determine whether minority status, acculturation, and self-construal are equally relevant to individuals from other Asian cultures and whether they have similar effects on career choice and behavior. In addition, many of these culture-specific variables are not, in fact, specific, to Asian Americans but apply more broadly to minorities in general. Variables such as filial piety and loss of face, which are more specific to Asian American culture, deserve attention. For example, some of the research cited in this chapter has already suggested that a stronger interdependent self-construal and concomitant emphasis on family have important implications for the career behavior of Asian Americans (e.g., Hardin et al., 2001; Tang et al. 1999); looking at the more specific construct of filial piety may further elucidate these relationships. Loss of face may also prove to be an important culture-specific variable in predicting career behavior. For example, how does a concern with loss of face affect variables such as career interests, preferred work environments, or managerial styles? Variables specific to subgroups within the broader Asian Americans population also deserve attention in future research. For example, the caste system is very important to career choice and mobility in India; research investigating the impact of caste on the career behavior of Asian Indians in the United States would be useful.

As cultural validity and cultural specificity studies begin to accumulate, the question then becomes how to combine and integrate the knowledge from these two different approaches. One model for undertaking this integration, called the *cultural accommodation model*, has been proposed by Leong and his colleagues (Leong & Serafica, 2001; Leong & Tang, in press). According to Leong and Tang (in press), the proposed cultural-accommodation approach involves three steps: (a) identifying the cultural gaps or cultural blind spots in an existing theory that restrict the cultural validity of the theory, (b) selecting current culturally specific concepts and models from cross-cultural and ethnic minority psychology to fill in the cultural gaps and accommodate the theory to racial and ethnic minorities, and (c) testing the culturally accommodated theory to determine if it has incremental validity above and beyond the culturally unaccommodated theory.

The first step of this cultural-accommodation model is directly based on the cultural validity studies we reviewed and proposed in this chapter. In some instances, the Western-based models of career psychology will be found to be culturally valid and more than adequate when directly applied to racial and ethnic minority groups. In other instances, some of the cultural validity studies will find problems and inadequacies in these Western-based models. These gaps will serve as clues to the missing cultural elements in the Western-based models. In the second step, a critical analysis of these studies from a cross-cultural perspective would then be able to identify potential culture-specific variables that can be used to address these gaps and cultural lacunae in the Western-based models. Finally, when a theory or model with demonstrated cultural validity problems has accommodated certain culture-specific variables to improve its level of cultural validity, then an empirical test of the incremental validity provided by the culture-specific variables can then be conducted.

Just as one cannot assume that a Western-based theory or model of career psychology is automatically going to work for racial and ethnic minority groups, one cannot assume that certain culture-specific variables being added in the cultural-accommodation approach are automatically going to improve the cultural validity of the theories and models in question. It is quite conceivable that different versions of a culturally accommodated model will have to be tested before the best set of variables can be found. This is the essence of the cultural-accommodation approach proposed by Leong and his colleagues (Leong & Serafica, 2001; Leong & Tang, in press) to integrate the cultural validity and cultural specificity studies discussed in this chapter.

FUTURE RESEARCH DIRECTIONS

- Studies of both cultural validity and cultural specificity are needed. The former is concerned with testing the validity of Western models and theories of career development with racial and ethnic minority groups, whereas the latter attempts to identify cultural unique variables for increasing researchers' understanding of the vocational behavior of culturally different populations.
- When examining Western theories, such as Holland's (1985) and Super's (1957), one finds that there often are cultural gaps in these models when applied to racial and ethnic minority groups. Such limitations remind one to proceed cautiously when using these models in providing career counseling to these clients. For example, whereas the structure of Holland's model may transfer to other cultural groups, expected relations to external criterion variables have yet to be found consistently. Super's model is conceptually biased toward an individualistic conception of career development that fails to account for the collectivistic orientations of many Asian and Asian American groups (e.g., the role of the family is neglected).
- Preliminary research with Asian Americans has found that culture-specific variables, such as minority status, acculturation, filial piety, and self-construal, may be significant moderators of career assessment and intervention with this particular ethnic minority group.
- Further research on these and other yet-to-be-identified culture-specific variables will help researchers develop culturally relevant and appropriate career counseling models for Asian American clients.
- As more and more data are collected on both cultural validity and cultural specificity, it will be important to develop a cultural-accommodation model to integrate both sets of findings to guide career assessment and intervention.

REFERENCES

Bandura, A. (1986). *Social foundations of thought and action: A social cognitive theory.* Englewood Cliffs, NJ: Prentice Hall.

Berry, J. W. (1976). *Human ecology and cognitive style: Comparative studies in cultural and psychological adaptation.* New York: Sage/Halsted.

Berry, J. W. (1980). Acculturation as varieties of adaptation. In A. Padilla (Ed.), *Acculturation: Theories, models and some new findings* (pp. 9–25). Boulder, CO: Westview Press.

Crites, J. O. (1965). Measurement of vocational maturity in adolescence: I. Attitude test of the Vocational Development Inventory. *Psychological Monographs, 79*(2, Whole No. 595).

Crites, J. O. (1978). *Career Maturity Inventory: Theory and research handbook.* Monterey, CA: CTB/McGraw-Hill.

Crites, J. O., & Savickas, M. L. (1995). *Career Maturity Inventory sourcebook.* Clayton, NY: ISM Information Systems Management, Inc., Careerware.

Cross, W. E., Jr. (1971). The Negro-to-Black conversion experience: Toward a psychology of Black liberation. *Black World, 20,* 13–27.

Day, S. X., & Rounds, J. (1998). Universality of vocational interest structure among racial and ethnic minorities. *American Psychologist, 53,* 728–736.

Day, S. X., Rounds, J., & Swaney, K. (1998). The structure of vocational interests for diverse racial–ethnic groups. *Psychological Science, 9,* 40–44.

Farh, J., Leong, F. T. L., & Law, K. S. (1998). Cross-cultural validity of Holland's model in Hong Kong. *Journal of Vocational Behavior, 52,* 425–440.

Fouad, N. A., Harmon, L. W., & Borgen, F. H. (1997). Structure of interests in employed male and female members of US racial–ethnic minority and nonminority groups. *Journal of Counseling Psychology, 44,* 339–345.

Hales, L. W., & Fenner, B. J. (1973). Sex and social class differences in work values. *Elementary School Guidance and Counseling, 8,* 27–32.

Hales, L. W., & Fenner, B. J. (1974). *Ohio Work Values Inventory.* Athens, OH: Kuder.

Hardin, E. E., Leong, F. T. L., & Osipow, S. H. (2001). Cultural relativity in the conceptualization of career maturity. *Journal of Vocational Behavior, 58,* 36–52.

Haverkamp, B. E., Collins, R. C., & Hansen, J. I. (1994). Structure of interests of Asian-American college students. *Journal of Counseling Psychology, 41,* 256–264.

Helms, J. E. (1993). An overview of Black racial identity theory. In J. E. Helms (Ed.), *Black and White racial identity* (pp. 9–32). Westport, CT: Praeger.

Hofstede, G. (1980). *Culture's consequences: International differences in work-related values.* Beverly Hills, CA: Sage.

Holland, J. L. (1985). *Making vocational choices: A theory of vocational personalities and work environments.* Englewood Cliffs, NJ: Prentice Hall.

Holland, J. L., Daiger, D. C., & Power, P. G. (1980). *My Vocational Situation: Description of an experimental diagnostic form for selection of vocational assistance.* Palo Alto, CA: Consulting Psychologists Press.

Hsia, J. (1988). *Asian Americans in higher education and at work.* Hillsdale, NJ: Erlbaum.

Lent, R. W., Brown, S. D., & Hackett, G. (1994). Toward a unified social cognitive theory of career and academic interest, choice and performance. *Journal of Vocational Behavior, 45,* 79–122.

Leong, F. T. L. (1985). Career development of Asian Americans. *Journal of College Student Personnel, 26,* 539–546.

Leong, F. T. L. (1991). Career development attributes and occupational values of Asian-American and European-American American college students. *Career Development Quarterly, 39,* 221–230.

Leong, F. T. L. (1997). Cross-cultural career psychology: Comments on Fouad, Harmon, and Borgen (1997) and Tracey, Watanabe, and Schnieder (1997). *Journal of Counseling Psychology, 44,* 355–359.

Leong, F. T. L., Austin, J. T., Sekaran, U., & Komarraju, M. (1998). An evaluation of the cross-cultural validity of Holland's theory: Career choices by workers in India. *Journal of Vocational Behavior, 52,* 441–455.

Leong, F. T. L., & Brown, M. (1995). Theoretical issues in cross-cultural career development: Cultural validity and cultural specificity. In W. B. Walsh & S. H. Osipow (Eds.), *Handbook of vocational psychology: Theory, research and practice* (pp. 143–180). Mahwah, NJ: Erlbaum.

Leong, F. T. L., & Chou, E. L. (1994). The role of ethnic identity and acculturation in the vocational behavior of Asian Americans: An integrative review. *Journal of Vocational Behavior, 44,* 155–172.

Leong, F. T. L., & Serafica, F. C. (1995). Career development of Asian Americans: A research area in need of a good theory. In F. T. L. Leong (Ed.), *Career development and vocational behavior of racial and ethnic minorities* (pp. 67–102). Mahwah, NJ: Erlbaum.

Leong, F. T. L., & Serafica, F. (2001). Cross-cultural perspective on Super's career development theory: Career maturity and cultural accommodation. In F. T. L. Leong & A. Barak (Eds.), *Contemporary models in vocational psychology: A volume in honor of Samuel H. Osipow* (pp. 167–205). Mahwah, NJ: Erlbaum.

Leong, F. T. L., & Tang, M. (in press). A cultural accommodation approach to career assessment with Asian Americans. In K. Kurasaski, S. Sure, & S. Okazaki (Eds.), *Asian American mental health: Assessment, theories and methods.* Dordrecht, The Netherlands: Kluwer.

Leong, F. T. L., & Tata, S. P. (1990). Sex and acculturation differences in occupational values among Chinese American children. *Journal of Counseling Psychology, 37,* 208–212.

Leung, S. A., Ivey, D., & Suzuki, L. (1994). Factors affecting the career aspirations of Asian Americans. *Journal of Counseling and Development, 72,* 404–410.

Luzzo, D. A. (1992). Ethnic group and social class differences in college students' career development. *Career Development Quarterly, 41,* 161–173.

Markus, H. R., & Kitayama, S. (1991). Culture and the self: Implications for cognition, emotion, and motivation. *Psychological Review, 98,* 224–253.

Osipow, S. H. (1975). The relevance of theories of career development to special groups: Problems, needed data, and implications. In J. S. Picou & R. E. Campbell (Eds.), *Career behavior of special groups: Theory, research, and practice* (pp. 9–22). Columbus, OH: Merrill.

Parham, T. A., & Helms, J. E. (1985a). Attitudes of racial identity and self-esteem in Black students: An exploratory investigation. *Journal of College Student Personnel, 26,* 143–147.

Parham, T. A., & Helms, J. E. (1985b). The relationship of racial identity attitudes to self-actualization of Black students and affective states. *Journal of Counseling Psychology, 32,* 431–440.

Rounds, J., & Tracey, T. J. (1996). Cross-cultural structural equivalence of RIASEC models and measures. *Journal of Counseling Psychology, 43,* 310–329.

Singelis, T. M. (1994). The measurement of independent and interdependent self-construals. *Personality and Social Psychology Bulletin, 20,* 580–591.

Sue, D. W. (1975). Asian Americans: Social psychological forces affecting their lifestyles. In J. S. Picou & R. E. Campbell (Eds.), *Career behavior of special groups.* Columbus, OH: Charles E. Merrill.

Sue, S., & Okazaki, S. (1990). Asian-American educational achievements: A phenomenon in search of an explanation. *American Psychologist, 45,* 913–920.

Sue, S., & Sue, D. W. (1973). Chinese-American personality and mental health. In S. Sue & N. N. Wagner (Eds.), *Asian-Americans: Psychological perspectives* (pp. 111–124). Palo Alto, CA: Science and Behavior Books.

Suinn, R. M., Rickard-Figueroa, K., Lew, S., & Vigil, P. (1987). The Suinn–Lew Asian Self-Identity Acculturation Scale: An initial report. *Educational and Psychological Measurement, 47,* 401–407.

Super, D. E. (1957). *The psychology of careers.* New York: Harper.

Swaney, K. B. (1995). *Technical manual: Revised unisex edition of the ACT interest inventory (UNIACT).* Iowa City, IA: American College Testing.

Tang, M., Fouad, N. A., & Smith, P. L. (1999). Asian Americans' career choices: A path model to examine factors influencing their career choices. *Journal of Vocational Behavior, 54,* 142–157.

Tracey, T. J. G., Watanabe, N., & Schnieder, P. L. (1997). Structural invariance of vocational interests across Japanese and American cultures. *Journal of Counseling Psychology, 44,* 346–354.

Triandis, H. C., Bontempo, R., Villareal, M. J., Asai, M., & Lucca, N. (1988). Individualism and collectivism: Cross cultural perspectives on self in group relationships. *Journal of Personality and Social Psychology, 54,* 323–338.

Triandis, H. C., Leung, K., Villareal, M. J., & Clack, F. L. (1985). Allocentric versus idiocentric tendencies: Convergent and discriminant validation. *Journal of Research in Personality, 19,* 395–415.

Woo, D. (2000). Glass ceilings and Asian Americans: The new face of workplace barriers. Walnut Creek, CA: AltaMira.

6
CULTURE-SPECIFIC ECOLOGICAL MODELS OF ASIAN AMERICAN VIOLENCE

GORDON C. NAGAYAMA HALL

More useful than simply identifying ethnic similarities and differences in rates of behavior is to understand culturally specific determinants of behavior and the effects of behavior in specific cultural contexts (Hall, Bansal, & Lopez, 1999). The purpose of this chapter is to identify culture-specific influences and the ecological context of Asian American violence. I use Triandis's (1996) definition of *culture* as shared attitudes, beliefs, norms, roles, and self-definitions. Culture is also the variability that exists between groups and societies (S. Sue, 1991). *Ethnicity* is a cultural variable that is more specific to a particular social context. For example, Japanese Americans and Chinese Americans are two different ethnic groups; however, they may share some cultural values (e.g., filial piety) that are common to Asian American culture. Culturally relevant constructs are more important in understanding behavior than is ethnicity, because culture is more comprehensive and proximal to behavior than is ethnicity. A term that I do not

Preparation of this chapter was supported by National Institute of Mental Health Grant R01 MH58726.

use is *race* because of the lack of a consensus on its definition among both psychologists and anthropologists (Yee, Fairchild, Weizmann, & Wyatt, 1993).

There is a paucity of research on violence among Asian Americans (Lum, 1998), so accurate rates of violence in this group are unknown. No prevalence or incidence studies of violence in large, representative samples of Asian Americans have been conducted. Official statistics generally suggest low rates of Asian American violence (Chen & True, 1994). These official statistics may have created a general impression that Asian Americans are not involved in violent crime (Esqueda, 1997). Nevertheless, official sources also suggest that violence is a problem for some Asian American groups. For example, disproportionately high rates of domestic violence among Asian American immigrants have been identified (Huisman, 1996; Ima & Hohm, 1991). Although immigrants face many stressors that may contribute to violent behavior, it is unknown whether rates of violence are actually higher among immigrants or if the higher rates are at least partially a function of greater scrutiny by public authorities of immigrants than of other groups (Chen & True, 1994). For example, the behavior of refugees on welfare, including violent behavior, may be closely monitored by officials. Violence, however, is not necessarily endemic among Asian immigrants. In a randomly selected community sample of Vietnamese immigrants that presumably is more representative than populations that are likely to be under scrutiny by public authorities, participants indicated disproportionately low rates of domestic violence (Segal, 2000).

Violent behavior usually comes to public attention when it is reported by victims. Asian American violence may not be detected, because many Asian Americans are reluctant to seek help. For example, Asian Americans may be less likely than other ethnic groups to report child sexual abuse to authorities (Rao, DiClemente, & Ponton, 1992). There is a stigma associated with help-seeking, particularly for issues of domestic violence, among many Asian Americans (Lum, 1998; Song, 1996). Bringing victimization issues to public attention may be viewed as bringing disgrace to the family (Chen & True, 1994). Violence may be considered family business and not the business of outsiders. It is unfortunate that an Asian American community's response to domestic violence may be to not believe the victim or to blame him or her for provoking the abuse (Rao et al., 1992). Self-blame for a perpetrator's actions may also occur among survivors. When Asian American women do seek help, family violence issues may not be disclosed initially (Norton & Manson, 1992). Thus, it may be extremely difficult to accurately detect Asian American violence by means of the standard methods that have been used with other ethnic groups. Some researchers may even be reluctant to address issues of family violence; this reluctance may stem from fears of creating a stereotype of Asian American families as excessively violent (Lum, 1998).

The lack of attention to Asian American violence may create the perception that violence is not a serious issue in the Asian American community. Indeed, there is evidence that Asian American women and men themselves are less worried about family violence than are members of other ethnic groups (Campbell, Masaki, & Torres, 1997). It is unknown whether the actual rates are lower or if these low rates are a function of definitions of *violence* among some Asian Americans that may differ from definitions among non-Asian groups. One perception is that when Asian Americans are involved in violence they are perceived as victims at the hands of non-Asians. Indeed, hate crimes against Asian Americans by non-Asian groups appear to be increasing (Young & Takeuchi, 1998). There is some evidence that Asian American homicide victims are not killed by other Asian Americans and that most of the perpetrators are strangers (Chen & True, 1994). With increased interethnic social contact, including dating and marriage, violence against Asian Americans by non-Asians may increase (Root, 1996). Nevertheless, the most common forms of violence in Asian American communities involve Asian Americans as both perpetrators and victims.

Stereotypes of Asian Americans as hard working, conscientious, and trouble free may cause their problems to be overlooked (Cartledge & Johnson, 1997). Some people in non-Asian communities may take a hands-off approach to Asian American violence because it is viewed as a problem of the Asian American community that has no bearing on the larger non-Asian community. Some people perpetually view Asian Americans as foreigners, no matter how long or for how many generations Asian Americans have lived in the United States. Thus, problems in the Asian American community are not necessarily viewed as "American" problems. This general lack of concern about issues of Asian American violence may imply that Asian Americans are less important than other groups (Root, 1996).

Are rates of violence among Asian Americans different than rates among members of other ethnic groups? Violent behavior is not unique to any group and is likely to be a problem for all ethnic groups. Domestic violence has been documented in Asian countries (Lum, 1998). Thus, there is a historical and cultural precedent for Asian American violence. Rates of physical and sexual violence among Asian Americans are similar to the rates in other ethnic groups (Foo & Margolin, 1995; Hall, Sue, Narang, & Lilly, 2000; Koss, Gidycz, & Wisniewski, 1987; Mills & Granoff, 1992; Urquiza & Goodlin-Jones, 1994).

What is the optimal method of assessing violent behavior among Asian Americans? Given the cultural proscriptions in many Asian American communities against reporting violence, research in which participants remain anonymous (e.g., when they are assessed in large groups and their identities are unknown) is likely to yield more accurate results than research in which participants' identities are known (e.g., individual interviews). A common method of assessing violent behavior in couples is to interview both members of the couple for purposes of corroboration. However, there is evidence of strong correspondence between perpetrator and victim reports of violence ($rs = .53–.58$), such that the reports of one partner may be adequate (Moffitt et al., 1997). Asian Americans may be particularly reluctant to report violent behavior if their partners also are participating in research and may have knowledge of their responses. Although participants may be told that their responses are confidential, partners participating in the same research project may query one another about their responses. Such discussions might provoke additional violence if one partner believes that the other cast him or her in a negative light. Thus, when researching violence, assessing individual Asian Americans in an anonymous manner may be desirable for both methodological and ethical reasons.

Most studies on rates of violence have combined subgroups of Asian Americans into a single group (Foo & Margolin, 1995; Hall et al., 2000; Koss et al., 1987; Mills & Granoff, 1992; Urquiza & Goodlin-Jones, 1994). However, there is much variability among Asian American groups; this is reflected in different rates of disorders across Asian American ethnic groups (Uehara, Takeuchi, & Smukler, 1994). As discussed earlier, some Asian American immigrant groups may experience more violent behavior than other Asian American groups. Ethnicity, however, is likely to be a distal predictor of behavior, including violent behavior (Holtzworth-Munroe & Stuart, 1994; Koss et al., 1987; S. Sue & Zane, 1987). There are likely to be constructs other than ethnicity that are more powerful determinants of violent behavior.

CULTURE-SPECIFIC INFLUENCES ON ASIAN AMERICAN VIOLENCE

Risk Factors

Asian American cultures are heterogeneous and comprise more than 29 distinct groups (L. C. Lee, 1998); however, there are some commonalities across groups. The traditional family structure for Americans whose background is in East Asia has its origins in Confucian values, which prescribe a patriarchal hierarchy (Bradshaw, 1994). Women and girls are expected to serve male family members (Chen & True, 1994). Domestic, subservient roles are prescribed for females in Southeast Asian (e.g., Vietnam, Cambodia) and South Asian (e.g., India) cultures as well (Almeida, 1996; Leung & Boehnlein, 1996). Asian Americans differ from overseas Asians insofar as Asian Americans are influenced by both Asian and Western cultures and values. Male dominance in Asian American groups may be expressed subtly, such as giving wives the illusion of influence, or blatantly, such as treating wives as property and not tolerating wives' refusal of sex (Ho, 1990). Male dominance certainly exists in non-Asian American cultures; however, one important difference is that in other cultures in which there is male dominance, power is negotiable, whereas in traditional Asian American cultures it is not (D. Sue, 1996). For example, European American culture is male dominated, but gender roles occasionally become fluid, as when competent women assume leadership roles. In many Asian American cultures gender roles are more rigid and not subject to negotiation and change. It is unfortunate that some Asian American women believe that a gender double standard is acceptable and excuse men's aggressive behavior as their prerogative as men. Patriarchal influences in Asian American cultures may make females vulnerable and put them at risk for being victimized by males (Hall, Windover, & Maramba, 1998). Prescriptions for male dominance and female submissiveness in Asian American groups are likely to result in most violence being perpetrated by males against females (Chen & True, 1994). Many Asian American females live in a state of domestic captivity (Root, 1996).

Gender role stereotypes of Asian American men within and outside the Asian American community are emasculating. One common stereotype of Asian American males is that they are effeminate and asexual (Espiritu, 1997). Some Asian American men may attempt to dispel this stereotype and assert their masculinity by means of violence. At the other extreme is the stereotype of the evil, sexist Asian American man who is intent on raping women, particularly European American women (Espiritu, 1997). This stereotype may directly promote Asian American men's violence. Gender role stereotypes of Asian American women may also create a risk for victimization. Images of Asian American women as subservient, innocent, fragile, and childlike in combination with images of them as sexually exotic may be particularly attractive to potential perpetrators of violence (Root, 1995). Asian American women may be perceived by perpetrators as less powerful than other women and less likely to defend themselves or to report violence. Asian American women who internalize these stereotypes may have difficulty taking action if they are victimized. For many perpetrators, fear of being caught deters them from being aggressive (Malamuth, 1988). Thus, Asian American women may be more attractive than others to some perpetrators because of a perception that they will be less likely to be caught for victimizing these women. Of course, these are stereotypes, and a perpetrator's perceptions of a person, and even a person's stereotypic behavior, are not invitations for violence (Hall, 1996).

Confucian values also emphasize the acceptance of fate, which could also serve as a risk factor for violence (Bradshaw, 1994). Some Asian American victims may view their victimization as their fate and believe that they can do nothing to change their fate. There is some evidence that a minority of physically abused Asian American women leave their homes after being abused (Song, 1996). Moreover, some Asian cultures view suffering with dignity as a strength. Fatalistic thinking may be particularly maladaptive when a perpetrator claims to have a problem that he cannot control, or when he or she unsuccessfully attempts treatment. Such circumstances may elicit unwarranted sympathy and may reinforce the belief that the perpetrator's violent behavior must be tolerated or accepted (Gondolf, 1988). Some victims may also feel that it is their responsibility to change the perpetrator's violent behavior (Lum, 1998). A strong sense of obligation to their husbands and to maintaining an intact family may prevent some Asian American women from leaving an abusive marriage. Divorce may be viewed by many Asian Americans as bringing shame to the family and may not be viewed as an option (Masaki & Wong, 1997). Indeed, Asian Americans have lower rates of divorce than any other American ethnic group (U.S. Census Bureau, 1997).

Another relevant Buddhist concept in many East Asian (e.g., Japan, China, Korea) cultures is *karma* (Yeung & Lee, 1997). Karma is often confused with fate but is a somewhat different concept; it is the idea that acts have consequences that span several lifetimes. Thus, it is possible that the current victim of violence once caused the perpetrator suffering in the current lifetime or in a previous one. Although the concept of karma is one of cause and effect, because most people are unable to recall the events from previous lives they cannot definitively establish the true causes of events. Thus, people with this worldview tend to accept the current condition rather than concern themselves with the question of cause and effect (i.e., they accept events as being caused by fate or karmic retribution). A related Buddhist concept is *yuan*, the idea that current relationships are a continuation of attachments from previous lives and, as such, are to be treasured (Chang & Holt, 1991; Yang, 1995). Such concepts involving the permanence of relationships may explain why some Asian American victims may accept violence and seek to maintain a relationship despite abuse. In a positive sense, such a view of permanency may be a motivation for the perpetrator to change, because from this perspective violence could inflict damage on the future of a permanent relationship. The influence of these traditional Buddhist concepts on Asian Americans' behavior is unknown. Nevertheless, these Asian conceptions of interrelatedness and the permanence of relationships are quite different than Western concepts of individual responsibility and beliefs that the consequences of individual acts may be temporary and that relationships too may be temporary.

One method of attempting to escape the role of servitude is for Asian American women to date and marry outside the Asian American community. Of course, there are many other reasons for intermarriage. Among Asian Americans, rates of intermarriage are much higher for women than for men (S. M. Lee & Yamanaka, 1990; Mok, 1999). However, to the extent that rates of violence are not significantly different across ethnic groups, interethnic relationships do not necessarily reduce an Asian American woman's chances of being victimized. Stereotypes of Asian American women as docile and submissive are also held outside the Asian American community (Root, 1995). For many Asian American women traumatized by violence, the trauma is insidious insofar as they cannot simply escape it by leaving a violent relationship (Root, 1992). Many Asian American women may view themselves as constantly having an inferior status inside and outside their communities, regardless of the context of dyadic relationships. In other words, an Asian American woman may leave a relationship or enter a new one, but her status as an Asian American woman does not change.

Across Asian American groups there is an emphasis on behaviors that promote interdependence (Uba, 1994). There is a strong emphasis on interpersonal harmony and cooperation with others, and blending in with the group is of utmost importance. Individuals tend to be identified with groups, such as their families and extended families, and individual behavior is regarded as a reflection on the whole group. Group norms tend to be explicit, and individuals are concerned about their social standing. Shame is used to curb deviant behavior. Deviant behavior may result in loss of face for the individual as well as the group with which he or she is affiliated. Loss of face is the threat of the loss of one's social integrity. Asian Americans tend to be much more concerned about loss of face than are European Americans (Zane, 1991).

Group norms concerning violence may be very influential among Asian Americans. The African proverb that it takes a village to raise a child is applicable to interdependent cultures, such as Asian American cultures. The Rev. Jesse L. Jackson, Sr., in his 1999 keynote address to the American Psychological Association, asserted that a violent village raises a violent child. Violent behavior by males may be tolerated or even accepted in some Asian American cultural contexts and is thus normative (Bradshaw, 1994; Tomita, 1999).

Recent evidence suggests that sexually aggressive Asian American men are concerned about loss of face and hold misogynous beliefs (Hall et al., 2000). Hall et al. (2000) examined self-reported sexual aggression among 91 Asian American and 377 European American college students. For Asian Americans, concern about loss of face was a risk factor among those who held misogynous beliefs. Thus, sexually aggressive Asian American men may believe that it is manly to hold negative attitudes toward women and to be sexually aggressive. To not be aggressive against women would be unmanly and would result in loss of face. It is interesting that Asian Americans born in the United States did not differ on the measures in the study from those born in Asia, which suggests that acculturation may not eliminate the effects of Asian cultures for many Asian Americans. However, the role of acculturation in Asian American violence has not been adequately investigated.

Conversely, European American men's sexual aggression was determined primarily by misogynous beliefs, with interpersonal variables not being predictive of sexual aggression (Hall et al., 2000). Loss of face was not associated with European American men's sexual aggression. Thus, Asian American men are more influenced by group and cultural norms about violence. Decisions to engage in violent behavior for European Americans tended to be appraised on an individual basis as a function of situational characteristics, such as perceived provocation (Astor, 1994; Bettencourt & Kernahan, 1997; Crick & Dodge, 1994; Dodge, Price, Bachorowski, & Newman, 1990).

Some European American men's violent behavior may be influenced by its effects on their reputation in a social context. The contributions of a cohesive social context to violent behavior has been examined in European American "cultures of honor" (Cohen, 1998). In cultures in which violent behavior is not entirely deviant and there is a tightly knit social structure, violent behavior may be deemed an appropriate means of defending one's honor. A man who is insulted but does not retaliate may perceive himself as harming his masculine reputation (Cohen, Nisbett, Bowdle, & Schwarz, 1996; Nisbett, 1993). Culture-of-honor traditions persist more in the U.S. South and West than in the North (Cohen, 1998; Nisbett, 1993). Cultures of honor developed in the South and West in reaction to the lack of social organization when these areas were frontier regions. In the absence of effective law enforcement and social order, cultures of honor evolved as a form of self-protection. These frontier communities became reorganized to accept violence as acceptable under conditions of provocation. Reputation and honor currently are more critical in stable, cohesive communities than in contexts in which individuals are more autonomous (Cohen, 1998). In communities that do not have culture-of-honor traditions, community cohesiveness (e.g., residential stability, being married, having a family) is associated with less violence. Conversely, in communities in which there is a culture-of-honor tradition, cohesiveness is positively associated with violence (Cohen, 1998). Many Asian American communities are similar to these non-Asian communities in that they are stable, cohesive, and tightly knit. Maintaining honor, or one's reputation, is analogous to loss of face in Asian American communities. Community perceptions of violence as deviant or relatively normative may determine its likelihood. Thus, the effects of loss of face and similar constructs on violent behavior are not necessarily specific to Asian Americans.

To the extent that disclosing family problems outside the family could result in loss of face, some Asian Americans may be reluctant to seek help for domestic violence (Bradshaw, 1994; Ho, 1990; Lum, 1998). It is unfortunate that the victim's family often may ignore the problem or be invested in maintaining the status quo in an effort to save face (Dasgupta & Warrier, 1996; Huisman, 1996). Even when some elderly parents want to intervene on behalf of an adult daughter, they may be ineffective because of cultural barriers and disruption of traditional authority structures (Root, 1998). Asian American women who seek services for abuse may do so as a last resort, sometimes after years of abuse (Lum, 1998). A lack of bilingual mental health services and anti-immigrant sentiment among some nonimmigrants are barriers for immigrants (Campbell et al., 1997). Even when culturally sensitive mental health centers exist, they may not have adequate resources to serve all the clients who need services (Campbell et al., 1997; Lum, 1998).

Immigrant women and children may be particularly susceptible to violence because of rejection in the new community and dependence on men (Bradshaw, 1994; Huisman, 1996; Ima & Hohm, 1991; Lum, 1998; Masaki & Wong, 1997; Rao et al., 1992). Sixty percent of a sample of immigrant Korean women in Chicago reported having been physically abused (Song, 1996). This abuse was most frequent and severe during the initial years following immigration. Immigrants and other Asian Americans isolated in predominantly non-Asian communities may feel particularly dependent on Asian American men because of a lack of access to Asian American communities (Lum, 1998; Root, 1998). Immigrant men may experience stressors, such as downward employment mobility relative to their status in Asia, that may cause them to displace their anger onto women and children (Masaki & Wong, 1997; Song, 1996; cf. Comas-Diaz, 1995). War trauma for Southeast Asian immigrants may result in them taking out their frustrations on family members (Chen & True, 1994).

Physical punishment is acceptable among some Asian American immigrants, and this may result in the low rates of reporting of Asian American child abuse (Chen & True, 1994; Ho, 1990). Physical punishment may be a way for some immigrants to attempt to re-establish control over their children when the children become influenced by persons outside the family (Chen & True, 1994). Physical abuse of children may be more likely than child sexual abuse (Ima & Hohm, 1991; Lum, 1998); nevertheless, rates of child maltreatment differ across Southeast Asian immigrant groups. For example, a negligible incidence of child maltreatment has been found among Hmong families, which has been attributed to supportive Hmong community networks in the United States.

Protective Factors

It would be easy to conclude from the foregoing discussion that the patriarchal and interdependent aspects of Asian American cultures make violence inevitable. However, the rates of violence across Asian American ethnic groups are unlikely to be different than they are for other ethnic groups. This means that a minority of Asian Americans are involved as perpetrators and victims of violence.

Patriarchy in and of itself does not necessarily lead to violence against women and children. One aspect of collectivist patriarchal systems in interdependent cultures is the patriarch's responsibility to care for those in his group. This sense of patriarchal responsibility may differ between interdependent and independent cultures (Hall, 1996). Thus, an abusive patriarch may be viewed as failing to fulfill his responsibility to care for his subordinates.

Interdependence may also contribute to impulse control among Asian Americans (Hall et al., 1998). Violence in collectivist groups is not an isolated act involving two unconnected individuals (Hall & Barongan, 1997); rather, it upsets interpersonal harmony. In collectivist contexts violence may be considered an act against a family, a group, or a whole community. For example, in Japanese culture, because violence upsets interpersonal harmony it is viewed as a last resort only when the grievance is severe and other solutions have been exhausted (Johnson, 1993). If there is disapproval of violence in a collectivist context, then violent behavior is likely to be deterred. To be violent would be deviant, which would result in loss of face for the individual and his or her group. Thus, a functional Asian American family and community may offer much social support as a buffer against stress and violence (Bradshaw, 1994; Lum, 1998).

The brevity of this section on protective factors relative to the previous section on risk factors reflects the amount of attention researchers have paid to these areas. As in other areas of clinical psychology, much more attention has been paid to psychopathology and interventions than to prevention. Much more work is needed on understanding and enhancing the protective aspects of Asian American cultures against violence and other forms of psychopathology.

CULTURE-SPECIFIC MODELS OF ASIAN AMERICAN VIOLENCE

Perpetrator Models

A comprehensive model of Asian American violence should incorporate individual, interpersonal, and ecological approaches. Although there is evidence of interpersonal influences in Asian American violence, in most instances the decision to engage in violence ultimately occurs at the individual level and does not involve multiple perpetrators. Thus, the perpetrator is responsible for violence, and the perpetration of Asian American violence should be conceptualized at the individual level. Perpetration should be considered independently of victimization, as perpetrator and victim characteristics appear to be orthogonal. Although there is a dearth of data on Asian American perpetrators of violence, it is likely that constructs found to be relevant predictors in other populations—including misogynous attitudes, issues of power and control, and traditional masculine socialization—are also predictive of Asian American violence. Interventions at the individual level should involve a redefinition of masculinity that includes empathy and cooperation. These characteristics are consistent with Asian American socialization and with the socialization of most females in society (Hall & Barongan, 1997).

To place the responsibility for violence on the individual perpetrator does not preclude the possibility of interpersonal influences. Asian American men's violence may be influenced by the opinions of peers, parents, and authorities (Hall et al., 2000). If these groups disapprove of violence, then Asian Americans risk loss of face by becoming violent. A violent act becomes a violation of the whole group rather than an isolated act against an individual (Hall & Barongan, 1997). Conversely, tolerance or approval of violence as manly by Asian American reference groups may facilitate it. The relative influence of general Asian American cultural values that affect violence, such as interdependence and loss of face, may vary across Asian American ethnic groups (e.g., Japanese Americans, Vietnamese Americans, Filipino Americans). Thus, understanding how specific reference-group influences supplement individual influences is critical in Asian American violence. Violence intervention research should be culturally sensitive (e.g., multilingual, multicultural) and should consider solutions at the group level. For example, family elders and community leaders may be mobilized into shaming a perpetrator about his or her violence (Bradshaw, 1994; Ho, 1990; Masaki & Wong, 1997). Other contexts for intervention include schools, churches, fraternities, and community and professional organizations. It is unfortunate that the traditions of some of these groups may encourage the sexism that is associated with violence.

The influence of the broader ecological context on Asian American men's violence also should be considered. Negative stereotypes of Asian American men are generated within and outside the Asian American community (Espiritu, 1997). Resentment of these negative stereotypes may create a ripe breeding ground for the hostility and misogynous beliefs associated with violent behavior. The general American societal emphasis on violence as a method of establishing masculinity is likely to influence Asian American males. Some Asian American men may victimize individuals whom they perceive to be vulnerable as a means of demonstrating their power and manhood. Even positive stereotypes of Asian American men may cause some men to become violent in an effort to dispel being stereotyped. Although there is no direct evidence that stereotypes influence Asian American men's violence, there is evidence that discrimination causes stress among Asian American men. Asian American service personnel during the Vietnam war were subjected to discrimination because of their physical resemblance to the enemy, and this discrimination resulted in stress beyond that of being in combat (Abueg & Chun, 1996; Loo, 1994). It is possible that the societal context of stereotyping also affects Asian American men's violence.

Victim and Survivor Models

Comprehensive models are also needed to understand Asian American victims and survivors of violence. Care and sensitivity need to be exercised such that victims are not conceptualized as being responsible for being victimized. Emphases on interpersonal conceptual models of violence and on interdependence in Asian American cultures create a risk for implicating the victim as causing violence. Individual models of violent victimization allow the consideration of victim issues independently of perpetrator issues and decrease the likelihood that victims will be blamed. Coping mechanisms of survivors of violence should be the focus of the research. Risk factors for violence are best studied among perpetrators, for whom there are well-established risk characteristics, rather than among victims, for whom specific characteristics are not associated with risk for victimization. Thus, violence prevention with women could focus on their perceptions of risk factors among potential perpetrators and on how effective women are at avoiding high-risk situations.

Interpersonal influences are important with regard to community responses to victimization. Some Asian American communities may view violence as tolerable or acceptable and may attempt to silence or blame victims. Such responses are likely to interfere with coping. Some Asian American victims fear losing face by reporting and seeking help for being victimized. Conversely, if the community perceives violence as interfering with family and general community functioning, and not simply a private matter, then help seeking may be conceptualized as a benefit to the family and community (Ho, 1990). An individual's level of attachment to the community is also an important consideration. Socially isolated individuals and families may be at greater risk for violence than those who are involved in communities (Belsky, 1993; Lum, 1998; Root, 1998). Nevertheless, attachment to a misogynous, violent community is a risk factor for violence. As with perpetrators, the relative influence of general Asian American values relevant to violence may vary according to Asian American ethnic community. Shelters and mental health services for victims should be culturally sensitive and should incorporate community resources. Interventions should emphasize that violence is not the victim's fault and that it is not the victim's responsibility to change the perpetrator's behavior. Prevention of violence could include public consciousness-raising, discussion groups, and focus groups (Ho, 1990). Some Asian Americans may need to be educated regarding what defines violence and the impact of violence on victims, told that violence is against the law, and educated about legal recourse for violence (Lum, 1998). However, such education may primarily attract persons who are already sensitized to the issues. Thus, prevention must also be incorporated into wider community contexts, such as schools, churches, and other community organizations. It is critical that both Asian American men and women are involved as leaders and participants in violence-prevention efforts so that violence is appropriately viewed as a man's problem as well as a woman's problem.

Societal context also contributes to violence against Asian Americans. Asian American women are (a) women in a male-dominated society,

(b) Asian Americans in an Asian American community that is male dominated, and (c) Americans in an American society in which they are minorities (Bradshaw, 1994; Root, 1995). Thus, Asian American women are devalued in most of the contexts in which they function. Traditional American feminine socialization is consistent with traditional Asian American feminine socialization. Both encourage female submission, which may be associated with a victim role. Although such socialization may be viewed as maladaptive, it will not simply disappear for Asian American women as a function of interventions. Culturally sensitive researchers must understand the cultural context of Asian American violence and develop approaches that are culturally compatible. For example, a certain amount of submission may be appropriate with responsible authority figures who care about the welfare of their subordinates. A violent authority figure could be conceptualized as losing his or her status of authority, because his or her actions violate the welfare of the group. In such instances, submission may also be conceptualized as contributing to the group's demise. As with Asian American men, there exist specific detrimental stereotypes of Asian American women within Asian American communities and, more generally, in society.

Asian Americans currently number more than 12 million and proportionally are the fastest growing ethnic minority group in the United States. There is a disproportionately small amount of public attention given to Asian American violence, which is likely to be as much of a problem in the Asian American community as it is in any other. Researchers can help promote understanding of a serious problem that has been largely ignored within and outside the Asian American community. A better understanding of Asian American violence may facilitate the development of culturally sensitive interventions and prevention.

FUTURE RESEARCH DIRECTIONS

The investigation of violence among Asian American adults is in its relative infancy. The following are critical issues that warrant future attention.

- Accurate rates of Asian American violence are unknown. Asian Americans unfortunately have not been analyzed as a separate group in most community and national surveys of violence. Moreover, it is important to examine specific Asian American ethnic groups (e.g., Chinese Americans, Filipino Americans, Vietnamese Americans) rather than combining subgroups of Asian Americans into a single group. Anonymous self-report of violence may be the most effective way to establish accurate rates of Asian American violence, as face-to-face interviews may cause many Asian Americans to be reluctant to honestly report violence.

- The cultural context of Asian American violence needs to be considered. Issues of power and gender roles may differ from culture to culture among Asian American ethnic groups, and these issues are often conceptualized quite differently in these cultures as opposed to how they are conceptualized in Western cultures. Adherence to group norms is highly influential for many Asian Americans. Existing models of violence that are based on individual-level explanations may fail to fully account for Asian American violence.

- The protective aspects of Asian American cultures need to be more fully investigated. It would be easy to misinterpret the patriarchal and traditional gender role aspects of Asian American cultures as risk factors for violent behavior; in some Asian American contexts these cultural aspects may strengthen the families and communities and may be protective factors against violence.

- Research on Asian American violence should be theoretically informed. For this to occur, theories of Asian American violence need to be developed. Comprehensive theories of Asian American violence must include conceptualizations of cultural issues as well as of the sociopolitical aspects of being an Asian American in the United States, including minority status and discrimination.

REFERENCES

Abueg, F. R., & Chun, K. (1996). Traumatization stress among Asians and Asian Americans. In A. J. Marsella, M. J. Friedman, E. T. Gerrity, & R. M. Scurfield (Eds.), *Ethnocultural aspects of posttraumatic stress disorder: Issues, research, and clinical applications* (pp. 285–299). Washington, DC: American Psychological Association.

Almeida, R. (1996). Hindu, Christian, and Muslim families. In M. McGoldrick, J. Giordano, & J. K. Pearce (Eds.), *Ethnicity and family therapy* (2nd ed., pp. 395–423). New York: Guilford Press.

Astor, R. A. (1994). Children's moral reasoning about family and peer violence: The role of provocation and retribution. *Child Development, 65,* 1054–1067.

Belsky, J. (1993). Etiology of child maltreatment: A developmental–ecological analysis. *Psychological Bulletin, 114,* 413–434.

Bettencourt, B. A., & Kernahan, C. (1997). A meta-analysis of aggression in the presence of violent cues: Effects of gender differences and aversive provocation. *Aggressive Behavior, 23,* 447–456.

Bradshaw, C. K. (1994). Asian and Asian American women: Historical and political considerations in psychotherapy. In L. Comas-Diaz & B. Greene (Eds.), *Women of color: Integrating ethnic and gender identities in psychotherapy* (pp. 72–113). New York: Guilford Press.

Campbell, D. W., Masaki, B., & Torres, S. (1997). "Water on rock": Changing domestic violence perceptions in the African American, Asian American, and Latino communities. In E. Klein, J. Campbell, E. Soler, & M. Ghez (Eds.), *Ending domestic violence: Changing public perceptions/Halting the epidemic* (pp. 64–87). Thousand Oaks, CA: Sage.

Cartledge, G., & Johnson, C. T. (1997). School violence and cultural sensitivity. In A. P. Goldstein & J. C. Conoley (Eds.), *School violence intervention: A practical handbook* (pp. 391–425). New York: Guilford Press.

Chang, H., & Holt, R. (1991). The concept of *yuan* and Chinese interpersonal relationships. In S. Ting-Toomey & F. Korzenny (Eds.), *Cross-cultural interpersonal communication* (pp. 28–57). Newbury Park, CA: Sage.

Chen, S. A., & True, R. H. (1994). Asian/Pacific Island Americans. In L. D. Eron, J. H. Gentry, & P. Schlegel (Eds.), *Reason to hope: A psychosocial perspective on violence and youth* (pp. 145–162). Washington, DC: American Psychological Association.

Cohen, D. (1998). Culture, social organization, and patterns of violence. *Journal of Personality and Social Psychology, 75,* 408–419.

Cohen, D., Nisbett, R. E., Bowdle, B. F., & Schwarz, N. (1996). Insult, aggression, and the Southern culture of honor: An "experimental ethnography." *Journal of Personality and Social Psychology, 70,* 945–960.

Comas-Diaz, L. (1995). Puerto Ricans and sexual child abuse. In L. A. Fontes (Ed.), *Sexual abuse in nine North American cultures: Treatment and prevention* (pp. 31–66). Thousand Oaks, CA: Sage.

Crick, N. R., & Dodge, K. A. (1994). A review and reformulations of social information-processing mechanisms in children's social adjustment. *Psychological Bulletin, 115,* 74–101.

Dasgupta, S. D., & Warrier, S. (1996). In the footsteps of "Arundhati": Asian Indian women's experience of domestic violence in the United States. *Violence Against Women, 2,* 238–259.

Dodge, K. A., Price, J. M., Bachorowski, J., & Newman, J. P . (1990). Hostile attributional biases in severely aggressive adolescents. *Journal of Abnormal Psychology, 99,* 385–392.

Espiritu, Y. L. (1997). *Asian American men and women.* Thousand Oaks, CA: Sage.

Esqueda, C. W. (1997). European American students' perceptions of crimes committed by five racial groups. *Journal of Applied Social Psychology, 27,* 1406–1420.

Foo, L., & Margolin, G. (1995). A multivariate investigation of dating aggression. *Journal of Family Violence, 10,* 351–377.

Gondolf, E. W. (1988). The effect of batterer counseling on shelter outcome. *Journal of Interpersonal Violence, 3,* 275–289.

Hall, G. C. N. (1996). *Theory-based assessment, treatment, and prevention of sexual aggression*. New York: Oxford University Press.

Hall, G. C. N., Bansal, A., & Lopez, I. R. (1999). Ethnicity and psychopathology: A meta-analytic review of 31 years of comparative MMPI/MMPI–2 research. *Psychological Assessment, 11,* 186–197.

Hall, G. C. N., & Barongan, C. (1997). Prevention of sexual aggression: Sociocultural risk and protective factors. *American Psychologist, 52,* 5–14.

Hall, G. C. N., Sue, S., Narang, D. S., & Lilly, R. S. (2000). Culture-specific models of men's sexual aggression: Intra- and interpersonal determinants. *Cultural Diversity and Ethnic Minority Psychology, 6,* 252–267.

Hall, G. C. N., Windover, A. K., & Maramba, G. G. (1998). Sexual aggression among Asian Americans: Risk and protective factors. *Cultural Diversity and Mental Health, 4,* 305–318.

Ho, C. K. (1990). An analysis of domestic violence in Asian American communities: A multicultural approach to counseling. In L. S. Brown & M. Root (Eds.), *Diversity and complexity in feminist therapy* (pp. 129–150). New York: Haworth.

Holtzworth-Munroe, A., & Stuart, G. L. (1994). Typologies of male batterers: Three subtypes and the differences between them. *Psychological Bulletin, 116,* 476–497.

Huisman, K. A. (1996). Wife battering in Asian American communities. *Violence Against Women, 2,* 260–283.

Ima, K., & Hohm, C. F. (1991). Child maltreatment among Asian and Pacific Islander refugees and immigrants. *Journal of Interpersonal Violence, 6,* 267–285.

Jackson, J. L., Sr. (1999, August). *Remaining vigilant: Changing the house.* Keynote address delivered at the 107th Convention of the American Psychological Association, Boston.

Johnson, F. A. (1993). *Dependency and Japanese socialization: Psychoanalytic and anthropological investigations into* amae. New York: New York University Press.

Kaptchuk, T. J. (1983). *The web that has no weaver: Understanding Chinese medicine.* Chicago: Congdon and Weed.

Koss, M. P., Gidycz, C. A., & Wisniewski, N. (1987). The scope of rape: Incidence and prevalence of sexual aggression and victimization in a national sample of higher education students. *Journal of Consulting and Clinical Psychology, 55,* 162–170.

Lee, L. C. (1998). An overview. In L. C. Lee & N. W. S. Zane (Eds.), *Handbook of Asian American psychology* (pp. 1–20). Thousand Oaks, CA: Sage.

Lee, S. M., & Yamanaka, K. (1990). Patterns of Asian American intermarriage and marital assimilation. *Journal of Comparative Family Studies, 21,* 287–305.

Leung, P. K., & Boehnlein, J. (1996). Vietnamese families. In M. McGoldrick, J. Giordano, & J. K. Pearce (Eds.), *Ethnicity and family therapy* (2nd ed., pp. 295–306). New York: Guilford Press.

Loo, C. (1994). The Asian American Vietnam veteran: Race-related trauma and PTSD. *Journal of Traumatic Stress, 7,* 637–656.

Lum, J. (1998). Family violence. In L. C. Lee & N. W. S. Zane (Eds.), *Handbook of Asian American psychology* (pp. 505–525). Thousand Oaks, CA: Sage.

Malamuth, N. M. (1988). A multidimensional approach to sexual aggression: Combining measures of past behavior and present likelihood. In R. A. Prentky & V. L. Quinsey (Eds.), *Human sexual aggression: Current perspectives* (pp. 123–132). New York: New York Academy of Sciences.

Masaki, B., & Wong, L. (1997). Domestic violence in the Asian community In E. Lee (Ed.), *Working with Asian Americans: A guide for clinicians* (pp. 439–451). New York: Guilford Press.

Mills, C. S. & Granoff, B. J. (1992). Date and acquaintance rape among a sample of college students. *Social Work, 37,* 504–509.

Moffitt, T. E., Caspi, A., Krueger, R. F., Magdol, L., Margolin, G., Silva, P. A., & Sydney, R. (1997). Do partners agree about abuse in their relationship? A psychometric evaluation of interpartner agreement. *Psychological Assessment, 9,* 47–56.

Mok, T. A. (1999). Asian American dating: Important factors in partner choice. *Cultural Diversity and Ethnic Minority Psychology, 5,* 103–117.

Nisbett, R. E. (1993). Violence and U.S. regional culture. *American Psychologist, 48,* 441–449.

Norton, I. M., & Manson, S. M. (1992). An association between domestic violence and depression among Southeast Asian refugee women. *Journal of Nervous and Mental Disease, 180,* 729–730.

Rao, K., DiClemente, R. J., & Ponton, L. E. (1992). Child sexual abuse of Asians compared with other populations. *Journal of the American Academy of Child and Adolescent Psychiatry, 31,* 880–886.

Root, M. P. P. (1992). Reconstructing the impact of trauma on personality. In L. S. Brown & M. Ballou (Eds.), *Personality and psychopathology: Feminist reappraisals* (pp. 229–265). New York: Guilford Press.

Root, M. P. P. (1995). The psychology of Asian American women. In H. Landrine (Ed.), *Bringing cultural diversity to feminist psychology: Theory, research, and practice* (pp. 265–301). Washington, DC: American Psychological Association.

Root, M. P. P. (1996). Women of color and traumatic stress in "domestic captivity": Gender and race as disempowering statuses. In A. J. Marsella, M. J. Friedman, E. T. Gerrity, & R. M. Scurfield (Eds.), *Ethnocultural aspects of posttraumatic stress disorder: Issues, research, and clinical applications* (pp. 363–387). Washington, DC: American Psychological Association.

Root, M. P. P. (1998). Women. In L. C. Lee & N. W. S. Zane (Eds.), *Handbook of Asian American psychology* (pp. 211–231). Thousand Oaks, CA: Sage.

Segal, U. A. (2000). A pilot exploration of family violence among nonclinical Vietnamese. *Journal of Interpersonal Violence, 15,* 523–533.

Song, Y. I. (1996). *Battered women in Korean immigrant families.* New York: Garland.

Sue, D. (1996). Asian men in groups. In M. P. Andronico (Ed.), *Men in groups* (pp. 69–80). Washington, DC: American Psychological Association.

Sue, S. (1991). Ethnicity and culture in psychological research and practice. In J. D. Goodchilds & D. Jacqueline (Eds.), *Psychological perspectives on human diversity in America* (pp. 51–85). Washington, DC: American Psychological Association.

Sue, S., & Zane, N. (1987). The role of culture and cultural techniques in psychotherapy: A critique and reformulation. *American Psychologist, 42,* 37–45.

Tomita, S. K. (1999). Exploration of elder mistreatment among the Japanese. In T. Tatara (Ed.), *Understanding elder abuse in minority populations* (pp. 119–139). Philadelphia: Brunner/Mazel.

Triandis, H. C. (1996). The psychological measurement of cultural syndromes. *American Psychologist, 51,* 407–415.

Uba, L. (1994). *Asian Americans: Personality patterns, identity, and mental health.* New York: Guilford Press.

Uehara, E. S., Takeuchi, D. T., & Smukler, M. (1994). Effects of combining disparate groups in the analysis of ethnic differences: Variations among Asian American mental health service consumers in level of community functioning. *American Journal of Community Psychology, 22,* 83–99.

Urquiza, A. J., & Goodlin-Jones, B. L. (1994). Child sexual abuse and adult revictimization with women of color. *Violence and Victims, 9,* 223–232.

U.S. Census Bureau. (1997). Selected characteristics of the population by race: March 1997. Retrieved March 30, 2002 from http://www.bls.census.gov/cps/pub/1997/int_race.htm

Yang, K. S. (1995). Chinese social orientation: An integrative analysis. In T. Y. Lin, W. S. Tseng, & E. K. Yeh (Eds.), *Chinese society and mental health* (pp. 19–39). Hong Kong: Oxford University Press.

Yee, A. H., Fairchild, H. H., Weizmann, F., & Wyatt, G. E. (1993). Addressing psychology's problems with race. *American Psychologist, 48,* 1132–1140.

Yeung, W. H., & Lee, E. (1997). Chinese Buddhism: Its implications for counseling. In E. Lee (Ed.), *Working with Asian Americans: A guide for clinicians* (pp. 452–463). New York: Guilford.

Young, K., & Takeuchi, D. T. (1998). Racism. In L. C. Lee & N. W. S. Zane (Eds.), *Handbook of Asian American psychology* (pp. 401–432). Thousand Oaks, CA: Sage.

Zane, N. (1991, August). *An empirical examination of loss of face among Asian Americans.* Paper presented at the 99th Annual Convention of the American Psychological Association, San Francisco.

7

METHODOLOGICAL ISSUES IN MULTIRACIAL RESEARCH

MARIA P. P. ROOT

Several years ago, I (Root, 1998b) suggested that there is a line between old and new lines of inquiry about multiraciality. The repeal of the last anti-miscegenation laws occurred 2 years after changes in immigration laws in 1965 opened the doors to greater numbers of people emigrating from Asia. This period of time marks the beginning of the biracial baby boom that would be followed by a research boom on multiracial identity 30 years later.

Since the publication of the first empirically based edited text on multiracial identity, *Racially Mixed People in America* (Root, 1992b), the number of dissertations and master's theses focused on this topic have proliferated. This book made accessible contemporary seminal research in this area. The publication of several subsequent books and articles heralded an increase in both interest in the emerging multiracial cohort's identity process and in the number of multiracial people in college and graduate school who wanted to drive the conceptual process in understanding identity development. The latter explanation is consistent with postmodern or postpositivistic formulations, which question whether the researcher or the participants should be the authority. Thus, much of the emerging research is conducted by people of mixed heritage or people who have some close relationship with such individuals. This implies that the researcher influences the questions and the interpretation of data and that his or her presence may affect the data collection process.

The proliferation of research also occurred during a historical period in which racial classification in the decennial census was debated. In fact, for the first time in history, the 2000 U.S. Census included a multiple-choice check-off to the race question; 2.4% of the U.S. population used this option (U.S. Bureau of the Census, 2001). This historical event may significantly affect identification possibilities for multiracial people in the future as data presented by the media will facilitate the construction of race with multiple simultaneous possibilities and realities (Root, 1996). This timing of this event constitutes a historical variable for future research studies.

Although contemporary mixed race occurs at a higher rate in the different Asian American groups than in other ethnic groups, more attention has been paid to Black–White mixed heritage. Blackness has had a caste status that has been cemented by a rigid one-drop rule of classification; that is, if one has any African ancestry one is labeled Black (Davis, 1991). The one-drop rule originated in an attempt to protect Whiteness, a notion in and of itself that required the construction of a racial hierarchy. The principle of hypodescent operates to protect Whiteness; individuals of mixed race, and even individuals involved with those of a lower socioeconomic class, are assigned the lowest racial social status. The one-drop rule has extended beyond Black–White race mixing and has been applied to other mixed-heritage people. For example, Spickard (1989) noted that hundreds of children and adults of mixed heritage were interned during World War II because they were considered Japanese. However, I (Root, 2001) noted that there has been a transformation of the Asian race to a class variable from a caste variable, something that has not yet been uniformly extended to people of African American heritage. In its starkest contrast, conceptualizing race as a caste versus class marker has significant implications for the identity process in people of mixed Asian American heritage with European versus African heritage. This conceptual construction of race has implications for research on identity processes.

In this chapter I explore two significant aspects of methodology that are significant challenges in research with people of racially mixed heritage: sampling and the data collection methods. Conceptual issues must drive both.

CONCEPTUALIZING THE PROCESS OF IDENTITY FORMATION

Forty years of research have shown tremendous variation in the identities of people of mixed heritage. Conceptualizing the process of identity formation affects how these variations are interpreted and the types of models offered to explain identity resolution. Conceptualization affects both the types of research questions posed and the filter through which they are examined. For example, several contemporary studies of racially mixed people suggest that identity can be dynamic, changing situationally. One study that illustrated this simply and clearly is Stephan's (1992) study of racially mixed college students in Hawaii. She asked them about identity in five different situations and found that the majority of respondents provided different answers in different situations; no respondents gave the same response to all five scenarios. Approximately 15% of the respondents in one of her studies identified with a group with whom they did not inherit identity through the family. Furthermore, there are several different reasons one might identify oneself monoracially or monoethnically or multiracially or multiethnically. However, if one does not know that this is a normative process for many people of mixed heritage, the changing labels in different situations might be interpreted as identity confusion.

Prior to the development of this field of research, the prevailing models of ethnic and racial identity development were based largely on African American identity resolution. These stage models, suggested by researchers such as Cross (1981); Helms (1989); and D. R. Atkinson, Morten, and Sue (1989), were linear and hierarchical. This means that a stage further along in the process would suggest a more favorable stage of identity and be correlated with better adjustment. These models essentially suggest that an individual moves from internalizing the denigrating messages of the status quo to a stage of retreat and immersion into the racial and ethnic group of origin; this is catalyzed by an existential, often traumatic event that reveals the world to be unfair and racially biased. One eventually is able to emerge, aware of unjust biases in the world but able to constructively deal with the bias without internalizing negative stereotypes or projecting negative racial biases.

Stage models are appealing because they acknowledge a developmental process. For example, Gibbs (1987) and Gibbs and Hines (1992) have offered a developmental analysis of identity issues from an Eriksonian framework using a clinical sample. At its base is an assumption of some universal process affecting identity development in general. More often than not the models have been specifically derived from Black and White mixed-heritage people and based on underlying assumptions that a single race identifier is preferable or the guiding model for the process (Poston, 1990). Even more recent revisions of classic nigrescence models still have an underlying monoracial bias (Carter, 1995; Cross & Fhagen-Smith, 1996).

Miller (1992) challenged the assumption that the racial identity process is universal. In fact historical legacies and political meaning guide it. For example, I (Root, 2001) noted that whereas non-White racial status has until recently had a caste status, there has been a transformation of race to a class variable for some (but not all) racial groups. This explains continued opposition to Black–White and Asian–Black intermarriage more so than

Asian–White intermarriage and more concern for children of the former unions than those of the latter.

Kich (1982, 1992) has proposed a three-stage model of multiracial identity based on a sample of biracial Japanese Americans. He suggested that there is initially incongruence and dissonance between self- and others' perceptions. This stage reflects internalized oppression not dissimilar from initial stages in nigrescence models, although it is attributed to a much younger age. Kich suggested that because of the central issues of reference group and belonging to one from ages 3–10 years, this source of dissonance is a catalyst for a struggle for acceptance from age 8 to young adulthood. The resolution of this stage is acceptance of a bicultural and or biracial identity in late adolescence or adulthood. Although Kich's model may not fit all people of multiracial origins, it illustrates the underlying difference in assumptions in the process of identity between monoracial versus multiracial people. Whereas it is possible for a monoracial or monoethnic person to immerse him- or herself in the ethnic or racial community or to see such reference groups, multiracial people have not had this guaranteed source of refuge. In fact, seeking refuge in one's assumed ethnic group may perpetuate feelings of not belonging and result in authenticity tests to prove belonging in a way not encountered by monoracial or monoethnic members. Kich's explication of the identity process also suggests that some of this dissonance must be resolved early and is cumulatively fueled by everyday experience, not necessarily by a single existential event. I (Root, 1999) suggested that the process may be more circular, limited by the cognitive capacities of each emotional and cognitive developmental stage through which an individual moves. Thus, the dissonance an 8-year-old faces may be resolved differently than the dissonance a first-year college student experiences in negotiating her or his identity in a new environment.

Miller (1992) and Root (1990) have noted that the preponderance of models are linear; however, research suggests that the identity process for many people who claim a mixed identity is dynamic and nonlinear. Thus, stage models may have reduced explanatory power for many aspects of identity production among people who identify themselves as being of mixed race.

Monoracial-identity models are able to accommodate only a portion of some multiracial people's identity processes and thus cannot accommodate the multiracial identity. Such models do not kindly accommodate multiplicity, duality, situational ethnicity, or race. They were also developed on the basis of a population that was demographically very different 20–30 years ago. For example, Poston (1990) provided a strict translation of an earlier model of Cross's (1985) Black identity model. Several researchers identified with the development of monoracial models of identity development have now attempted to address the identity process of multiracial individuals in their models. However, these models follow psychology's tradition as attempting at face value to be apolitical when race is a highly political construct. Without an articulation of the historical contexts, roles, and regard of people of mixed race, underlying theoretical assumptions about how this racial identity process works will be outdated.

Miller (1992) explained how racial identity theories have assumed that one's ascribed identity and personal identity will be the same, which several researchers who have examined multiple-heritage participants found is not the case. Using participants in Honolulu, Duffy (1978) was the first to articulate a simultaneous dynamic identity as a possible normative articulation of identity for mixed-race people. Stephan (1992) articulated this further in her work on mixed-race Japanese, mixed-race Asians, and contemporary mixed-heritage adolescents of Mexican American heritage (Stephan & Stephan, 1989).

Departing from stage models, I (Root, 1990) emphasized the multiple variables that may give rise to different processes resulting in different resolutions of identity, such as family environment, place of birth, temperament, and so forth. I offered four resolutions of identity that were not sequential but grounded in historical context and adaptivity: (a) accept the default monoracial and monoethnic identity through a hypodescent process, (b) identify with multiple groups, (c) actively resolve a single racial or ethnic identity, and (d) identify as a new ethnic or racial group. On the basis of my subsequent research, 10 years later I added a fifth resolution of identity: adopt a symbolic race or ethnicity (Root, 1998a). Given that no single model can explain the path that the majority of people follow, I have continued to focus on the processes affecting identity development that would explain variations in identity. In subsequent work I offered an ecological framework for racial identity development (Root, 1999) in line with the contextual emphasis that researchers of multiracial populations have emphasized. In line with earlier articulations (Miller, 1992; Root, 1990; Stephan, 1992; Stephan & Stephan, 1989), ecological frameworks provide the greatest ability to explain multiple types of resolutions, simultaneous identities, situational race or ethnicity, and even identification with heritages that are not part of one's family lineage. This is normative phenomenology for some people of mixed heritage. By avoiding the pitfalls of declarative authority and hierarchical models, all identities are assumed to have some adaptive function. My Ecological Framework for Understanding Racial Identity Development accommodates a monoracial solution as well as multiracial solutions. Using a symbolic interactionist perspective from the sociology tradition, I look at the almost infinite numbers of interactions that influence the identity process, and I suggest that the main lenses of influence are gender, class, regional history of race relations, and community. However, any of the other lenses within the model can become a salient lens through which all experience is filtered or reinterpreted. For example, sexual orientation or sexual identity may be a lens through which gender and racial and ethnic identity are experienced and interpreted (Allman, 1996; Kich, 1996). Within these potential interactive frames the influences of family, traits, special skills, and generationally driven interactions within a community further interact to anticipate the possible generational solutions to racial and ethnic identity. Generational issues are important to Asian American communities in that they help people understand the tensions affecting a transition from Asian identified to Asian American identified. Generation also influences rates of intermarriage and has been catalogued extensively by Kitano (e.g., Kitano, Fujino, & Sato, 1998) over the years.

METHODOLOGY

One of the significant problems in multiracial research is that the findings are likely influenced by who is willing to participate in a study that is recruiting multiracial participants. Implicit in the advertisements is an assumption that at some level the potential participant identifies him- or herself as multiracial. The conclusions about multiracial identity would be strengthened if participants were included who might not identify themselves in this way. I (Root, 1998a) developed a methodological approach to this problem. I discuss this sampling method later in the chapter. An important finding emerged that has not been previously reported emerged from my study (Root, 1998a). A minority of respondents of European heritage manifested what Waters (1990) described in her study of European-origin people as *symbolic identity*. In my (Root, 1998a) study symbolic identity was manifested in racial identification as White with recognition and interest of ethnic roots but without attachment. Thus, the use of any ethnic identifiers was symbolic in the way Waters described it.

Sampling and methods of data collection are two significant issues for studies of multiracial respondents. I now consider these issues in depth.

Sampling

Non-Random Distribution of the Multiracial Population

In a previous publication, I noted that obtaining multiracial participants for research studies can be difficult and complex and can pose many threats and challenges to validity (Root, 1992a).

> These threats arise for several reasons: Multiracial people are nonrandomly distributed in the United States; they are a numerical minority in much of the mainland United States, especially among adult-age subjects; and identification and recruitment of multiracial subjects is complex. Additionally, a city's or region's history of racial mixing will affect the extent to which the sample is representative of other mixed-race samples. (p. 183)

People of mixed racial heritage and Asian American heritage do not occur randomly in the population (U.S. Bureau of the Census, 2001). Because the census data on race were released state by state, the percentages of people who checked more than one race vary between states and between counties within the same state (see Table 7.1). Whereas an average of 2.4% of the U.S. population indicated that they were multiracial in racial origin, this percentage ranged from a high of 21.4% in Hawaii to a low of 0.7% in Mississippi. In general, Western states had higher proportions of individuals who identified themselves as multiracial (4.3%). The Midwest (1.6%) and the South (1.8%) reported significantly lower figures. The Northeast (2.3%) and the mid-Atlantic states (2.4%) were in between (U.S. Bureau of the Census, 2001). The nonrandomly distributed multiracial population and households were already evident more than 10 years ago. Chew, Eggebeen, and Uhlenberg (1989) reported that 50% of children in multiracial households resided in the six states of California, Hawaii, Illinois, New York, Texas, and Washington. Thus, general random surveys in which one hopes to derive a large enough sample of people of mixed racial heritage may require an unwieldy process or a large number of respondents and thus not be cost effective (Stephan, 1992).

Identifying Participants by Surname

Identifying participants is complex. One method has been to use surnames in studies of intermarriage. Although many Asians of Chinese, Japanese, Korean, and Vietnamese heritage can be identified by surname, Filipinos are harder to identify, because many have Spanish surnames. However, the pattern of intermarriage for Asian Americans, based on Los Angeles County data patterns, suggests that Asian American women intermarry more frequently than do men (Kitano, Fujino, & Sato, 1998). This pattern of intermarriage coupled with the patriarchally based practice of women adopting their husband's surnames, has eliminated the surname as a reliable marker of potential participant recruitment.

Advertising and Snowball Methods

Straight advertising in various publications tends to recruit a limited sample (Hall, 1980; Root, 1998a). These ads usually indicate that they are looking for people to participate in a study of identity development or of life experiences associated with being mixed race. Some people with multiple racial heritages will likely not respond to such an ad, for many possible reasons. They may not think of themselves as mixed in terms of ethnic or racial identity. They may feel that the authenticity of their ethnic or racial identity may be threatened if friends or family know that they are participating in such a study. People of Latin, American Indian, Pacific Island, or Filipino ancestry who are typically regarded as mixed-race people may not feel compelled to respond in the same proportions as other people. Individuals who

TABLE 7.1

Percentages of People Who Checked More Than One Racial Signifier on the 2000 U.S. Census by State and Territory (U.S. Bureau of the Census)

State	%population	State	%population
Alabama	1.0	Nevada	3.8
Alaska	5.4	New Hampshire	1.1
Arizona	2.9	New Jersey	2.5
Arkansas	1.3	New Mexico	3.6
California	4.7	New York	3.1
Colorado	2.6	North Carolina	1.3
Connecticut	2.2	North Dakota	1.2
Delaware	1.7	Ohio	1.4
Florida	2.4	Oklahoma	4.5
Georgia	1.4	Oregon	3.1
Hawaii	21.4	Pennsylvania	1.2
Idaho	2.0	Rhode Island	2.7
Illinois	1.9	South Carolina	1.0
Indiana	1.2	South Dakota	1.3
Iowa	1.1	Tennessee	1.1
Kansas	2.1	Texas	2.5
Kentucky	1.1	Utah	2.1
Louisiana	1.1	Vermont	1.2
Maine	1.0	Virginia	2.0
Maryland	2.0	Washington	3.6
Massachusetts	2.3	West Virginia	0.9
Michigan	1.9	Wisconsin	1.8
Minnesota	1.7	Wyoming	1.8
Mississippi	0.7		
Missouri	1.5	District of Columbia	2.4
Montana	1.7	Puerto Rico	4.2
Nebraska	1.4		

Note. From U.S. Bureau of the Census (2001). http://www.census.gov/population/cen2000/phc-t6/.

have resolved identity issues may also not feel compelled to come forward and explore these issues.

Most researchers have combined advertising in various newspapers (college, city, ethnic community) with a *snowball* method. The snowball method recruits a very select group of participants; people known by one participant and often, also identifying as multiracial, recruit other people they know to the study, a friend, classmate, or family member. Whereas the snowball method enlarges the sample, it does not necessarily diversify the experiences, ages, or racial identities within the sample (e.g., Hall, 1980; Kich, 1982; King, 1997; Mass, 1992; Murphy-Shigematsu, 1986; Standen, 1996; Stephan, 1991; Stephan & Stephan, 1989; Thornton, 1983; Williams, 1992, 1996; Yoshimi, 1997). In fact, unless explicitly stated otherwise, one might assume that studies on mixed-race Asians used a snowball technique (e.g., Cauce et al., 1992; Root, 1998b). The snowball method has been widely used because of the difficulty in recruiting participants, because of nonrandom distribution of mixed-heritage people in the population; their hesitance to participate; the small proportion of the population from which the sample is drawn; and the limited research funding, if any, to carry out such research.

Generational Issues

The generation in which one grew up, reflected by age and influenced by history, also influences perceptions and possibilities in identity choices. For example, the increased tendency to identify oneself as multiracial has occurred among the younger generation. Although they still receive pressure to identify themselves according to the one-drop rule, they have a visible cohort with which to identify and share similar experiences. They are not isolated, as many people of mixed-race Asian heritage were previously. School-age mixed-race Asian Americans are a significant proportion of most Asian American communities in this country. In fact, in a recent sociological study, the percentage of one's Japanese heritage has become an issue for contestants in the annual Cherry Blossom Queen Pageant (King, 1997). As the rates of intermarriage for Japanese Americans increases for both women and men over several generations, issues about percentage of heritage have become part of open discussions as to what might be the minimum required percentage to represent the Japanese American community in such pageants. Similarly, some adult Japanese American basketball leagues specify a blood quantum to participate.

Another generational issue is the national origins of one's parents. Among people born during or just after the U.S. military presence in Asian countries because of World War II or the Korean War, mothers were usually from Asia and often were non-English speaking. Japan, Korea, and the Philippines were the major sources of Asian brides. Currently, the majority of interracial marriages involve two persons both raised, if not born, in the United States, who do not experience themselves as foreigners and do not need their children to act as interpreters or cultural liaisons (Root, 1997). This changes for people the experience of growing up. Nationality and American culture are not issues between or within families. When mothers are foreigners, they are less frequently from Japan and more frequently than in the past from the Philippines or Korea (Thornton, 1992) or other Asian countries.

Use of Control Groups

Conventional research design has insisted on control groups. The appropriateness of a control group must be considered in light of the research questions posed—and if a control group is used, who exactly constitutes the appropriate control group (Cauce et al., 1992; Root, 1998b)? Not using one reflects not a lack of rigor but more likely a lack of utility given the focus of the study (e.g., Hall, 1980; Kich, 1982; Murphy-Shigematsu, 1986; Thornton, 1983). A rationale must be provided rather than an assumption that a research study will be better or more valid because a control group was used. In a study of Asian American and African American adolescents, Cauce et al.

(1992) used monoracial Asian Americans and monoracial African Americans as control groups, because they seemed to share similar experiences being treated as children of color. This was not intended as a study of multiracial Asian Americans or African Americans.

Primary Versus Secondary Sampling

Stephan (1992) noted that if one wanted to collect information about ethnic identity, one should do this by means of primary data collection, as secondary analysis is fraught with problems. For example, knowing that a person is of mixed heritage does not necessarily give one information about how that person identifies him- or herself. Census figures should not be equated with whether people publicly or personally identify themselves as multiracial or are indeed multiracial. For example, only 4.2% of Puerto Rico's widely acknowledged multiracial population reported this (U.S. Bureau of the Census, 2001). Stephan (1992) concluded and strongly recommended that the identification of a sample regarding ethnic identity must be a primary data collection process to facilitate appropriate questions.

Importance of Nonclinical Samples

In line with much of the research on identity development, the initial research has used nonclinical samples (cf. Root, 1992b). The use of nonclinical samples has been essential to establish the range of possible identities. For example, without research that revealed that mixed-heritage identity, situational identity, or symbolic identity could be associated with good adjustment, observing these choices only in clinical samples may lead one to rely on older, pathological interpretations of confusion or self-hatred as the only explanations for these choices.

College, Community, and Restricted Samples

There are significant conceptual issues to be considered in whether a researcher pursues a college sample versus a community sample. The latter does not exclude college students. It potentially includes a wider range of people in terms of socioeconomic, racial, and age characteristics. However, in contrast to early contemporary studies of racially mixed people that drew samples from the community or from multiple cities (e.g., Hall, 1980, 1992; Kich, 1982, 1992; Murphy-Shigematsu, 1986; Thornton, 1983), recent studies of mixed-heritage people involve convenience sampling that is usually limited to college samples.

College samples represent a fairly homogeneous age and developmental stage that affects identity development on several planes (e.g., race, ethnicity, gender, and sexuality). Sometimes, these restricted age range and sample characteristics can be helpful and offer some useful information and preliminary hypothesis for further research (Mass, 1992; Stephan, 1992).

College-age students undoubtedly provide a richness of dynamic experience influencing the identity process. However, the identities they choose do not necessarily reflect the identities they will have 10 years later. In my study of biracial siblings (Root, 1998a) who ranged in age from 18 to 55, I specifically asked them how they identified at various life stages. A prominent feature of the results was the impact of life events and developmental milestones on the identity process: death of a parent, reconciliation with family members, marriage, illness, birth of children, a move from or to a community, and so forth. Conclusions based on such restricted samples are limited. For example, a friend of Hawaiian ancestry living in Hawaii noted that, because he was born before Hawaii became a state, he was recorded ethnically in vital statistics as Hawaiian, Chinese, and Portuguese. When Hawaii became a state, he was an "other," according to the U.S. government census, although he was still recorded multiply in vital statistics in Hawaii's records. He eventually was categorized as an Asian/Pacific Islander on the basis of preference rules and U.S. rules of race. Now he has an option for multiple identification.

Whereas one must be cautious in using restricted samples, specific hypotheses would require a restricted sample to answer specific questions or test hypotheses. For example, I (Root, 1999) reported on the impact of having to negotiate one's identity in college, particularly at a large college away from one's home community. At a young age, older brothers and sisters and parents often negotiate one's identity in the community. This conscious negotiation process in college, away from family, creates a very conscious process of how race works at a very personal level for many young Asian Americans, who report few if any encounters with racial prejudice in their home communities. They may encounter the racial or ethnic authenticity tests (Root, 1990, 1998a). These oppressive rituals provide a gatekeeping function to determine whether someone is "Asian enough." These tests are put to mixed-race Asians more frequently than to monoracial Asians; the person creating the tests controls the rules and the criteria. In the most unfortunate circumstances, hatred of Whiteness must be demonstrated or caricatures of a stereotyped Asian American must be displayed.

This active negotiation of identity in the college and young adult years has been explored in dating relationships of college women. Twine (1996), although studying young women of African and European heritage, noted that in college these women were negotiating racial and ethnic identity and affiliation through the men they chose to date. Women who dated African American men had more access to and acceptability in the African American community than women who dated men of other ethnicities. It is likely that this Gender × Ethnicity interaction prevails for Asian Americans, too; a woman's identity in a patriarchally organized society continues to be marked more by her partner's social location than vice versa.

Williams (1992) also used restricted samples to explore factors influencing identity formation in mixed-race Japanese Americans of European and African heritage who have lived on U.S. military bases in Japan. This restricted sampling allowed her to provide a rich sociological description of factors affecting identity and resolution of identity in this unique milieu.

Controlling for the Effect of an Asian or Asian American Parent

In some studies, the gender of the Asian parent has been controlled, making sampling that much more restricted and the results more specific. For example, Standen (1996) limited his participants to people with Korean mothers; Hall (1980) limited her study to Japanese and Japanese American mothers and African American fathers; Thornton (1983) further restricted his participant pool by limiting his study to Japanese mothers from Japan and African American fathers.

Leveraged Sampling

The Biracial Sibling Project increased the diversity of a sample used to explore gender, ethnic, and racial identity development through the methodology of sibling recruitment, or *leveraged sampling* (Root, 1998a). One sibling would respond to the ad in a community-employment newspaper (serving interests across several ethnic communities and classes) or one of the city's two main newspapers. To be accepted into the study, the respondent had to obtain the agreement of one other sibling to participate (Root, 1998a). In multiracial families, siblings often identify differently from one another. So, for example, in a Japanese African American household with three siblings, one sibling may identify ethnically as Japanese American, another as African American, and another as mixed. Likewise, in a Filipino White household, two siblings may identify differently, one as mixed, one as White (symbolic identity) with Filipino heritage. If there were more siblings within the same family, others identities might emerge. However, by recruiting a sibling who may not have even been interested in responding to such an ad, the diversity of the sample increased. This type of recruitment, although it bears a resemblance to the snowballing method, uses leverage of sibling participation to allow the interested sibling to participate. In snowballing methods leverage is not a qualification for participation.

Heterogeneous Versus Homogeneous Samples

The racial and ethnic mixture of a sample can be important. In some of the original contemporary classic studies, the researchers were very specific in making cross-study comparisons more possible by obtaining the samples within similar time frames. Japanese Americans have constituted the vast majority of study participants in studies of multiracial people of Asian descent. For example, Hall and Thornton have used participants of African and Japanese heritage (Hall, 1980, 1992; Thornton, 1983). Murphy-

Shigematsu (1986) used biracial people of Japanese American heritage, as did Kich (1982). Stephan used people of mixed heritage in Hawaii of Japanese descent (cf. Stephan, 1992). Mass (1992) used Japanese American college students of mixed heritage. Williams (1992) used Japanese Americans who had lived on military bases. In a more recent study, Standen (1996) used only Korean White participants. Keeping the ethnicity of the Asian group the same allows for discussion of specific cultural attitudes, beliefs, and values as they influence the identity process.

Is it ever OK to reduce ethnicity to race? If one is studying race and not intending to study or interpret one's results in light of culture or ethnicity, then it might be possible to use groups of different Asian heritage mixes with White or Black (or both) ancestry. However, researchers invariably find a result that suggests some difference between groups but do not have the statistical or conceptual power because of either the nature of the interview or the numbers of participants to understand whether a finding is generalizable or is idiosyncratic to the study. For example, whereas Grove (1991) limited her study to people of Asian and European heritage, she included people of various Asian ethnicities and found some possible differences in trends, but the subsamples were too small to draw confident conclusions from emerging trends.

Given the history of race relations in the United States, and the notions of racial and ethnic purity among some ethnic Asians, the combination of Asian heritage with Black or White parentage yields different experiences (Root, 2001; Williams, 1992). The specific Asian ancestry may make a difference for reflection of how much mixing has occurred in that group, often guided by generation in this country; the historical context of mixing, such as colonization (Root, 1996); and the proportion of that particular community that is mixed.

Geography and Generalizability

Geographic location is important to the context of racial and ethnic experiences. Location interacts with history and guides school, neighborhood, and community experiences of race. For example, being of mixed heritage in Honolulu is a different experience than being of mixed heritage in Los Angeles. Both experiences will be quite different from those of someone of mixed Asian heritage raised in Minneapolis (Root, 1999). Geographic differences affect the generalizability of findings. For example, making sense out of the 2000 U.S. Census figures regarding proportions of people who checked more than once race seems to reflect an attitudinal history toward race mixing (see Table 7.1).

Data Collection

In research with people of mixed heritage, two major methods of primary data collection are (a) interview and (b) paper-and-pencil measures. Each of these can reflect qualitative or quantitative methods. The narrative and the focus group, which are qualitative methods, have gained increasing popularity. A critique of each of these methods follows. It is interesting to note that some researchers have used different data collection methods for different participants to increase their sample size. For example, Tomishima (1999) allowed participants for the qualitative part of her study to choose whether they wanted to take part in an in-person interview, an electronic-mail narrative, or a written narrative. These are three very different methodologies with different strengths and weaknesses. Small numbers of participants still permit a researcher to test and build theories, but they do not provide the confidence to test specific hypotheses. However, Tomishima's study allowed trends to emerge, because it was theoretically grounded.

Regardless of the method of data collection, the conceptual framework is important in guiding the data collection and interpretation. For example, if I (Root, 1998a) had used a framework ensconced in the racial politics of hypodescent, certain questions would not have been asked. If a White identity for racially mixed participants meant confusion, shame of their ethnic heritage, or if there were some other conventional explanation for people who have transgressed conventional lines of race, I would have missed the opportunity to hear and question about the emerging phenomenon of symbolic identity in contemporary times, the reconstruction of Whiteness. Instead, I found that White identity and symbolic ethnicity seemed to be associated with having significant acceptance by and access to White relatives, isolation from the ethnic community not necessarily by choice but by geographic location, growing up in a foreign country in which race is constructed and assigned meaning differently than in the United States, infrequent contact with ethnic relatives because of geographic location, class markers as middle class, or some combination of these (Root, 1998a). It was not limited to people of Asian and European ancestry, and not predictable by phenotype. White identity bore no resemblance to the phenomenon of passing (Bradshaw, 1992; Daniel, 1992), or pretending to be White and denying one's racial heritage.

Bias Versus Objectivity

Denzin (1994) observed that there is an art to interpretation that is ensconced in the political. Claims of unbiased research are almost a stance of the past. He noted that

> the social sciences today face a crisis of interpretation, for previously agreed-upon criteria from the positivist and postpositivist traditions are now being challenged. . . . This crisis has been described as poststructural and postmodern, a new sensibility regarding the social text and its claims to authority. Describing this new situation, Richardson (1991) observes, "The core of [this] sensibility is doubt that any discourse has a privileged place, any method or theory a universal and general claim to authoritative knowledge" (p. 173). (Denzin, 1994, p. 501)

The contemporary research on mixed-heritage Asian Americans does not claim objectivity; instead, it has used the rationale of an insider perspective from which to develop the initial questions and spontaneous follow-up questions. It further uses an insider perspective to consider possibilities for interpretation filtered through the lived experience of mixed heritage.

Open Ended Interviews

Interviews are constructed from a conceptual framework and bias. Some biases are more constricting than others. In a qualitative study in line with ethnographic research, an interviewer may pose few but open-ended questions to obtain the greatest depth and breadth of data possible (Fontana & Frey, 1994); for example: "Tell me about how you identify yourself ethnically and what influences have been significant to your determination of identity." From there, each participant may be asked a very different set of questions determined by their unique responses. Interviews such as this require an artistry often unappreciated by the untrained person or person wedded to empirical designs using quantitative analysis (Sandelowski, 1993). Such interviews are much more difficult than they appear to be.

Purely qualitative designs oftentimes refuse to permit a hypothesis to be posed, on the basis of the argument that the hypothesis influences the data collection and poses an authority that undermines the reality of voices and feelings of respondents, which are the valid data—even more so than the researcher's interpretation (Denzin, 1994). The data analysis can be difficult as the researcher's lens becomes paramount to the analysis and selection of themes to be reported emerging from the interviews. Even with computerized programs for scoring interviews, sifting through the data can be formidable and requires significant listening skills, data reduction experience, and talent. Keywords are not enough to capture the process by which some people of mixed heritage report on their relational racial or ethnic selves. Sandelowski (1993) emphasized the skill and art required of data reduction.

Structured Interviews

In contrast to open-ended interviews, structured-interview studies pose definite hypotheses to be confirmed or disconfirmed and a predetermined and finite of set of questions to be posed to each respondent (Fontana & Frey, 1994). Questions outside of these are posed only for clarification of an ambiguous response to the immediate question. The types of structured questions already have codifiable answers or are asked in a way that are codifiable without much reduction of the response; for example: "How old were you when you first became aware of your ethnic heritage?" If the respondent says, "Between 6 and 8," then the interviewer may clarify, "To the best of your recollection, could you give me a single age—6, 7, or 8?" or "Is there a memory that helps you determine this age?" The latter question is asked not in hopes of eliciting rich data but in helping increase the confidence the individual has in asserting his or her answer. Another structured question might be "How do you racially identify yourself when you are at a party with friends?" Some of these answers will lend themselves to parametric analysis and others to nonparametric analysis. The answers are not usually as rich, because the questions do not typically encourage such richness. On the basis of the interviewer's responses, and on when he or she seems satisfied to move on with the interview, the respondent becomes aware that a finite answer, rather than a narrative, is sought. This expectation shapes the data provided.

Semistructured Interviews

In semistructured interviews, each participant is posed the same set of questions guided by a hypothesis; however, unique questions may follow each one. For example, each respondent may be asked "Please divide up your life into critical time periods." I (Root, 1998a) used this question in my study of biracial siblings and followed it with a set of further determined questions, such as "What were critical influences or events affecting your awareness of your race or ethnicity during this period of time?" and "Why?" From there, the questions were open ended within each timeframe. In the analysis, responses must often be reduced across respondents and thus some of the immediate idiosyncratic richness is lost. However, selected narrative responses to questions are used to illustrate some of the richness and meaning behind a response, particularly when it represents a repetitive theme.

Narratives

Narratives sometimes assume a stance such as the open-ended interview, and they can be taped or written; for example: "Write a page on an important experience that shaped your racial or ethnic identity." However, the interview method has been reduced to simplicity. Seldom are people trained to derive the maximum amount of data possible from the method. Narrative analysis has been loosely defined, if it is defined at all (Manning & Cullum-Swan, 1994). However, regardless of definition, it shares with ethnographic types of open-ended interviews the notion that data derive from the perspective of the teller rather than an authoritative source such as society or the researcher (Manning & Cullum-Swan, p. 465). In reality, if one is focusing on ethnic or racial identity, then the researcher will need to direct the respondent to this subject matter, which may then place the narrative out of context and a different response may be obtained than if the question were totally open ended.

Focus Groups

Focus groups also have gained popularity. There are guidelines for this methodology. The researcher poses some open-ended questions or conducts the process in a semistructured way. However, the facilitator or interviewer is a participant–observer, as in any interview to some extent (P. Atkinson &

Hammersley, 1994). When the researcher chooses to move the group to another question, whom he or she allows to elaborate, whether he or she establishes ground rules for interaction, whether interruptions are allowed, if the researcher participates by offering personal examples to encourage people to talk—all influence the process of a focus group. Skill in group facilitation and process is useful to conduct a focus group skillfully, maximizing the data that may unfold in a finite amount of time.

Written Questionnaires

Paper-and-pencil questionnaires are useful for obtaining more contained answers and answers that are already in codifiable form, which is useful for quantitative analysis. For example, they allow quick gathering of demographic information, some family information, and so forth. Some of the information that might be derived from a structured interview can be obtained with paper-and-pencil questions. These answers are often less subject to interpreter bias if the questions are asked in specific ways; for example: "How do you ethnically identify yourself?" "How do you think your mother identifies you ethnically?" and "How does your father identify you ethnically?" However, the richness of data obtained in open-ended or semistructured interviews is not possible. Paper-and-pencil questionnaires can be useful when combined with interviews. For example, one can compare situational responses to identity questions in an interview with the responses from a scored identity questionnaire.

Influences of the Researcher

Even a researcher who uses grounded-theory methods (Strauss & Corbin, 1994) and gives authority to the voice of participants still has a bias at some level. She or he will have a lens that affects what he or she studies, how he or she hears responses, what responses he or she deems important for posing additional questions, and the meaning he or she gleans from responses across participants.

No researcher yet has directly explored how the phenotype, ethnicity, or race of the researcher influences data collection with multiracial respondents. The researcher and his or her bias are significant variables in research on multiracial people. Given the reception of or pressures surrounding identity issues in some ethnic communities, the researcher will want to consider his or her influence, particularly in interviews. This is especially important when participants are declaring racial identity in certain contexts. For example, if the participant wants to impress the interviewer or needs his or her acceptance (Kich's [1982] Stage 2), they may not declare a multiracial identity. Declarations of such identities have often been met in society with hostility, rejection, misinterpretation, and even ridicule (Nakashima, 1992).

Just as the counseling literature has explored same-ethnicity or same-race matches and associated some differences in clinical outcome or diagnosis with the match, match may be an issue for certain types of interview questions with people of mixed heritage. No one has ever explored this issue systematically; however, thinking that the laboratory never exists totally separate from the real world, I have chosen my interviewers carefully. They need to have examined their assumptions and biases about race and toward mixed-race people. The following qualities will facilitate artful interviewing: an open attitude; exceptional interviewing competence; knowledge of the possible meanings of nuances in answers; sensitivity to places at which to ask further questions or clarifications of answers so that meaning is assigned by the interviewee when possible; competence in the multiracial identity literature; and constructive coping with personal experiences of a racially mixed phenotype, stereotyping, and or discrimination. A combination of most of these qualities allows the interviewer to conduct the interview with credibility. She or he has a better chance of conveying openness and the ability to understand the possible variations in response that the participant might give without hostility or judgment. Subsequently, the researcher is acknowledged as a participant observer who influences the process of research regardless of whether he or she wants to (P. Atkinson & Hammersley, 1994).

SUMMARY

I have reviewed several of the challenges facing researchers who want to explore identity issues in populations of mixed heritage, with a particular focus on Asian Americans. The conceptual framework guides the questions and whether or when certain types of identifications are adaptive, normative, or problematic. I also provided a critique of interview formats and the limitations and possibilities associated with each one. Last, I explored methods of data collection as the last layer before analysis that determines the quality of data the researcher will obtain. Researchers are challenged to combine scientific methods of inquiry, whether qualitative or quantitative, with creativity. Both types of method demand skills, rigor, knowledge, and challenges to the racial assumptions with which most researchers have been raised. The ultimate validity check may be member validation. Do the findings ring true when checked by members of the group studied (Sandelowski, 1993)? Given the social constructions of race, findings about identity or identifications may vary across studies because of the multiplicity of interactive variables shaping identity for a situation (Root, 1999). However, if one's findings ring true with members of the group studied, and are replicable across researchers, one has accomplished valid research.

FUTURE RESEARCH DIRECTIONS

At least four significant implications follow from this chapter.

- The increased presence of multiracial Asian Americans challenges "racial purity" as a necessary condition for Asian American identity (Root, 1998b). How will researchers determine whether to include or exclude research participants who identify themselves as Asian American who are multiracially or multiethnically identified?
- With so many researchers uneducated about the multiracial experiences and the prejudicial attitudes toward multiracial people, how will these biases be held in check in research studies?
- It is problematic to translate monoracial-identity models into multiracial-identity models. Such a translation does not occur in process, because the multiracial person is often deemed not fully Asian American or only half Asian American. Thus, the assumption of refuge into the community of origin is not guaranteed.
- The class versus caste status associated with Asian versus African heritage must be considered in researching multiracial Asian American identity (Hall, 1980; King & DaCosta, 1996; Root, 2001; Thornton, 1983; Williams, 1992). Caste restrictions may add to the identity-resolution process, perception of choices, or struggle with acceptance.

Enough preliminary research has been conducted to generate myriad questions for the future. More than ever, researchers need a return to some well-reasoned methodology. This includes paying attention to sampling issues, such as the use of restricted versus nonrestricted samples. Rationales need to be provided for considering Asian Americans of different ethnic groups a homogeneous versus heterogeneous sample. Gender differences in identity need to be explored. Last, to replicate findings or understand existing findings, researchers need to use significant samples of people of ancestry other than Japanese American. This allows researchers to understand how historical, cultural, economic, immigration, and phenotypic variables affect the identity process. I am concerned that if researchers do not provide well-reasoned rationales for their methodological approaches to research of mixed-race identity that much of this research will be useless. This will open the door for researchers unfamiliar with the nuances of multiracial experiences to translate models and apply conceptualizations and interpretations that may be at best incomplete and at worse invalid. With tighter and conventional methodology, however, the findings from these studies could become the truth even if they are not conceptually valid. Researchers must return to more rigorous methodology to answer the questions that pilot research has posed.

REFERENCES

Allman, K. M. (1996). (Un)natural boundaries: Mixed race, gender, and sexuality. In M. P. P. Root (Ed.), *The multiracial experience: Racial borders as the new frontier* (pp. 277–290). Thousand Oaks, CA: Sage.

Atkinson, D. R., Morten, G., & Sue, D. W. (1989). *Counseling American minorities: A cross-cultural perspective.* Dubuque, IA: William C. Brown.

Atkinson, P., & Hammersley, M. (1994). Ethnography and participant observation. In N. K. Denzin & Y. S. Lincoln (Eds.), *Handbook of qualitative research* (pp. 248–261). Thousand Oaks, CA: Sage.

Bradshaw, C. K. (1992). Beauty and the beast: On racial ambiguity. In M. P. P. Root (Ed.), *Racially mixed people in America* (pp. 77–88). Newbury Park, CA: Sage.

Carter, R. T. (1995). *The influence of race and racial identity in psychotherapy: Toward a racially inclusive model.* New York: Wiley.

Cauce, A. M., Hiraga, Y., Mason, C., Aguilar, T., Ordonez, N., & Gonzales, N. (1992). Between a rock and a hard place: Social adjustment of biracial youth. In M. P. P. Root (Ed.), *Racially mixed people in America* (pp. 207–222). Newbury Park, CA: Sage.

Chew, K., Eggebeen, D. & Uhlenberg, P. (1989). American children in multiracial households. *Sociological Perspectives, 32,* 65–85.

Cross, W. E., Jr. (1981). Black families and Black identity development. *Journal of Comparative Family Studies, 19,* 341–350.

Cross, W. E., Jr. (1985). Black identity: Rediscovering the distinction between personal identity and reference group orientation. In M. B. Spencer, G. K. Brookins, & W. R. Allen (Eds.), *Beginnings: The social and affective development of Black children* (pp. 155–172). Hillsdale, NJ: Erlbaum.

Cross, W. E., Jr., & Fhagen-Smith, P. (1996). Nigrescence and ego identity development: Accounting for differential Black identity patterns. In P. Pederson, J. G. Dragrens, & W. J. Lonner (Eds.), *Counseling across cultures* (pp. 108–123). Thousand Oaks, CA: Sage.

Daniel, G. R. (1992). Passers and pluralists: Subverting the racial divide. In M. P. P. Root (Ed.), *Racially mixed people in America* (pp. 91–107). Newbury Park, CA: Sage.

Davis, F. J. (1991). *Who is Black? One nation's definition.* University Park: Pennsylvania State University Press.

Denzin, N. K. (1994). The art and politics of interpretation. In N. K. Denzin & Y. S. Lincoln (Eds.), *Handbook of qualitative research* (pp. 500–515). Thousand Oaks, CA: Sage.

Duffy, L. K. (1978). *The interracial individuals: Self-concept, parental interaction, and ethnic identity.* Unpublished master's thesis, University of Hawaii.

Fontana, A., & Frey, J. H. (1994). Interviewing: The art of science. In N. K. Denzin & Y. S. Lincoln (Eds.), *Handbook of qualitative research* (pp. 361–376). Thousand Oaks, CA: Sage.

Gibbs, J. T. (1987). Identity and marginality: Issues in the treatment of biracial adolescents. *American Journal of Orthopsychiatry, 57*, 265–278.

Gibbs, J. T., & Hines, A. M. (1992). Negotiating ethnic identity: Issues for Black–White biracial adolescents. In M. P. P. Root (Ed.), *Racially mixed people in America* (pp. 223–238). Newbury Park, CA: Sage.

Grove, K. (1991). Identity development in interracial, Asian/White late adolescents: Must it be so problematic? *Journal of Youth and Adolescence, 20*, 617–628.

Hall, C. C. I. (1980). *The ethnic identity of racially mixed people: A study of Black-Japanese.* Unpublished doctoral dissertation, University of California, Los Angeles.

Hall, C. C. I. (1992). Please choose one: Ethnic identity choices for biracial individuals. In M. P. P. Root (Ed.), *Racially mixed people in America* (pp. 250–264). Newbury Park, CA: Sage.

Helms, J. E. (1989). Considering some methodological issues in racial identity research. *The Counseling Psychologist, 17*, 227–252.

Kich, G. K. (1982). *Eurasians: Ethnic/racial identity development of biracial Japanese/White adults.* Unpublished doctoral dissertation, Wright Institute Graduate School of Psychology.

Kich, G. K. (1992). The developmental process of asserting a biracial, bicultural identity. In M. P. P. Root (Ed.), *Racially mixed people in America* (pp. 304–317). Newbury Park, CA: Sage.

Kich, G. K. (1996). In the margins of sex and race: Difference, marginality, and flexibility. In M. P. P. Root (Ed.), *The multiracial experience: Racial borders as the new frontier* (pp. 263–276). Thousand Oaks, CA: Sage.

King, R. C. (1997). Multiraciality reigns supreme? Mixed race Japanese Americans and the Cherry Blossom Queen Pageant. *Amerasia Journal, 23*, 113–129.

King, R. C., & DaCosta, K. M. (1996). Changing face, changing race: The remaking of race in the Japanese American and African American communities. In M. P. P. Root (Ed.), *The multiracial experience: Racial borders as the new frontier* (pp. 227–244). Thousand Oaks, CA: Sage.

Kitano, H. H. L., Fujino, D. C., & Sato, J. T. (1998). Interracial marriages: Where are the Asian Americans and where are they going? In L. C. Lee & N. W. S. Zane (Eds.), *Handbook of Asian American psychology* (pp. 233–260). Thousand Oaks, CA: Sage.

Manning, P. K., & Cullum-Swan, B. (1994). Narrative, content, and semiotic analysis. In N. K. Denzin & Y. S. Lincoln (Eds.), *Handbook of qualitative research* (pp. 463–477). Thousand Oaks, CA: Sage.

Mass, A. I. (1992). Interracial Japanese Americans: The best of both worlds or the end of the Japanese American community? In M. P. P. Root (Ed.), *Racially mixed people in America* (pp. 265–279). Newbury Park, CA: Sage.

Miller, R. L. (1992). The human ecology of multiracial identity. In M. P. P. Root (Ed.), *Racially mixed people in America* (pp. 24–36). Newbury Park, CA: Sage.

Murphy-Shigematsu, S. L. (1986). *The voices of Amerasians: Ethnicity, identity and empowerment in interracial Japanese Americans.* Unpublished doctoral dissertation, Harvard University.

Nakashima, C. L. (1992). An invisible monster: The creation and denial of mixed-race people in America. In M. P. P. Root (Ed.), *Racially mixed people in America* (pp. 162–178). Newbury Park, CA: Sage.

Poston, W. S. C. (1990). The biracial identity development model: A needed addition. *Journal of Counseling and Development, 69,* 152–155.

Root, M. P. P. (1990). Resolving "other" status: Identity development of biracial individuals. In L. Brown & M. P. P. Root (Eds.), *Diversity and complexity in feminist theory and therapy* (pp. 185–205). New York: Haworth.

Root, M. P. P. (1992a). Back to the drawing board: Methodological issues in research on multiracial people. In M. P. P. Root (Ed.), *Racially mixed people in America* (pp. 181–189). Newbury Park, CA: Sage.

Root, M. P. P. (Ed.). (1992b). *Racially mixed people in America.* Newbury Park, CA: Sage.

Root, M. P. P. (1996). The multiracial experience: Racial borders as a significant frontier in race relations. In M. P. P. Root (Ed.), *The multiracial experience: Racial borders as the new frontier* (pp. viii–xxviii). Thousand Oaks, CA: Sage.

Root, M. P. P. (1997). Multiracial Asians: Models of ethnic identity. *Amerasia Journal, 23,* 29–42.

Root, M. P. P. (1998a). Experiences and processes affecting racial identity development: Preliminary results from the Biracial Sibling Project. *Cultural Diversity and Mental Health, 4,* 237–247.

Root, M. P. P. (1998b). Multiracial Americans: Changing the face of Asian America. In L. C. Lee & N. W. S. Zane (Eds.), *Handbook of Asian American psychology* (pp. 261–287). Thousand Oaks, CA: Sage.

Root, M. P. P. (1999). The biracial baby boom: Understanding ecological constructions of racial identity in the 21st century. In R. Hernandez-Sheets & E. R. Hollins (Eds.), *Racial and ethnic identity in school practices: Aspects of human development* (pp. 67–90). Mahwah, NJ: Erlbaum.

Root, M. P. P. (2001). *Love's revolution: Interracial marriage in America.* Philadelphia: Temple University Press.

Sandelowski, M. (1993). Rigor or rigor mortis: The problem of rigor in qualitative research revisited. *Advances in Nursing Sciences, 16,* 1–8.

Spickard, P. R. (1989). *Mixed blood: Intermarriage and ethnic identity in twentieth-century America.* Madison: University of Wisconsin Press.

Standen, B. C. S. (1996). Without a template: The biracial Korean/White experience. In M. P. P. Root (Ed.), *The multiracial experience: Racial borders as the new frontier* (pp. 245–259). Thousand Oaks, CA: Sage.

Stephan, C. W. (1991). Ethnic identity among mixed-heritage people in Hawai'i. *Symbolic Interaction, 14,* 261–277.

Stephan, C. W. (1992). Mixed-heritage individuals: Ethnic identity and trait characteristics. In M. P. P. Root (Ed.), *Racially mixed people in America* (pp. 50–63). Newbury Park, CA: Sage.

Stephan, C. W., & Stephan, W. G. (1989). After intermarriage: Ethnic identity among mixed heritage Japanese-Americans and Hispanics. *Journal of Marriage and the Family, 51,* 507–519.

Strauss, A., & Corbin, J. (1994). Grounded theory methodology: An overview. In N. K. Denzin & Y. S. Lincoln (Eds.), *Handbook of qualitative research* (pp. 273–285). Thousand Oaks, CA: Sage.

Thornton, M. C. (1983). *A social history of a multiethnic identity: The case of Black Japanese Americans.* Unpublished doctoral dissertation, University of Michigan.

Thornton, M. C. (1992). The quiet immigration: Foreign spouses of U.S. citizens, 1945–1985. In M. P. P. Root (Ed.), *Racially mixed people in America* (pp. 64–76). Newbury Park, CA: Sage.

Tomishima, S. A. (1999). *Factors and experiences in biracial and biethnic identity development.* Unpublished doctoral dissertation, University of Utah.

Twine, F. W. (1996). Heterosexual alliances: The romantic management of racial identity. In M. P. P. Root (Ed.), *The multiracial experience: Racial borders as the new frontier* (pp. 291–304). Thousand Oaks, CA: Sage.

U.S. Bureau of the Census. (2001). Census.gov/population/ph-tbl.

Waters, M. C. (1990). *Ethnic options: Choosing identities in America.* Berkeley and Los Angeles: University of California Press.

Williams, T. K. (1992). Prism lives: Identity of binational Amerasians. In M. P. P. Root (Ed.), *Racially mixed people in America* (pp. 280–303). Newbury Park, CA: Sage.

Williams, T. K. (1996). Race as process: Reassessing the "What are you?" encounters of biracial individuals. In M. P. P. Root (Ed.), *The multiracial experience: Racial borders as the new frontier* (pp. 191–210). Thousand Oaks, CA: Sage.

Yoshimi, J. (1997). Hapas at a Los Angeles high-school: Context and phenomenology. *Amerasia Journal, 23,* 130–147.

EPILOGUE:
TOWARD THE FUTURE OF ASIAN
AMERICAN PSYCHOLOGY

GORDON C. NAGAYAMA HALL, SUMIE OKAZAKI,
AND DONNA K. NAGATA

The chapters in this book illustrate the breadth and depth of Asian American psychology. Theory and research on Asian Americans are beginning to develop in many areas of psychology. Although there are unique challenges in each area, there are also some common issues that face the field.

As discussed in the Introduction, *Asian American* is a concept and identity that is unique. Asians residing in Asia have contact primarily with other Asians in their own ethnic groups. Although cross-cultural research that examines cultural differences between people in Asia and those in North America can offer some insight into the cultural origins of Asian Americans, it cannot adequately address the complexities of being an Asian in America (Hall & Maramba, 2001). Asians in America share cultural similarities with people in Asia as well as with people in the United States, yet these similarities with people from two cultures make Asian Americans different from those of either culture.

Asian Americans are heterogeneous in terms of cultural backgrounds and history in the United States. However, most of the research reviewed in this book does not address potential differences among the Asian American ethnic groups. For example, cultural constructs, such as interdependence and loss of face, may function somewhat differently and may vary in prominence across different Asian American ethnic groups. Although there exist some commonalities in Asian cultures from the same region, such as

East Asia, with its roots in Confucian ideology, one cannot assume that such commonalities generalize to other South Asian and Southeast Asian cultures.[1]

In some cases, the rarity of interethnic Asian American comparisons may stem from an absence of studies on particular groups. Most of the research in this book involves Americans with East Asian and Southeast Asian backgrounds; there is a dearth of theory and research on South Asian Americans. Without more investigations on Americans of South Asian descent, researchers will not understand the full spectrum of Asian American psychology or the potential for interethnic comparisons.

There is also great variability in the religious and spiritual practices among Asian American ethnic groups. For example, Protestant churches play an important role in the lives of many Korean Americans and Chinese Americans (Tan & Dong, 2000), whereas many Filipino Americans tend to be Catholic (Lin, Demonteverde, & Nuccio, 1990), and some Southeast Asian Americans practice combinations of animist beliefs and ancestor worship (Bliatout, 1993). However, relatively little attention has been paid to this important source of variation in the psychological experiences and functioning among Asian American individuals. Trimble (1990) argued that research that compares a combined Asian American group with another group obscures the diversity within Asian Americans. We recognize the inherent methodological difficulty in conducting culturally sensitive research with a diverse population group such as Asian Americans (Okazaki & Sue, 1995), yet we also recognize that the field of Asian American psychology has matured to the point where more research that examines multiple Asian American ethnic groups and more sources of within-group variability (e.g., spirituality, acculturation, socioeconomic class, bicultural identity) will help inform the field as to what may be general cultural influences as well as what may be ethnic-specific cultural influences.

Asians in the United States are faced with the task of navigating at least two cultures to thrive in their families, ethnic communities, and in the broader non-Asian society (LaFromboise, Coleman, & Gerton, 1993). Such cultural navigation is salient not only to the two thirds of Asian Americans who were born in Asia but also to many people of Asian ancestry who were born in the United States. Phenotypic as well as cultural characteristics often prevent Asian Americans from fully assimilating into the American mainstream, even if their families have been in the United States for multiple generations. Thus, theory and research in the field of Asian American psychology need to address issues of ethnic and cultural identity. The mechanisms that cause Asian Americans to retain an Asian cultural identity, to

---

[1]There are, of course, important differences among cultural groups within any particular region. For a detailed discussion of the differences in social orientations between Chinese and Japanese peoples, both of which have often been characterized as collectivistic or interdependent, see Dien (1999).

acculturate to a non-Asian identity, and to develop varying degrees of a bi-cultural identity are not adequately understood. Moreover, as Tsai, Chentsova-Dutton, and Wong (chapter 2) and Root (chapter 7) discuss in their chapters, cultural identity may be domain specific in that levels of acculturation may differ according to a particular context (e.g., language use, social affiliations). There is also limited information on how Asian American acculturation is similar to and differs from that of other non-Asian immigrants (e.g., Fuligni, 1998).

In addition to issues of Asian American identity, much work is necessary on the multiple identities of Asian Americans, including dimensions of culture, gender, sexual orientation, class, and geographic region, as Root discusses in chapter 7. In a recent discussion of the various models of acculturation, Flannery, Reise, and Yu (2001) proposed that Asian American acculturation often involves *ethnogenesis*, or an emergence of a new cultural identity that is shaped by the distinctive experience of life in America. Flannery et al. further presented a new tridirectional model of acculturation, in which the two axes representing home and host orientations are obliquely rotated, with an added third dimension representing ethnogenesis. These recent advances in the conceptual and methodological models of Asian American acculturation and identity promise a continued vibrancy in the science of Asian American psychology.

Much theory and research on Asian Americans have examined cultural issues. Relatively little research, however, has addressed issues associated with Asian American minority status. Being the target of discrimination is an experience that distinguishes Asian Americans from most European Americans and from most Asians in Asia. There is evidence that Asian American college students perceive personal discrimination significantly more than European Americans do (Crocker, Luhtanen, Blaine, & Broadnax, 1994) but less so than African Americans or Latino/Latina Americans (Sears, Citrin, Cheleden, & van Laar, 1999). Issues of discrimination may be more prominent for Asian Americans in social contexts in which they constitute a small minority versus in multicultural social contexts (Tsai, Mortensen, Wong, & Hess, in press). Regardless of its relative impact, discrimination limits Asian Americans' opportunities in society and relegates Asian Americans to limited societal niches. Hall suggests in chapter 6 that extreme stereotypes of Asian American men as either nonmasculine or violent may play a role in Asian American men's violence. In their chapter on career psychology, Leong and Hardin (chapter 5) suggest that Asian Americans may not choose or persist in certain careers because of limited access to these careers for Asian Americans. Thus, many Asian Americans may believe that they are not capable of succeeding in stereotypically non-Asian careers. More theory and research are needed to understand the influence of ethnic minority status on Asian Americans and how the effects of ethnic minority status are similar and different between Asian Americans and other ethnic minority groups.

In addition, the relationships of Asian Americans to other ethnic groups in a multicultural society are poorly understood.

Another common thread in this book is an emphasis on methodological issues. Okazaki (chapter 1) and Tsai et al. (chapter 2) detail in their chapters innovative experimental methods to examine issues of identity. On the other hand, the research reviewed in Root's (chapter 7) and Iwamasa and Sorocco's (chapter 4) chapters has relied heavily on interviews, focus groups, and self-report measures. In fact, Root argues that qualitative methods may be better suited than quantitative methods for studies of multiracial identity. The challenge for future researchers in the field of Asian American psychology lies in reconciling the theoretical questions with appropriate methodology, using multiple methods to approach the question at hand, and creating innovative tools and methods when existing approaches are not suitable.

The development of new measures that assess unique aspects of Asian Americans' experiences is also necessary for the advancement of the field. For example, Zane's (1991) measure of loss of face and Tsai and Ying's bidimensional cultural orientation measures appear to have particular utility among Asian Americans. Another culturally related methodological issue involves the unit of analysis. Traditional American psychology has focused on the individual; However, for many Asian Americans, family, community, and cultural context are as important as the individual. As suggested in Okazaki's (chapter 1), Okagaki and Bojczyk's (chapter 3), Hall's (chapter 6), and Root's (chapter 7) chapters, ecological approaches that consider the individual in context are important for a comprehensive understanding of Asian Americans. The field currently lacks conceptual and methodological tools to incorporate the nuanced effects of sociopolitical, historical, and geographical locations and of the neighborhoods and communities on Asian American individual and families. This is certainly an area that is ripe for scientific innovation that would have an impact beyond Asian American psychology.

The title of this book calls attention to the "science" within Asian American psychology. How do the chapters of this volume help readers to understand the current status and future direction of science in Asian American psychological research? From a conceptual perspective, the contributions remind us of the complexities inherent in the study of Asian Americans and the importance of tempering our desire for scientific precision with the need for cultural and ecological understanding. At the same time, many of the chapters highlight the significant progress that has already occurred in the field. Numerous studies now evaluate the applicability of previous research (based largely on non-Asian American groups) to Asian Americans. These efforts have important implications not only for Asian American psychology but also for general psychology as a whole. The sheer increase in the number of studies that focus on specific Asian American psychological issues also signals the growing presence and evolution of the field. In addition, several chapters describe innovations in the methodologies that are used in these studies. Cultural priming, physiological measures, and sociometric ratings are now being added to the paper-and-pencil and interviewing data collection approaches that have typified the field in the past, and explicit strategies for collecting data with Asian Americans are now being proposed. Taken together, these exciting developments characterize a thriving and expanding field of scholarship. Our hope is that this book will stimulate the further development of theory and research in Asian American psychology as it continues to advance in the 21st century.

REFERENCES

Bliatout, B. T. (1993). Hmong death customs: Traditional and acculturated. In D. P. Irish, K. F. Lundquist, & V. J. Nelsen (Eds.), *Ethnic variations in dying, death, and grief: Diversity in universality* (pp. 79–100). Washington, DC: Taylor & Francis.

Crocker, J., Luhtanen, R., Blaine, B., & Broadnax, S. (1994). Collective self-esteem and psychological well-being among White, Black, and Asian college students. *Personality and Social Psychology Bulletin, 20,* 503–513.

Dien, D. S. (1999). Chinese authority-directed orientation and Japanese peer-group orientation: Questioning the notion of collectivism. *Review of General Psychology, 3,* 372–385.

Flannery, W. P., Reise, S. P., & Yu, J. (2001). An empirical comparison of acculturation models. *Personality and Social Psychology Bulletin, 27,* 1035–1045.

Fuligni, A. J. (1998). Authority, autonomy, and parent–adolescent conflict and cohesion: A study of adolescents from Mexican, Chinese, Filipino, and European backgrounds. *Developmental Psychology, 34,* 782–792.

Hall, G. C. N., & Maramba, G. G. (2001). In search of cultural diversity: Recent literature in cross-cultural and ethnic minority psychology. *Cultural Diversity and Ethnic Minority Psychology, 7,* 12–26.

LaFromboise, T. D., Coleman, H. L. K., & Gerton, J. (1993). Psychological impact of biculturalism: Evidence and theory. *Psychological Bulletin, 114,* 395–412.

Lin, K., Demonteverde, L., & Nuccio, I. (1990). Religion, healing, and mental health among Filipino Americans. *International Journal of Mental Health, 19,* 40–44.

Okazaki, S., & Sue, S. (1995). Methodological issues in assessment research with ethnic minorities. *Psychological Assessment, 7,* 367–375.

Sears, D. O., Citrin, J., Cheleden, S. V., & van Laar, C. (1999). Cultural diversity and multicultural politics: Is ethnic balkanization psychologically inevitable? In D. A. Prentice & D. T. Miller (Eds.), *Cultural divides: Understanding and overcoming group conflict* (pp. 35–79). New York: Russell Sage Foundation.

Tan, S., & Dong, N. J. (2000). Psychotherapy with members of Asian American churches and spiritual traditions. In P. S. Richards & A. E. Bergin (Eds.), *Handbook of psychotherapy and religious diversity* (pp. 421–444). Washington, DC: American Psychological Association.

Trimble, J. E . (1990). Ethnic specification, validation prospects, and the future of drug use research. *International Journal of the Addictions, 25,* 149–170.

Tsai, J. L., Ying, Y., & Lee, P. A. (2000). The meaning of "being Chinese" and "being American": Variation among Chinese American young adults. *Journal of Cross-Cultural Psychology, 31,* 302–332.

Zane, N. (1991, August). *An empirical examination of loss of face among Asian Americans.* Paper presented at the American Psychological Association Convention, San Francisco.

AUTHOR INDEX

Numbers in italics refer to listings in the reference sections.

Lucca, N., 95, *103*, 144, *152*
Luhtanen, R., 25, *36*, 197, *199*
Lum, J., 154, 155, 158, 161, 162, 164, *168*
Lum, O., *130*
Lustina, M. J., *99*
Luzzo, D. A., 146, *151*

Maassen, G. H., 51, *62*
Maccoby, E. E., 69, 70, *101*
Madden, T., 48, *63*
Magdol, L., *169*
Malamuth, N. M., 157, *169*
Manning, P. K., 186, *191*
Manson, S. M., 154, *169*
Maramba, G. G., 157, *168*, *199*
Marcia, J. E., 46, *63*
Margolin, G., 155, 156, *167*, *169*
Markus, H. R., 15, 22, *36*, 53, *62*, *63*, 134, 144, 145, *151*
Marsella, A. J., *129*
Marshall, J. R., 28, *34*
Martin, J. A., 69, 70, *101*
Martinez, R. O., 48, *63*
Martzke, J. S., 29, *34*
Masaki, B, 155, 158, 161, 163, *167*, *169*
Masaki, H., 116, *129*
Mason, C., *190*
Mass, A. I., 178, 180, 183, *191*
Masse, L. C., *63*
Matute-Bianchi, M. E., 86, *102*
McConaughy, S. H., 26, *33*
McCoy, K., 17, 27–29, *38*
McFarland, B., *36*
McKinley, J. C., 121, *128*
McNeilly, M., 29, *33*
Menendez, A., *128*
Menon, T., 21, *35*
Miller, G. A., 31, *36*
Miller, J. G., 8, *10*
Miller, R. L., 173–175, *191*
Mills, C. S., 155, 156, *169*
Mink, I. R., 48, *62*
Minn, J. Y., 17, *37*
Miranda, C., 53, *64*
Miyake, K., *34*
Mizokawa, D. T., 82, 86, *102*
Moffitt, T. E., 156, *169*
Mok, T. A., *169*
Moon, A., 116, *129*
Morera, O. F., 16, *38*
Morishima, J. K., xvi, *xviii*, 82, *102*
Morris, M. W., 20, 21, *35*, *100*

Morris-Prather, C. E., 30, *36*
Morten, G., 173, *190*
Mortensen, H., 56, 58, *64*, 197
Moss, E. M., 29, *36*
Mounts, N., 69, *103*
Muir, D. W., *36*
Murdaugh, C., *130*
Murphy-Shigematsu, S. L., 178–180, 182–183, *192*
Myerhoff, B., 43, *63*

Nagata, D. K., 16, *36*
Nakashima, C. L., 187, *192*
Narang, D. S., 155, *168*
National Center for Education Statistics, 83, *102*
National Institutes of Health, 117, *129*
Nesdale, D., 48, *63*
Newman, J. P., 160, *167*
Nguyen, L., *63*
Nguyen, N. A., 74, 75, 95, *102*
Nihira, K., 48, *62*
Nisbett, R. E., 18, *34*, 160, *167*, *169*
Nitschke, J. B., 28, *35*
Noguchi, M., 116, *129*
Norton, I. M., 154, *169*
Nuccio, I., 196, *199*

Okagaki, L., 70, 71, 85, 86, *102*
Okazaki, S., xvi, *xvii*, 16, 17, 26–28, *36*, *37*, 47, *61*, 68, 83, *103*, 140, *152*, 196, *199*
Olmedo, E. L., 59, *63*
Olstad, R. G., 82, *102*
Omowale, N., 30, *36*
Opton, E., Jr., 29, *36*
Ordonez, N., *190*
Osato, S., 116, *128*
Osipow, S. H., 136, 137, *150*, *152*
Oster, H., *34*

Padilla, A. M., 59, *63*
Pang, V. O., 82, *102*
Parham, T. A., 141, *152*
Park, K. B., 17, *37*, *129*
Park, S. Y., 59, *62*
Parsons, O. A., 29, *37*
Passel, J. S., 73, *100*
Patel, N., 72, *102*
Paulhus, D. L., 47, *63*
Paulino, A., 43, *62*
Pelham, B. W., 15, 22, 23, *35*, *37*

SUBJECT INDEX

Caretaker fathers, 73
Caste system, 148
Caste variables, 172, 173
CBOs. *See* Community-based organizations
Center for Epidemiologic Studies Depression
    Scale (CESD—10), 121
Central Americans, 122
Checking homework, 88
Checklists, 118
Cherry Blossom Beauty Queen Pageant (San
    Francisco), 7, 179
Chiao shun (training a child), 71
Chicago, 161
Children
    abuse of, 161
    acculturation of, 73–74
    continuous monitoring and guidance of,
      71
    and ethnic identity, 46
    and homework, 92–93
    and intimacy, 116
    liaison role of, 75
    and math performance, 23, 24
    moral development of, 79–80
    parents' role in education of, 85–89
    sexual abuse of, 154
    social development of, 73–76
    and sociometric task, 51
    and sports activities, 93
    work values of, 144
China, 4, 69
Chinatown (San Francisco), 52
Chinese Americans, xi, 5
    caregiving among, 116
    collectivistic value orientation of, 144
    college completion rates of, 84
    couples studies of, 29
    and cultural influences, 45
    and cultural orientation, 47
    depression in, 121
    dialects spoken by older, 109
    and emotion, 45
    and ethnic identity, 54
    expressive behavior of, 27
    generational status of older, 108
    and language, 59
    and mental health, 44, 48
    and mental health treatment, 44
    parent-adolescent relationships of, 76–
      77, 95–96, 98
    and parents' role in children's educa-
      tion, 87–89

and peer delinquency, 81
preschool, 92–93
social development of, 83
social roles of, 53–55
and underlying beliefs about intellectual
    performance, 86
work values of, 142–143
Chinese Canadians, 47
Chinese (in Netherlands), 49
Choices, career. *See* Career choices
Civil rights movement, xi, 47
Class variables, 172, 173
Cognition
    cultural, 19–20
    social, 18–25, 33, 137–138
Cognitive development, 83–94
    limitations of current knowledge on,
      93–94
    and parental expectations, 84–85
    and psychosocial maladjustment, 91–
      92
    and socialization, 86–89
    and underachievement, 89–92
    and underlying beliefs about intellectual
      performance, 85–86
Coherence, sense of, 45, 81
Cohesiveness, family, 86
Collaborative relationships, 122–125
Collective self, 20–21
Collective Self-Esteem Scale, 25
Collectivism, 21, 162. *See also* Individual-
    ism—Collectivism
Collectivist orientation, 81, 91
College completion, rates of, 83–84
College samples, 180–181
Commitment (to community), 114
Communication
    with parents, 76
    with school personnel, 90
    trangenerational, 111
Community-based organizations (CBOs),
    122–125
Community environment, 108
Community samples, 180
Compromise, 145–146
Computer science lessons, 88
Conformity, 71
Confucian ethics and values, 69
    and acceptance of fate, 157–158
    and patriarchal hierarchy, 156–157
Consciousness raising, 164
Context, 57–59, 71

East Asia, 4
Ecological context of men's violence, 163
Ecological Framework for Understanding Racial Identity Development, 175
Education. *See also* academic achievement, academic orientation.
    about violence, 164
    and career choices, 140
    college, 83–84
    and dropout rates, 91
    emphasis on, 86
    level of, 108, 109, 116
    parents' level of, 91
    parents' role in, 87–89
    underachievement and prior, 91
Effort, 86
Elder abuse, 116
Elderly. *See* Older adults
Elders, respect for, 75
Electromyograph measurements, facial, 29
Electrophysiological studies, 28
Emotional expression, 27, 45
Emotional facial behavior, 52
Emotions, 107
Employment
    adolescent, 87–88, 92
    and domestic violence, 161
    and work environment, 141, 142
Engaged fathers, 73
English (language), 20–21
Environment
    for academic achievement, 88
    for career success, 138
    Eurocentric work, 141, 142
    personality and work, 133–136
    role of, in child development, 79–80
    structuring of home, 87
Ethnic American traditions, 108
Ethnic identity, 108
    achieved stage of, 46
    changing, 54
    cultural influences on researchers' notions of, 53–54
    definition of, 42
    development of, 81–82
    directions for future research on, 60–61
    existing literature on, 46, 48–49
    and mental health, 48–49
    methodological issues in study of, 49–60
    and multirace, 173–175
    pan-Asian American, 6

    and peer relationships, 80
    Phinney's model of, 46, 48
    priming of, 23–25
    social context influencing, 57–59
    value of studying, 42–45
Ethnicity
    definition of, 153
    of older Asian Americans, 107, 108, 111
    priming of, 24
    situational, 174
Ethnic minority research, 3
Ethnic socialization, 82
Eurocentric work environments, 141, 142
European Americans, 116
    and career psychology, 134–136
    and elder abuse, 116
    and MMPI effectiveness, 121
    parent-adolescent relationships of, 76–77
    and parental expectations, 85
    and parents' role in children's education, 87–89
    and peer relationships, 80
    and self-realization, 142–143
    as term, 5
    and underlying beliefs about intellectual performance, 86
    and violence, 159–160
Exercise programs, 109
Expectations
    parental, 84–85
    student, 89
    student vs. parental, 91
Expressive behavior, 27
Extracurricular lessons, 86–88
Eye contact, 123

Face, saving, 18–19
    and acculturation, 47
    and career psychology, 148
    and moral development, 78–79
    and older adults, 107
    and violence, 159, 160, 163
Facial Action Coding System, 52
Facial electromyograph measurements, 29
Familialism, 54
Family(-ies)
    and career choice, 138
    cohesiveness of, 86
    context of, 71
    and domestic violence, 160–161
    and older adults, 109, 116

Honolulu, 175

Ideas—data, 142
Identity
    ascribed, 175
    Asian American, 6
    bicultural, 174
    biracial, 174
    ethnic. *See* Ethnic identity
    gender, 23–25
    personal, 175
    priming of, 19–25
    racial, 175
    symbolic, 176
    vocational, 137, 145
Identity confusion, 173
Identity formation, 172–176
Idiocentric individuals, 144
Illness, 109
Immigrant Chinese. *See* Chinese immigrants
Immigrants, 42
    Cambodian, 86
    Chinese, 44, 45, 48, 68–69
    college completion rates of, 84
    and cultural influences, 45
    and depression, 48
    domestic violence among, 154
    Filipino, 86
    and generational conflict, 74–75
    and mental health treatment, 44
    Mexican, 86
    and underlying beliefs about intellectual
        performance, 86
    Vietnamese, 48, 74–75, 79–80, 86, 154
Immigration
    involuntary, 75, 109
    motivation for, 109
    reasons for, 109
Immigration status, 108
Impression management, 47
Incentives, culturally appropriate, 124–125
Income
    and college completion rates, 84
    and older Asian American needs, 111
    research population's level of, 123
Independence, 137, 144–146
India, 4, 73, 134, 148
Indifferent parenting, 69
Indigenous heritage, 111
Individualism—collectivism, 21–22, 47,
        144–145, 147
Individuation, 77

Indulgent parenting, 72
Informant reports, 26
Informed-consent documents, 119
In-group friendships, 81
Inouye, Daniel, 107
Insecurity, 72
Integrationists, 140–142
Intelligence, 85–86
Interdependence, 137, 144, 146, 159, 162
Intergenerational conflict, 43
Intermarriage, 158–159, 173–174
Internalization, 141
Internment, Japanese American, 107, 172
Interpersonal relationships, 124
Interracial marriage, xiii, 7
Intervention studies, 119–120
Interviews, 50
    with older Asian Americans, 113–117,
        119, 121, 122
    open ended, 185
    semistructured, 186
    structured, 185–186
    and violence research, 155–156
Intimacy with children, 116
Involuntary immigration, 75, 109
Involvement
    in career choices, 146
    child development and parental, 71
    of fathers, 73
    parental, in school, 88
Irish Americans, 43
Italian Americans, 43

Jackson, Jesse L. Sr., 159
Japan, 4, 22
    Asian brides from, 179
    and Confucian ethics, 69
    military bases in, 182
Japanese
    and ethnic identity, 53
    and stressful films, 29
    and violence, 162
Japanese African Americans, 182
Japanese American Citizens League, 7
Japanese Americans, xi, 5–7
    anxiety/depression conceptions of older,
        116, 118, 123
    biracial, 174
    and caregiving, 109, 116, 121–122
    college completion rates of, 84
    depression in, 120
    and elder abuse, 116

ethnic socialization of, 82
generational status of older, 108
intermarriage of, 179
internment of, 107, 172
intervention studies for older, 120
and mixed-race studies, 182–183
and MMPI effectiveness, 121
older, 109, 113, 114, 116, 118, 120, 122–125
parent-adolescent relationships of, 98
and parental responsibility for academic achievement, 85
and parents' role in children's education, 87–89
and peer delinquency, 81
at Seinan Senior Citizens' Center, 122–125
self-concept of, 82
social development of, 83
and underlying beliefs about intellectual performance, 86
World War II veterans' prejudice against, 107
Japanese (language), 67
Jen (personage), 96
Jewish Americans, 43
Job performance, evaluation of, 145
Jobs, adolescent (employment), 87–88, 92
Job satisfaction, 136, 141–142
Job stress, 141–142

Karma, 78, 158
Khmer Americans
and moral development, 78–79
parenting by, 71–72
underachievement of, 90, 91
Khmer Buddhist traditions, 78
King, Rodney, 7, 107
Knowing the child before he knows himself, 71
Knowledge of mainstream society, 90, 91, 94
Korea, 4
Asian brides from, 179
and Confucian ethics, 69
Korean Americans, 5, 7
college completion rates of, 84
domestic violence among, 161
and elder abuse, 116
and ethnic identity, 54
family support of older adult, 116
generational status of older, 108
and Los Angeles riots, 7, 107

and mixed-race studies, 182
and MMPI effectiveness, 121
and parents' role in children's education, 88–89
and peer delinquency, 81
self-concept of, 82
social development of, 83
and underlying beliefs about intellectual performance, 86
Koreans (in China), 59
Korean War, 179
Korean White Americans, 183
Krou khmae (ritual specialist), 72

Language, 20–21
and acculturation, 59
and development, 67
and generational status, 108
linguistic preferences, 59
and older Asian Americans, 108, 109, 111
and parental authority, 75
and research design, 113
and sense of coherence, 45
surveys and understanding of, 118, 119, 121
and underachievement, 89, 90, 94
Language classes, 88, 89, 93
Laos, 4, 90
Laotian Americans
college completion rates of, 84
underachievement of, 90
Latino Americans, 85
Learning disabilities, 90
Lee, Wen Ho, 6
Leveraged sampling, 182
Liaison role of children, 75
Life events, impact of, 181
Life expectancy, 110
Life satisfaction, 48, 49
Limiting contact with non-Asian Indians, 76
Linguistic preferences, 59
Local-knowledge model, 68, 72
Longitudinal studies, 16
Los Angeles, 46, 49, 54, 114, 120, 142
Los Angeles riots, 7, 107
Loss of face. See Face, saving

Majority culture, 56, 60
Maladjustment, 91–92
Male dominance, 156–157
Male primacy, 116

Managerial parental involvement in school, 88

Managerial skills, 145

Marginalists, 141

Marital partners, 54

Marriage
  interethnic, 158–159
  interracial, xiii, 7, 173–174
  and violence, 158–159

Materialistic attitudes, 75

Materials, buying extra, 88

Math classes, 89

Math performance, 23–25, 83
  and maladjustment, 91
  of men/women, 97
  and priming techniques, 58
  of Southeast Asian Americans, 84, 90
  and underlying beliefs about intellectual performance, 86

Math-related fields, 140

Maturity, career, 137, 145

Meal services, 109

Men
  and career psychology, 134
  math scores of, 97

Mental health/illness, 48–49
  of older Asian Americans, 111
  older Asian Americans' conceptions of, 116

Mental health services
  and compliance with treatment, 44
  and cultural sensitivity, 164
  and domestic violence, 160–161

Methodologies, xiii, 13–33
  and future research directions, 32–33
  and measurement, 26–30
  need for expanded, 17–18, 30–32
  and older adult research, 111–113
  social cognition as basis for, 18–25
  traditional, 15–16

Mexican Americans, 49
  ethnic socialization of, 82
  mixed-heritage, 175
  and underlying beliefs about intellectual performance, 86

Mid-old cohorts, 109–110

Minneapolis, 58–59

Minnesota Multiphasic Personality Inventory (MMPI), 121

Minority group status, 57, 107, 139–140

Minority-specific factors (of career psychology), 132–133

Mixed-heritage Mexican Americans, 175

Mixed-race Asians, 175

Mixed-race Japanese, 175

MMPI. *See* Minnesota Multiphasic Personality Inventory

Mobility, upward, 141

Modesty, 145

Money, values about, 142

Monitoring
  of children, 71
  of schoolwork, 87

Monoethnic identity, 173, 175

Monoracial identity, 173–175

Mood, 49

Mood disorders, 17

Moral development, 78–80

Morale, 116

Moratorium stage (of ethnic identity), 46

Mothers
  and child development, 74–75
  foreign-born, 179
  and mixed-race studies, 182

Motivation
  to immigrate to U.S., 109
  of researcher, 112
  and underlying beliefs about intellectual performance, 86

Multiculturalism, 47

Multicultural organizations, 142

Multicultural psychology, 8

Multicultural society, xii

Multiethnic identity, 173

Multigroup Ethnic Identity Measure, 42

Multiple-choice items, 118, 119

Multiple components of self-concept, 81–82

Multiplicity, 174

Multiracial identity, 173

Multiracial individuals, xiii

Multiracial research, 171–189
  directions for future research on, 188–189
  and identity formation, 172–176
  methodology of, 176–188
  recruitment methods for, 176–179

Music lessons, 88, 89, 93

Myanmar, 4

My Vocational Situation, 145

Narratives, 186

National Assessment of Educational Progress, 83

National Institutes for Health, 119

National origin, 111, 179
Native Hawaiians, 80, 105
Neglectful parenting, 69
Nepal, 4
Neurasthenia, 17
Neuroscience, affective, 28
Nigrescence models, 173, 174
Nisei Week, 108
Nonverbal behavior, 26–28
Nurturing, 71
Nutritional needs, 111

Obedience, 71, 72
Object orientation, 142
Obligation to others, 69
Observing the child, 71–72
Occupational segregation, 139, 141–142
Occupational status, 108
Ohio Work Values Inventory, 142
Older adults, 105–127
    case example of research of, 122–125
    depression concepts among, 116
    depression in, 120–121
    directions for future research on, 126–127
    and discrimination, 107–108
    heterogeneity of Asian American, 108–110
    methodological issues in research of, 111–113
    number of, 105
    research designs for study of, 113–122
Old-old cohorts, 109–110
Omiyage (gift giving), 124
One-drop rule of classification, 172
Open ended interviews, 185
Openness, 59
Organization, understanding the, 125
Orientation (in decisional process), 146
Origin, national, 111, 179
Out-group friendships, 81
Overseas Asians, 4, 134
Overseas-born Asian Americans, 47
Overseas Chinese, 68–69
Overseas East Asians, 17
Overseas Japanese, 22

Pacific Islanders, 4, 105
Pakistan, 4
Pan-Asian American ethnic identity, 6
Paper-and-pencil questionnaires, 187
Parent-adolescent relationship, 76–77, 95–96, 98

Parental authority, undermining of, 75, 79
Parental control, 68–69
Parental demandingness, 69, 71
Parental involvement and support, 71
Parental responsibility, 85–89
Parental responsiveness, 69
Parenting, 69–73
    authoritarian, 69–71
    authoritative, 69, 70
    indifferent, 69
    indulgent, 72
    by Khmer Americans, 71–72
    neglectful, 69
    permissive, 69, 70, 72
Parenting styles model, 69
Parents
    caring for older, 79, 109
    educational level of, 91
    well-being of, 91
Participation in culturally relevant activities, 59
Past lives, 72, 78, 158
Patriarchal hierarchy, 156–157, 161–162
Peers
    assistance of, 80
    delinquency of, 81
    and development, 51
    relationships with, 80–81
    and underachievement, 89
Permissive parenting, 69, 70, 72
Persistence, 86
Personage (*jen*), 96
Personal collection of data, 124
Personal identity, 175
Personality—work environment theory, 133–136
Philadelphia, 43, 89
Philippines, 4, 179
Physical health, 111
Physical punishment, 75, 161
Physical violence, 155
Physiological measures, 28–30, 52
Pilot data, collection of, 124
Place of birth, 44, 47
Political constructs, 175
Political ideology, 56, 59
Political persecution, 109
Political refugees, 75
Postfigurative culture, 111
Postfigurative role loss, 111
Posttraumatic stress disorder, 29, 109
Poverty, 84

gender, 156–157
liaison, of children, 75
postfigurative, loss, 111
of researcher, 112
social. *See* Social roles
of wise elders, 111
of women, 157

Samoan Americans, 84
Sampling, 180
San Diego (California), 90
San Francisco, 7, 48, 52, 59
San Francisco Bay area, 43, 45, 46, 53, 58–59
Saving face. *See* Face, saving
School achievement. *See* Academic achievement
School functions, attending, 88
School systems, familiarity with, 94
Science-related fields, 140
Seinan Senior Citizens' Center (Los Angeles), 122–125
Selective acculturation, 59
Self-blame (for abuse), 154
Self-cognition, 19–23
Self-concept, 81–82
Self-construal, 144–147
Self-Construal Scale, 146
Self-efficacy, 132, 138, 143
Self-esteem
    in adolescents, 77
    basis of, 144–145
    and ethnic identity, 48, 49
Self-realization, 142–143
Self-reports
    with questionnaires, 15
    of violence, 159
Self-stereotyping, 23–24
Semistructured interviews, 186
Senior citizen's day programs, 109
Separationists, 141, 142
Setting rules for afterschool time, 88
Sexual abuse, child, 154
Sexual aggressiveness, 159
Sexual orientation, 111
Sexual violence, 155
Shame (to families), 89. *See also* Facing, saving
    and divorce, 158
    and violence, 159, 163
Shelters, 164
Siblings

biracial, 181
    recruitment of, 182
Sister role. *See* Brother/sister role
Situational ethnicity, 174
Size of print, 119
Skin conductance responses, 29
Small work groups, 80
Snowball method of recruitment, 178–179
Social activities, 109
Social addresses, 67
Social affiliation preferences, 59
Social anxiety, 26–28
Social cognition, 18–25, 33
Social cognitive theory, 137–138
Social development, 68–83
    autonomy, development of, 76–78
    and ethnic identity, development of, 81–82
    limitations of current knowledge on, 83
    and moral development, 78–80
    and parent-child relationship, 73–76
    and parenting, 69–73
    and peer relationships, 80–81
Socialization, 78–80, 82
Socializing, 50
Social Phobia and Anxiety Inventory, 28
Social phobics, 28
Social roles, 53, 54
Social services, 111
Social skills, 86
Social status, 111
Social support for older adults, 108, 109, 116
Socioeconomic status (SES), 48
    and career psychology, 138
    of older Asian Americans, 108, 109
Sociometric task, 51
Solitude, 142
Somatic symptoms, 17, 92
Son role. *See* Daughter/son role
South Asia, 4
South Asian Americans, *see* Asian Indian Americans.
Southeast Asia, 4–5
Southeast Asian Americans
    generational status of older, 108
    underachievement of, 84, 90
    and underlying beliefs about intellectual performance, 86
Southerners (American), 18–19
Specific Affect Coding System, 27
Spiritual well-being, 72
Sports activities, 89, 93

Sri Lanka, 4
Stereotype threat, 97
Stereotyping, xi, 141–142
    multiracial, 173
    self-, 23–24
    and violence, 155, 157–159, 163
Sterotype boosting, 24
Strengthening of Intergenerational/Intercul-
    tural Ties in Immigrant Chinese
    American Families, 43
Stress, 17
    and domestic violence, 161
    and ethnic identity, 49
    job, 141–142
    and maladjustment, 92
    and nonverbal behavior, 28
    from stereotyping, 163
Stressful films, 29
Structural parental involvement in school,
    88
Structured interviews, 185–186
Structuring of home environment, 87
Submission, 165
Substance use, 80
Success, academic, 91
Suinn—Lew Asian Self-Identity Accultura-
    tion Rating Scale, 42, 142
Super's vocational development theory, 136–
    137
Support, parental, 71
Surnames, 177
Survey studies, 113, 117–119
Symbolic identity, 176
Sympathetic nervous system, 28–29

Task satisfaction, 142
Television, 79, 87
Tenure, 145
Terminology, 4–5
Tests of authenticity, 174, 181
Thai Americans, 94
Thailand, 4
Thanking research population, 125
Thank you notes, 124
Time for homework, 87
Tolerance, 58
Torture, 109
Touch, 123
Traditional beliefs, 73
Traditionalists, 141
Traditional values, 112–113
Traditions, ethnic American, 108

Training a child *(chiao shun)*, 71
Traits, 53, 54
Transgenerational culture, 111

Underachievement, academic, 84, 89–92
UNIACT. *See* Unisex Edition of the ACT
    Interest Inventory
Unidimensional model (of cultural orienta-
    tion and acculturation), 46–47
Unisex Edition of the ACT Interest Inven-
    tory (UNIACT), 134–135
United States, as multicultural society, xii
University of California, 141
Upward mobility, 141
U.S. Bureau of the Census, 4
U.S. military, 179, 182, 183

Values
    and generational conflict, 74–75
    impact of Asian American, 82
    of older Asian Americans, 112–113
    and parenting, 69
    and priming, 58, 97
    work, 142–144
Verbal scores
    of African Americans, 97
    of Southeast Asian Americans, 90
Veterans, Vietnam, 29
Victimization issues, 154, 163–164
Video recording, 27–28
Vietnam, 4
Vietnamese Americans, 5, 48, 49, 79–80, 107
    and caregiving research, 122
    college completion rates of, 84
    domestic violence among, 154
    and generational conflict, 74–75
    generational status of older, 108
    and parents' role in children's educa-
        tion, 87
    and role of environment in child devel-
        opment, 79–80
    social development of, 83
    and underlying beliefs about intellectual
        performance, 86
Vietnam veterans, 29
Violence, Asian American, 153–166
    and acceptance of fate, 157–158
    culture-specific influences on, 156–162
    culture-specific models of, 162–165
    directions for future research on, 165–
        166
    domestic violence, 154–156, 160–161

and patriarchal hierarchy, 156–157
protective factors for, 161–162
risk factors for, 156–161
sexual violence, 155
varying definitions of, 155
Vocational development theory, 136–137
Vocational identity, 137, 145

Welfare, refugees on, 154
Well-being, 17
and ethnic identity, 49
of parents, 91
Whiteness (term), 172
Widowhood, 43, 110
Women
and career psychology, 134
and domestic violence, 154, 160–161
dropout rates of, 91

and math performance, 23–25
math scores of, 97
and math tests, 58
violence and roles of, 157
Workbooks, buying extra, 88
Work environment
Eurocentric, 141, 142
and personality, 133–136
Work identification, 22
Work values, 144
World War II, 6, 107, 172, 179

Yes-no formats, 122
Young-old cohorts, 109–110
Yuan, 158

Zung Self-Rating Depression Scale, 121

ABOUT THE EDITORS

Gordon C. Nagayama Hall is professor of psychology at the University of Oregon–Eugene. He received his PhD in clinical psychology from Fuller Theological Seminary in 1982. He was previously a professor of psychology at Kent State University and the Pennsylvania State University. His research interests include the cultural context of psychopathology, particularly sexual aggression. Dr. Hall has received grants from the National Institute of Mental Health to study culture-specific models of men's sexual aggression and to study monocultural versus multicultural academic acculturation. He recently coauthored *Multicultural Psychology* (2002) with Christy Barongan. Dr. Hall was president of the American Psychological Association's Society for the Psychological Study of Ethnic Minority Issues (Division 45) and has received the Distinguished Contribution Award from the Asian American Psychological Association.

Sumie Okazaki received her PhD from the University of California–Los Angeles, in 1994. From 1995 to 1999 she was an assistant professor of psychology and Asian American studies at the University of Wisconsin–Madison. Since 1999, she has been an assistant professor of psychology at the University of Illinois at Urbana–Champaign. She is on the editorial board of the journal *Cultural Diversity and Ethnic Minority Psychology* and *Journal of Personality and Social Psychology*. She has received a Mentored Career Development Award from the National Institute of Mental Health, a Young Investigator Award from the National Alliance for Research in Schizophrenia and Depression, and an Early Career Award for Distinguished Contribution from the Asian American Psychological Association. In her research she uses a multimethod approach to examine emotions and emotional distress among Asian Americans.